GENESIS: Fact or Fiction?

by JONN DOUGHE

Note for Librarians: a cataloguing record for this book that includes Dewey Decimal Classification and US Library of Congress numbers is available from the Library and Archives of Canada. The complete cataloguing record can be obtained from their online database at:

www.collectionscanada.ca/amicus/index-e.html

ISBN 1-4120-3874-X

TRAFFORD

Offices in Canada, USA, Ireland, UK and Spain

This book was published *on-demand* in cooperation with Trafford Publishing. On-demand publishing is a unique process and service of making a book available for retail sale to the public taking advantage of on-demand manufacturing and Internet marketing. On-demand publishing includes promotions, retail sales, manufacturing, order fulfilment, accounting and collecting royalties on behalf of the author.

Book sales for North America and international:

Trafford Publishing, 6E–2333 Government St.,
Victoria, BC V8T 4P4 CANADA
phone 250 383 6864 (toll-free 1 888 232 4444)
fax 250 383 6804; email to orders@trafford.com

Book sales in Europe:

Trafford Publishing (UK) Ltd., Enterprise House, Wistaston Road Business Centre,
Wistaston Road, Crewe, Cheshire CW2 7RP UNITED KINGDOM
phone 01270 251 396 (local rate 0845 230 9601)
facsimile 01270 254 983; orders.uk@trafford.com

Order online at:

www.trafford.com/robots/04-1682.html

10 9 8 7 6 5 4 3

Prologue

The Bible remains the best-selling non-fiction book in the world and it exists as the foundational truth for billions of individuals through many religious groups. Some groups or denominations that serve the same God, from the same Bible, confuse the foundational truths when they cannot find any parts of the Bible on which they can agree. This problem is common, but can be solved by knowing more about the Bible. Jesus Christ was born into a world that was so fanatical about the man-made traditions and trappings of religion that they did not know him, the main character of God's Book. The purpose of my book is to point out many of the basic truths of God's word that must be understood in order to serve God on his terms.

The Book of Genesis is under attack. Ironically, some of these attacks are coming from among the groups who claim to know God. Genesis introduces a knowledge of God that must be accepted by everyone who truly wants to understand the Bible. Reject Genesis and you reject foundational truth. I pray that each reader of this book will use the Bible to prove and confirm each statement, reading and re-reading the scriptures if needed, until it is clear to you.

Introduction

The Book of Genesis is definitely a factual account of God's creation of and initial dealings with humanity. The teachings of Christ stand on the reality of Genesis along with all of the Old and New Testament writings. The fall of Adam in Chapter 3 of Genesis established God's word of salvation that became flesh at John 1:1–18, and taught humanity what God requires from those who overcome the fall. Take away Genesis and the historical man, Christ, will cease to exist. The foundation of human existence, purpose, weaknesses, strengths and opposition are developed in Genesis.

The major themes of the Bible—faith, hope, works, grace, repentance, salvation, mercy, love and so on—are introduced and demonstrated through the lives of the people in Genesis. Genesis is like the legs that the whole body of Holy Scripture stands on. It cannot be seen or accepted as a poem or insignificant writings by anyone who truly wants to understand the Bible.

The study of fossils and archaeology has created yet another unnecessary confusion between science and theology. Scientists who claim their recent discoveries make the Bible obsolete contend with theologians who claim the Bible has to be infallible for salvation to exist. The earth was covered with water after God created life on earth and in the oceans, yet man has not explored one percent of the oceans. It's quite possible that there are many deepwater creatures currently in the oceans that mankind has not yet seen. I would not accept unknown fossils as prehistoric until I studied the fossils of every unknown life form in the oceans, the skies, and on earth in order to rule out the possibility that unknown sea or animal life got trapped on earth through the flood. Understanding my book and the Bible should help clear up some of what people call controversy.

The Bible says the earth was created in the beginning with the rest of the Universe. The beginning could have been millions, billions or trillions of years ago. The Bible does not deal with anything from that beginning until God prepares the existing, water-covered earth for life as we have known it over the past 6,000 years or so.

If life existed on earth before man got here, God created it. If legitimate scientists have found fossil evidence of life unknown to our times, it does not create a controversy with the Bible. The Bible never said that life did not exist on earth prior to mankind, and theologians who don't know this need to learn it. A controversy is created by opposite positions on an issue. The Bible only deals with mankind and what they need to get to the next level of existence.

After studying and understanding the Bible from cover-to-cover, I can't find a basis for controversy on this issue. If earth was used for other life forms over perhaps billions of years of existence, these life forms are not physically linked to mankind. The only connection would be the same God as Creator; there are no missing links related to humans. God made perfect originals for the human race.

The danger here is in forcing people to choose between theology and true scientific facts when there is no need to. True science has no facts that disprove God as Creator of all things and no logical scientist will accept theories as facts. The careful observer must make a distinction between true and false science, then govern themselves accordingly.

The issue of human sexuality is on center stage in many countries of the world today. God made the original people of two genders—male and female. He blessed them with the power to reproduce by the seed carrier uniting with the fertile member of the pair that makes one set. He then commanded and empowered them to be fruitful and multiply.

God determined the reproductive role of each person in the family and made it obvious by what you see at birth.

The access to and occupation of the earth by Satan and his demonic hordes has given them power to attack and confuse the sex organs of some humans, before birth, in a physical way. Some may have both sex organs while others have none. Contrary to popular belief, God did not do this. Adam let Satan in and he has altered the perfection established by God. Jesus Christ could see the demons of Satan literally living in people and creating adverse results in their lives as he cast them out and overpowered Satan in the first battle of the ultimate war.

Any human may have to live with physical or mental problems just because they live in an imperfect world or suffer from the trespasses of others and their imperfections. In a case where a child is born with dual or no genitals, it is not wise to make a value judgement on that most innocent one or the immediate people around them. Wisdom may demand that you examine Satan's motives for putting such a weight on them. Do they have some talent that God has plans for?

I do not make the next statement as a medical professional, only a careful observer and, as such, a person might want to consider my suggestion at their own risk. If possible, the logical thing may be to, under the strict supervision of the best medical professional available, take time to allow the affected one to show through their actions what sex suits them best. Then, if medical science can provide surgical solutions, thank God for medical science and do the best you can. The person who has to go through this life with that condition should understand that they are not being punished for some sin they committed in life because they entered life with the condition. Satan did it.

Adam let Satan in and a lot of innocent people will have to find a way to get through this life with problems they did not create. The person who is blessed at birth with no physical problems, then decides God made an error by putting them in the wrong body, is choosing to create a different set of problems.

If Satan did not get to a person's body or mind at birth, that person must realize that Satan won't quit coming just because they are healthy. The struggle to keep Satan at bay is more difficult because Satan uses the power he gained over Adam to work through human flesh to gain his objectives. This is illustrated by Cain's situation in Chapter 4. The willingness of people to follow the lust of the flesh, the inspiration of some external influences and the raw power of Satan to tempt the flesh causes a lot of people to fall into lifestyles they cannot explain to God. God's destruction of Sodom and Gomorrah for their homosexual behavior is a most graphic example of how God ultimately deals with that issue.

God's laws of sexual morality at Leviticus 18 are necessary reading for anyone contemplating and/or supporting homosexual activity. Leviticus 18:22 clearly calls homosexuality an abomination and verses 25 through 30 spell out God's condemnation of nations that condone this and the other named sins. The New Testament confirms the condemnation of this sin. In Romans 1:18–32, Paul shows the character traits of people who give in to the temptations of Satan and force God to give them up. The persons, groups or nations that choose to ignore God's revealed will and written law are forcing God to defend his name against them.

Both Bible history and secular history have proven that these so-called sexual freedom movements are, in truth, some of Satan's better angling efforts. Satan catches a few by line, then sends them into society with some good "woe is me" victim's story, a story that may even be played up in some dramatic way that makes people show tolerance for the sin and compassion for people living the sin. Satan uses some people as bait to condition the majority of a society to embrace a sin pattern that will allow him to fish through that society with a net. Multitudes of people who would never commit the sin will question, or even doubt God's authority to call it sin and destroy their souls in the process.

The bottom line for this sin issue, and all other sin issues, is: continue to break the laws of acceptable human behavior and your society will eventually self-destruct. Add total disregard of the sacred directions for successful existence that come from the Bible, and your actions may force God to cut your society out like some cancerous growth that endangers His world. If people will apply the scriptures at Matthew 22: 37–39, and "love the Lord with all of your heart, soul and mind and thy neighbor as yourself," a lot of individual and societal problems will be solved.

Contents

CHAPTER 1

The Bible is not a fairy tale. The Bible is much more than a collection of wise sayings and rules. The Bible is God's way of communicating his message and method of salvation to dead humanity. The Bible is not based on theories. A theory can be defined as, "An idea, opinion, or guess. A coherent group of general propositions used as principles of explanation for a class of phenomena. An explanation that has not yet been proved true." The Bible deals with facts, facts that give a proven history of what was, what is and accurately identifies what is to come.

The most important, lengthy, mysterious and complicated book ever written is the Bible. The Bible has been the subject of a lot of wild stories—you cannot understand it. God never meant for man to understand the Bible. One particular passage may have a different meaning for everyone who reads it, and so on and so on. Think about it: to say God's only written communication to mankind that leads to his salvation is fixed so that mankind cannot understand it is to call God a liar, cheat, deceiver and every negative title that Lucifer, his arch enemy, has earned.

I am planning a series of communications that are designed to amplify the whole Bible so everyone can obtain a clear message from it. The question that still puzzles me after over thirty years of working in the Bible is where to start my study of the Bible to get a good understanding of it. My answer is usually in the form of this question: Where did you start reading every other book that you want to understand? The answer is always the same—I start reading the book at the beginning. Since the Bible is probably the longest and certainly the most complicated book you will ever read, why complicate it more by starting somewhere other than at the beginning? I am using the NEW KING JAMES VERSION, Thomas Nelson, Inc., (publisher).

I would ask you to turn to Chapter 1 of Genesis, verse 1.

> **Gen. 1:1 In the beginning God created the heavens and the earth.**

The first verse does not hinge on theory or guesswork about the origin of the Universe. God created it. You might wonder when God created the heavens and the earth, or Universe as we call it now. My objective here is only to prove the Universe existed prior to the six day-period we call Creation.

The first verse did not say when God created it. Based on what is written, the Universe could be millions, billions or trillions of years old. The first human thought is that the whole Universe was created to serve mankind, therefore its age would be slightly older than the 6,000 or so years from the creation of Adam. Theologians who see it this way without reading what is written, and scientest who claim they can prove otherwise, will be at odds until both read and understand what is clearly stated in Chapter 1.

The fact that the earth was not prepared for life as we know it suggests that it was used some other way, or was dormant, until God got ready to use it. All of the things that exist in the heavens existed before the beginning of the six-day period we call Creation. The earth also existed before that six-day period and it was covered with water. The Bible says the earth was completely dark at that time. The answer to a question about the age of the Universe can only be answered by its owner and Creator—God.

The size of the Universe would be the next logical question for most of us. The Universe is defined as the totality of known or supposed objects and phenomena throughout space, or everything that exists. Mankind can only guess about the complete size of the Universe. Scientists do not know if the Universe has a limited size. The best scientists, using the most up-to-date equipment in existence, have gathered enough data to feel safe making the following statements.

The Universe includes the earth and everything on it. It also includes everything in the solar system. All the stars, of which the sun is one, are part of the Universe. More than 100 billion stars are grouped in the shape of a giant circular galaxy called the Milky Way. The Milky Way is about 100,000 light years across. A light year is the distance that light travels in a year—about 5.88 trillion miles.

Studies of distant space with optical and radio telescopes show that there are at least as many galaxies in the Universe as there are stars in the Milky Way. Galaxies tend to be grouped together into clusters, and some clusters appear to be grouped into superclusters. Superclusters are the largest coherent (held together) structures yet discovered in the Universe.

The above information can be expanded from home encyclopedias, computers, or your local library. The point I want to make is that the earth, whose circumference is roughly 25,000 miles, would measure up to God's known Universe as less than one drop of rain would measure up to all of the oceans of the earth. The Satanically inspired arrogance of man, who mostly thought this planet was flat only 500 years ago, will lead him into eternal ruin if he does not accept the fact that earth is only one small piece of God's giant puzzle.

At II Corinthians 12:1-6, Paul said he was taken physically or spiritually to the 3rd heaven, which he later called Paradise, where he heard inexpressible words that are not lawful for a man to utter. We now know that our sun lights up the heavens around us. Is the 3rd heaven he refers to in another solar system and who is speaking these inexpressible words?

The fact that Lucifer, who was once a trusted servant of God, possibly an archangel, had already rebelled against God and incited one-third of the angels to do so before Adam was created should prove the existence of intelligent life prior to man (Rev. 12:4–9; Isa. 14:12–15). Whether there was any life on earth prior to man is not covered in the Bible. If there was, God created it. However, it has nothing to do with where human beings should be concentrating their time and efforts.

Earth, as we know it, is becoming unusable because of man's poor guardianship and will eventually be rendered incapable of sustaining life if some serious changes are not made soon. Man has advanced the art of war to a point where he can destroy life completely (Matt. 24:22). Whether life existed on earth before is a subject that should pale in comparison to how humans continue their existence right now.

Question: Does God move from one solar system to the next, recreating existing matter and giving it life? If so, is his objective to give life to a series of life forms that will obey and serve him? Answer: Unknown. What is known is that the creation of man and his immediate surroundings certainly prove God's desire to have obedient servants on earth. The fact that God tested Adam and Eve after Creation will bear that out.

A follow-up on God's creative process will show how the six days of work and one day of rest did not include the creation of angels previously mentioned, or whoever he refers to as us in the making of man in Genesis 1:26. The language clearly shows the existence of other life prior to man. How much other life or how long it existed prior to man will be answered by God when the mysteries of God are made known to mankind and we are allowed to see him as he is (Rev. 10:7). The order of creation of the whole Universe, as we currently know it, is not the focal point of Genesis 1 and 2. The Bible gives the Creation details as they relate to man and the system that serves his needs.

In Chapter 1 of Genesis, we find a detailed account of what we refer to as Creation. In verse 2, the earth, which existed, was without form and "darkness was on the face of the deep." This darkness was not what we know as darkness, with the lesser light of the moon ruling the night. The darkness was complete. No sight was possible in it.

The human mind generally tends to compare all things based on human ability. In other words, if you asked a panel of the greatest scientists on earth about the chances of duplicating the events of Genesis 1 and 2, they would probably look at all that man is, what man knows, what man has done and what man may be capable of doing in his future, then decide that it cannot be done. The scientists would be right in their opinion as long as they are using man, the created being, as the measuring rod.

Human beings, who at this point have never created anything at all, have invented things from what God created and are currently using most of those inventions in ways that might jeopardize the future of the planet. A reader who tries to figure Creation on the basis of the knowledge of man, the created being, is losing the whole point of the Bible. The Bible is authored by God and is designed to bring the knowledge of man upward to a better understanding of God.

The alternative to accepting God as Creator would be that all things exist by sheer luck, or that some explosion of unknown origin created order instead of chaos. A big bang theorist said it seems like there was nothing, then everything exploded into existence. The theory sounds like the very thing God did when he called Creation into existence, but the theorist refuses to accept God as the power behind it.

Absolutely nothing mysteriously evolved into everything without any power controlling it. Ancient Babylonians thought two giant monsters began to fight and carved out the Universe in the fight, but nobody knows where the monsters came from. Or, we can all find some of the many wild theories that are floating around, but none of them even makes common sense.

The only acceptable idea is that there are beings greater than man. The greatest being is God who can call matter into existence and create or recreate it simply by speaking. In verse 3, when God said, "Let there be light," he called it into existence and began to prepare an environment for life as man would come to know it, as stated in Genesis 1:3–8.

> Gen. 1:3 Then God said, "Let there be light"; and there was light.
>
> 4 And God saw the light, that it was good; and God divided the light from the darkness.
>
> 5 God called the light Day, and the darkness he called Night. So the evening and the morning were the first day.
>
> 6 Then God said, "Let there be a firmament in the midst of the waters, and let it divide the waters from the waters."
>
> 7 Thus God made the firmament, and divided the waters which were under the firmament from the waters which were above the firmament; and it was so.

8 And God called the firmament Heaven. So the evening and the morning were the second day.

The first day's work, in verses 3 through 5, covers activating our one major star, the sun, which scientists think is only one star out of 100 billion, and the lesser light, our moon.

The firmament is the heavens as we know them, the air or sky that divide the waters with the cloud system above and waters still covering the earth. This represents the second day's work.

God's work continues into the third day with the events that are covered in verses 9 through 13. In verse 9, God said, "Let the waters under the heavens be gathered together into one place, and let the dry land appear; and it was so." The sight of this act would no doubt be so overwhelming to a human being that they would have to acknowledge the power of God in the same way they do after some great storm or other overpowering situation that leaves people happy to be alive and readily thanking God for that privilege. They know a far greater power than man has acted. God names the earth and seas in verse 10, then proceeds with the living things.

The question of which came first, the chicken or the egg, has the beginning of its answer in verses 11 and 12. God calls into being the originals of plant life, all containing the seeds of reproduction within. Verses 14 through 19 deal with the events of Day 1, but the emphasis of Day 4 is how the light relates to times and seasons. The seeds are in place in the plants and now the earth is given the seasonal cycles for reproduction. On Day 5, God called all water-based creatures and fowls into life, all carrying the seeds of reproduction within.

A look at verse 22 reinforces the true power behind life, as we know it. God blessed his creations to multiply and they did. This is the same God that childless Abram and Sarai called on. This is the same God that childless Hannah called on in 1 Samuel 1:10-15. This is the same God who is the only one who can order reproduction.

Verses 24 through 31 cover Day 6. The rest of Creation was completed on this day. Verse 24 says God called all land-based animals into existence from the earth and gave them life by the sheer power of his word. The Creation of mankind will be different from all other living things. In verse 26, we find that God chose to create man in his image. The word image would make us think that God must look like a man, but Genesis 5:3 shows this image is spiritual in nature.

Adam had sons and daughters whose physical appearance has no bearing on how the word "image" is used here. Seth would bear the spiritual image of an obedient person whose line would produce Noah and the only survivors of God's judgement on a disobedient world through the flood. Adam compromised this image, or likeness, that had him created a little lower than the angels in Psalm 8:4–6. Paul, at Colossians 1: 15, talks about Jesus, the physical man, who is the image of the invisible God. If God is invisible, the image has to be the unseen spiritual side that God is referring to in regard to Adam.

The breath of God made Adam a living soul. This breath from God made man co-eternal with God. Man was designed and created to be in God's service forever. It was his duty to never dishonor or disobey his Creator in any way. Man was given guardianship over the earth and authority over all other living creatures. Verses 29 and 30 tell us that man and all other land-based creatures were created as vegetarians. The thought that being a vegetarian now has some spiritual value is false because after the flood, mankind is allowed to eat meat, as stated in Genesis 9:3.

But the idea that God created one creature to be food for another is put to rest here. It was after Adam lost dominion of the earth to Satan that creatures began to feed on weaker creatures. Chapter 11 of Isaiah identifies a time when Christ will rule the earth without the presence and influence of Satan, where the wolf shall dwell with the lamb at verse 6, the cow and the bear shall graze at verse 7, the nursing child shall play by the cobra's hole at verse 8, and so on. This leads people to think it represents a time that man has never known, when in fact, it mirrors the pre-Satanic earth.

Chapter 1 ends with God blessing all that he has created and he empowers all to be fruitful and multiply. In verse 31, God declares that all the work done during the six days was very good. At this point, we see the earth, its inhabitants, and immediate surroundings as perfect.

CHAPTER 2

Chapter 2 of Genesis opens with the author reviewing the actions of Chapter 1. There are several things to consider and review as we move forward. The six days used for the preparation and creation of life as we know it must be taken in its own context.

1. The Creation of heaven and earth here deals with the reactivation of our earth and its immediate surroundings, not the whole Universe.

2. The author (Moses, most likely) may or may not have put down the words and details in the exact order that they happened or were revealed to him, so we must not think the facts are incorrect because they are not presented in the order that we would expect.

3. If the whole Universe were the target of the Bible, it would probably mention other planets and possibly other created life forms. The fact that the Bible focuses only on things we are familiar with makes it obvious to me that God gave the Bible to mankind as a map out of his fallen state.

In verses 2 and 3, God seals the seventh day as holy and sets it apart as a day of worship and rest. The day of God still carries the same power today for those who call him Savior.

The creation of Adam gets more detailed in verse 7.

> Gen. 2:7 And the Lord God formed man of the dust of the ground, and breathed into his nostrils the breath of life; and man became a living being.

The Bible says man was created from the earth. Scientific facts say the human body is a copy of the earth, containing the reciprocal percentages of liquid, earth, minerals, and traces of the rarest elements known to science. Man here becomes co-eternal with God as God breathes the breath of life into him—he became a living soul.

The fact that all humans say or feel that life goes on, even after the earthen body has been put away, bears witness to God's imprint on man. Have you ever heard people discuss the whereabouts of a deceased person when they know exactly where that person's body is? Have you ever heard people talk about where they want to go—get this—when they die? How many times have you said or thought about your direction after you die?

The fact that man is a living soul and that soul is co-eternal with God, the soul must be accounted for after the body fails; this is buried deep in the subconscious mind of every human. That is the living soul bearing witness to God, its Creator, and it is not based on religion, creed, or race.

Verses 8 through 25 give us more details concerning the who, what, where, when, why and how of the Creation story covered in Chapter 1. Many scholars still think of the Garden of Eden as the place of man's creation, but verse 8 and verse 15 tell us that man was created elsewhere and put in the Garden of Eden.

Man is given a specific task in verse 15 and rules and restrictions in verses 16 and 17. Keep these verses in mind because they will become a key to understanding man's current plight.

> **Gen. 2:15 Then the Lord God took the man and put him in the Garden of Eden to tend and keep it.**
>
> **16 And the Lord God commanded the man, saying, "Of every tree of the garden you may freely eat;**
>
> **17 but of the tree of the knowledge of good and evil you shall not eat, for in the day you eat of it you shall surely die."**

In verses 18 through 21, we get more confirmation and details on the creation, naming, and guardianship of all land-based animals. The animals and Adam were created directly from the earth, but animals were animated, or given life, by the word or will of God. Adam was given the breath of God and he became a living soul, but Eve was created from living tissue and bone taken from Adam. This reproduction of a woman from the bone and tissue of a man is the first and only authorized recreation of a human being, and there was a successful transfer of the soul. The only being capable of making this move successfully is God.

The modern-day cloning technology that man has stumbled upon has a lot of problems and will have more when human cloning becomes a reality. I know human cloning has been banned in America. That only means it is illegal, which doesn't stop people from doing what they want to do in America. Some other countries have not even gone as far as banning it yet. I think you can safely say that, somewhere on today's earth, someone is actively trying to clone humans. The act is clearly beyond God's reason for man's existence. God has done a fine job as Creator and he does not need our help. Creation does not suffer until man disobeys God. The questions you could raise over the human cloning issue are too numerous to get into at length, but I will advance a few.

It is not clearly known how God arranged the transfer of the soul from the original created beings to their offspring, but it is obvious that both genders are in God's plan for reproduction. How do men using tissue samples from one person transfer the soul to their product? If man's product is not a living soul, then what is it? What does it do, this man that another man created? Who owns this created man? Do we refer to a man that another man created as an it or a he? Is it a mindless, no-souled, unfeeling, flesh machine? Who are the parents of this man-made man? Will it be used as a military article or what? I could go on and on, but you get the message here. If men cannot live together knowing they are alike, what on earth will they do with a life-form that is not really human?

The first man was not a mindless, grunting caveman who evolved from some unknown origin. He named all of God's creatures and had been given dominion over them. The scene in verses 19 and 20 present a world without fear, danger, struggles, or opposition of any kind. Verse 25 shows the innocence of the original couple: "And they were both naked, the man and his wife, and they were not ashamed." (I will amplify this verse in the next Chapter.)

Perfection, from God's point-of-view, is clearly seen here. Man has the clearest possible knowledge of his responsibility to nature, to other creatures on earth and his relationship with his mate. It is clearly spelled out in verse 24 that you leave the family that you came from to marry a mate and start your own family. One man with one woman, one wife with one husband, was God's original plan. The things that men did later with plural wives, harems, and concubines were not God's original plan. There were many other things done that God winked at and covered by the cross until the law came and clarified many of those things that man did not know.

CHAPTER 3

Genesis makes it clear that the fall of mankind was not God's desire. The testing of mankind's loyalty to and faith in the Creator was established by only one restriction in the midst of a multitude of prosperity and privilege. God, as Creator, has a plan for man to serve his Universe in some capacity, but there can be no questions about who man would serve.

The first test of loyalty came from Lucifer. The scriptures tell us that Lucifer is an angel who rebelled against God. The Bible also tells us that a full one-third of the angels in heaven joined Lucifer in this rebellion. The Bible does not give a detailed biography of Lucifer, but it is plain from scripture that he has miraculous powers on earth and ready-access to God.

In Chapter 3, we see the serpent identified as the most cunning of God's beasts of the field. The fact that Lucifer is in total control of the serpent is obvious when he engages Eve in a conversation at the forbidden fruit tree. The conversation that follows provides an in-depth look at how Lucifer can and will use whomever or whatever is available to turn God's creation against him (Gen. 3:1–7).

> Gen. 3:1 Now the serpent was more cunning than any beast of the field which the Lord God had made. And he said to the woman, "Has God indeed said, "You shall not eat of every tree of the garden?"

2 And the woman said to the serpent, "We may eat the fruit of the trees of the garden;

3 but of the fruit of the tree which is in the midst of the garden, God has said, "You shall not eat it, nor shall you touch it, lest you die."

4 Then the serpent said to the woman, "You will not surely die.

5 For God knows that in the day you eat of it your eyes will be opened, and you will be like God, knowing good and evil."

6 So when the woman saw that the tree was good for food, that it was pleasant to the eyes, and a tree desirable to make one wise, she took of its fruit and ate. She also gave to her husband with her, and he ate.

7 Then the eyes of both of them were opened and they knew that they were naked; and they sewed fig leaves together and made themselves coverings.

Note: Coverings are translated elsewhere as girding coverings or aprons.

In verse 1, Lucifer opens with a question that seeks to cast a doubt in Eve's mind about God's honesty and motives toward Adam and herself. In verses 2 and 3, Eve answers the question. However, in verse 3, she adds something to her answer that was not in God's command to Adam at Genesis 2:17, when God told him, "but of the tree of knowledge of good and evil you shall not eat, for in the day that you eat of it you shall surely die."

In following the order of the events, we find that Eve was probably not there when God commanded the man not to eat from that tree (Gen. 2:16). He did not say anything about touching that forbidden tree. Adam truly loved Eve. The only person who could have told Eve not to touch the unlawful tree was Adam. The Bible does not include the context of any conversation where Adam might have said, "Do not touch this tree."

The common opinion would be that Adam's love for Eve was so powerful and dedicated that he would not want her to even touch the tree that bore the forbidden fruit: That is love. It is also the biggest and most common mistake made by even the most devout Christians—adding to, or subtracting from, what God says (Rev. 22:18–19).

Lucifer, the most prolific misquoter of scripture since the world began, will always be waiting to take advantage of what you do not know. He even attempted to confuse Jesus by misquoting scriptures in Matthew 4:1–11. Follow me into a what if: What if the serpent is curled up in the tree while he is talking to Eve. (Verse 6 strongly suggests that the whole conversation took place at the tree.) Her well-meaning misinformation becomes a major negative to her because the serpent is in the tree and he did not die. In verse 4, when Lucifer says to the woman that she will not die for touching the tree, he looks like the proof of that. In the woman's mind, and based on the misinformation she accepted, God is not telling the truth.

That is how slick and slippery Lucifer is and that is how he deceives and takes advantage of the whole world. He uses what we do not know against us. He uses what we think we know against us. He uses what we almost know against us. He destroys us through our lack of the true knowledge of God (Hosea 4:6). How many times did Jesus warn or tell his apostles and disciples not to be deceived? Lucifer's ability to deceive, then and now, is still his most basic tool. Lucifer has an open door into the woman's mind now.

In verse 5, Lucifer accuses God of keeping them in the dark and keeping them from being as God. In verse 6, the temptation to disobey God has taken full bloom now because what began as a conversation has been transformed into a physical act of rebellion against God by the woman. She follows the flesh. Appetite—good for food. Eyes—pleasant to look at. Ego—desire for a wisdom that the Creator had forbidden. The woman of flesh who lived by the spirit has allowed another power to control and enter her spiritual psyche. The Satanic conversation and influence has become a very real physical power in her life and body now.

The Bible does not say whether or not Lucifer had ever tried to tempt Adam, but the fact that he had power over his wife made Adam a much easier target. Lucifer could and did employ his latest acquisition against Adam. Eve, his beloved spouse, would be used against her husband the same way the serpent was used against her.

Adam broke God's law. How significant is that? Referring to I Cor. 15:20-26, only two men are capable of affecting all humankind by their actions—Adam and Jesus Christ. The two representative men are directly from God. Adam is God's direct creation and Christ is his only begotten son. Adam breaks the bond of fellowship with God and, now that his eyes are opened, he and Eve see their nakedness.

I want to clarify Chapters 1 and 2 as they relate to Adam and Eve's vision. They had perfect vision before they ate the forbidden fruit. They had been designed to live forever as flawless beings with excellent vision and they could see that neither of them was wearing clothing or coverings of any kind. The question is, what happened to them and made them feel a need for cover? The answer is tied to what they learned when they ingested the knowledge of good and evil.

The knowledge of good and evil enabled them to experience lust when looking at each other's nakedness. Now they are the only creatures in the earth who crave sex from the newly acquired knowledge of lust instead of the God-ordained command to reproduce. In other words, the human sex drive is controlled by the type of lust that Satan used to make the great King David, a man after God's heart, watch a woman bathing and wind up murdering her husband to cover up his adultery with her, as stated in Chapter 11 of 2 Samuel.

We see the same lust driving the multibillion dollar pornography industry and all other media-hyped advertising lures that use the slogan "SEX SELLS," and riding it to the bank at the expense of society. Adam and Eve are now aware of good and evil, but they have no way to retain the good and control the evil. Lucifer had convinced them that they would be as God with this knowledge of good and evil and they never stopped to think it through.

God had not created them to be gods. God, the Creator, wanted them to serve him. Lust is steering the human sex drive now, so chastity rules are needed to keep people from all types of abusive, immoral sex acts. The position of man is futile. He has rendered himself incapable of providing the services that he was created for and he has given Lucifer access to the earth and power to tempt humanity through the newly acquired knowledge of good and evil.

The good or best thing for Adam to do would have been to obey God and pass the first test, then maybe he would have learned more about God's ultimate will for humanity. Mankind is currently trying to get back to the spot from which Adam fell.

The deadly consequences of Adam's fall are too numerous to go into here, but we must amplify these few.

> **1. Adam once enjoyed God's presence. Now, his guilt made him hide.**
>
> **2. Adam once was clean in heart and mind. Now, he is polluted in both.**
>
> **3. Adam and Eve's nakedness once was as natural as creatures today, in their natural state. Now, the temptations of the mind, along with the lust of the heart, have made nakedness a shameful thing to them.**

Another deadly consequence of Adam's fall is that the dominion mankind had over the earth, and the order to take care of it, is now in danger because of the power Adam and Eve surrendered to Lucifer when they disobeyed God. The earth is now the victim of every kind of pollution and mismanagement that people who put money ahead of posterity can get away with. The earth is man's only home and man is the worst enemy the earth has.

The fallen condition of mankind begins to come out under God's questions to Adam in verse 11: "And He said, "Who told you that you were naked? Have you eaten from the tree of which I commanded you that you should not eat?" Adam answers God in verse 12: "Then the man said, "The woman whom you gave to be with me, she gave me of the tree, and I ate."

The woman that God gave him, the beautiful female that Adam described in Genesis 2:23 as bone of his bone and flesh of his flesh, is now blamed as the one who gave him the fruit, as if to say, "God should have kept the woman or the woman should have kept the fruit." He left out the fact that he should have refused the fruit and kept his commandment from God.

Satan offered the second Adam, Jesus Christ, the glory of all the kingdoms of the world (Matt. 4:8–10), but he chose not to pass the duty of obedience to others. He was obedient unto death. Adam tries to dodge his responsibility by passing the fault for Eve onto God, then passing the fault for eating the fruit onto Eve. Eve tells about how she was beguiled by the serpent, but she cannot deny the fact that she clearly knew God's commandment, even if it had been altered.

The serpent whose body Satan used is the first to be cursed. He is cursed above all creatures. He and his offspring would crawl on their belly and eat dust for all time, in Gen. 3:14. I don't want the reader to be confused here by any of the many evolution "THEORIES" that people accept without evidence, or get caught up in the idea that the book of Genesis is just a poem, so I want to point out a few facts as we go along: Did God say snakes would crawl on their belly? How do snakes travel? Why do most people feel they should kill a snake whenever and wherever they see one?

Continuing to verse 16 (I will deal with verse 15 later), the passage covers the next to be cursed—the woman.

> **Gen. 3:16 To the woman He said: "I will greatly multiply your sorrow and your conception, In pain you shall bring forth children; Your desire shall be for your husband, And he shall rule over you."**

The birthing process would require a painful monthly cycle for conception. Childbirth would become a painful and risky undertaking. The woman is clearly put in subjection to the man and he is given leadership of the first and most effective social program ever invented—THE FAMILY. Ask yourself: Do women undergo a painful monthly cycle during childbearing years? Is childbearing risky and dangerous?

The third part of the curse for the female is that she is to "be in subjection to the husband and he shall rule over the wife." This means exactly what God said. That does not give a man the right to drive his wife and family like cattle; it compels him to lead by example, as a shepherd would. The wife who must rule her husband not only risks ruining her marriage, she also has challenged God with her act of disobedience.

God's word makes it so simple that a child could understand it and God simply will not fail and quit being the moral ruler and Creator of the whole Universe because people choose to disobey him. He has to be

God because no one else is qualified for the job. Do not let Satan talk you into standing against God's revealed word and think God cannot and or will not defend his word. God gives us a lifetime to figure that out. Then, you must die from the body and give God an account of how you chose to deal with what he said.

In 1 & 2 Timothy and Titus, Paul's pastoral epistles give the qualifications for New Testament ministers. Paul's revelation is clear in 1 Timothy 2:9–15.

> **1 Tim. 2:9 in like manner also, that the women adorn themselves in modest apparel, with propriety and moderation, not with braided hair or gold or pearls or costly clothing,**
>
> **10 but, which is proper for women professing Godliness, with good works.**
>
> **11 Let a woman learn in silence with all submission.**
>
> **12 And I do not permit a woman to teach or have authority over a man, but to be in silence.**
>
> **13 For Adam was formed first, then Eve.**
>
> **14 And Adam was not deceived, but the woman being deceived, fell into transgression.**
>
> **15 Nevertheless she will be saved in childbearing, if they continue in faith, love, and holiness, with self control.**

Any woman who says God called her to preach is calling God a liar. In verse 12, the type of woman who seeks to overthrow the man is referred to as a usurper. Paul is led back to the original curse and makes it plain that what God laid on humankind, because of their disobedience, is in effect until God removes it. The order of Satan's successful attack is no doubt the reason for God's actions. God's action is protective. People who choose to ignore God's order have challenged God in the same way that Satan did.

The woman gave in to temptation and was, no doubt, the only tool Satan could effectively use to get to the man. God placed them in the positions that he thought they were best suited for and he did not have to ask for permission. The commandment is tied to the self-inflicted curse and it is as plain as day: The man is commanded to lead within his family.

Because of Satan's presence the world is not ready to be what God intended. Spiritual warfare is being waged daily. The physical wars always come after the spiritual wars have been lost, as stated in James 4: 1–4.

> Jas. 4:1 Where do wars and fights come from among you? Do they not come from your desires for pleasure that war in your members?
>
> 2 You lust and do not have. You murder and covet and cannot obtain. You fight and war. Yet you do not have because you do not ask.
>
> 3 You ask and do not receive, because you ask amiss, that you may spend it on your pleasures.
>
> 4 Adulterers and adulteresses! Do you not know that friendship with the world is enmity with God? Whoever therefore wants to be a friend of the world makes himself an enemy of God.

The human family has to organize into a spiritual fighting force in order to survive. The man is head, priest, trainer, and front-line warrior for his home in the spiritual fight against Satan and his demonic army. The spiritual warfare is not fought with guns or bombs. The spiritual warfare is fought by having the family leader teach the family how to honor the Creator, reestablish contact with him through repentance, work toward the knowledge and faith needed to repel every attack that Satan makes on the family, pray for the spiritual success of all families and serve in true spiritual organizations—CHURCHES—that teach and promote these values.

The reason God put the man in charge is clearly spelled out by Paul in 1 Timothy 2:13–15. The idea that God, the Father, called a woman to be a church overseer goes against the revealed will of God, the Holy Spirit, and sounds like Satan tempting women again with something they think will make them wise. Obedience is the quality needed for those who wish to serve God at the next level. The next move on Satan's agenda is to use the woman to convince her man that God's words are not true and that some spirit (demonic, of course) called her to do something that God clearly said she should not do. Then, here we go again falling for the oldest trick in the book—literally, the oldest trick in the Book.

God's word will not fail because people choose not to obey it. The curse on the serpent affected its ability to ambulate and its social status among other creatures. The curse on the woman affected her body and position in the family. The curse on Adam affected everything else in Genesis 3:17–19.

> Gen. 3:17 Then to Adam He said, "Because you have heeded the voice of your wife, and have eaten from the tree of which I commanded you, saying, "You shall not eat of it:" "Cursed is the ground for your sake; In toil you shall eat of it all the days of your life.
>
> 18 Both thorns and thistles it shall bring forth for you, And you shall eat the herb of the field.
>
> 19 In the sweat of your face you shall eat bread, Till you return to the ground, For out of it you were taken; For dust you are and to dust you shall return."

Because Adam listened to his wife and flagrantly disobeyed the clearly known commandment of God, cursed is the ground because of him. The ground will not yield food without effort by those who eat it. The two humans are spiritually dead now and their bodies are no longer immortal. Their days are numbered and the end of their mortal lives is just a matter of time.

The condition Adam and Eve brought upon themselves will be the inheritance of their offspring, which is, with the exception of Jesus Christ, all of humanity. The co-eternal soul of man must still give account for his acts and deeds while in the body. The sin of this representative man opened a door to the evils that Satan brings upon all of humanity.

The most common question you hear when people suffer is, "Why did God bring a tragedy to me?" People must be careful not to blame God for problems they create for themselves, the problems Satan brings to you because you serve God, or the problems that come to all of us because we are currently living in an imperfect world.

Consider a man sitting on a curb after drinking too much and hitting an innocent child on a bike who has the right of way—and he wants to know why God did this to him? The truth is, God did not entice the man to drink and drive. Satan did. The man gave in to what he knew was illegal. The man was wrong. Satan orchestrated pain for the innocent, but we should blame Adam for letting him in.

Consider a confused young couple sitting in a hospital wondering why God let their child be the only one in the nursery that has severe birth defects. The two of them took all of the safety precautions and cannot figure out what happened. God did not hurt a child. If everything was done correctly in delivery, then Satan, who comes to steal, kill and destroy, did it and it did not have to be on account of how bad they are. It could be that Satan, who can see to the future, may have seen that God has some good thing for that couple to do and handicapped their child to try to stop them. Don't blame God for that. Satan did it, but Adam let him in. This is war.

The nature of the fight must be understood. Do bad things happen to good people? Of course they do—read the Book of Job. The careful student, counselor, or minister must always keep this in mind when trying to determine the cause of some tragedy. In verse 15, God reveals his course of action in the battle for humanity.

> **Gen. 3:15 and I will put enmity, Between you and the woman, And between your seed and her Seed; He shall bruise your head, And you shall bruise his heel."**

Satan would continue to tempt, entice, trick, confuse, lie to, lie on and lie about God's people from generation to generation. A virgin woman would bring forth a child that God, the Holy Spirit, would procreate. This man would be like Adam was before he fell. The second Adam would not be born with the sin sickness that sinful Adam passed to humanity. The sin sickness can be seen, even in children at an early age, when you note the natural tendency to do what is wrong. It takes work and discipline to do what is right.

Christ would have the same attributes of pre-fall Adam, but he would not have any of the advantages Adam had. Adam came into a world where everything was in his favor. He only had one restriction and no fear of death if he heeded it. Christ came into a world in which Satan had control. He was a fugitive before he was born and, unlike Adam, he had to live sinless and die to satisfy God's death sentence on sinful mankind.

In death, Satan bruised his heel, while Christ gave Satan a mortal head wound when he partook of death for humanity, defeated death and got up out of the grave. The person who does not want to take advantage of the soul-saving work of Christ must realize that one sin is all it takes to destroy their soul.

The promise of a Savior was made before the first generation was born and would stand as a beacon of hope for humanity. In other words, Jesus is the check that God wrote to cover the sins of the world. The sins of the worst human that ever lived is paid for by God's check, based on God's conditions—repent, love Christ, accept his law as law, deny self, learn his will, love both friends and enemies, be obedient to his word—and God's check will buy you eternal salvation.

Adam and Eve were driven out of the Garden of Eden to keep them from the tree of life. The tree of life is mentioned again for those who overcome the sin of this world in Revelations 22:1–3, and verse 3 tells of the time when the curse is over.

> **Rev. 22:3 And there shall be no more curse, but the throne of God and of the Lamb shall be in it, and His servants shall serve Him.**

A lot of Bible must be fulfilled before the end of the curse, but the believer's reward is knowing it will end, and service to God will be the overcomer's focal point.

The branch of every sinful, greedy, dishonest, lustful and ungodly act throughout human history leads back to Adam's act of disobedience as its roots. I have heard of national surveys taken that say most Americans, Christians included, have some doubts about the existence of Satan.

The same Bible that tells you about God also gives you the knowledge of and information on Satan, the devil, also known as Lucifer, the serpent and the dragon. Anyone who reads this book and fails to see the fruit and influence of Satan is simply rejecting reality. They will never understand the Bible they are rewriting in their minds because it is not real. The battle lines are clearly established with Satan's entry in this Chapter. The war will rage throughout the Bible until he is put down for good at Revelations 20:10.

God said Adam would surely die the day he ate the forbidden fruit. While the bible does not say how long Adam had lived before he ate the forbidden fruit, all indications are that most of his 930-year-life was lived after he disobeyed God.

Did God's words at Gen. 2:17 fail? Of course not. Adam died the spiritual death that day, leaving all human beings that came from him with the same basic need if they want to be saved. Nicodemus, the religious Pharisee who came to Jesus by night to acknowledge his Godly origin, John 3, had to learn what all people need to know. To clearly understand spiritual rebirth, read John 3: 1-21 with special attention to verses 3 through 10.

Spiritually dead and physically dying Adam, and we who are born of dying flesh and able to reproduce in the flesh, must be born again of God's spirit to get back on eternal basis with God.

Adam's failure made Christ's success a must for those who accept him. The term *born again Christian*, is established on these facts and as spiritually inspired Peter stated at Acts 4:12, Jesus Christ is the only name given among men that we can call on to be saved.

CHAPTER 4

In Chapter 4 of Genesis, we can see a graphic example of how losing the spiritual warfare within oneself leads to physical acts of aggression. This lesson is taught by the well-known story of the struggles between Cain and Abel, two of the many children of Adam and Eve.

The Bible does not say how many other sons and daughters Adam and Eve had, or whether any of these other sons and daughters lived during Cain and Abel's narative. This chapter of Genesis only mentions three sons of Adam and Eve, but it is obvious from Genesis 5:3–4 that other sons and daughters were born to the first couple. In fact, I have read commentaries that say Adam and Eve were the direct parents of at least 56 children. I cannot prove this from scripture and I am not aware of oral tradition or historical data that supports that number. All I can say is that it would have been relatively easy for people who lived as long as they did to have that many children.

According to the first two verses of Genesis 4, Cain was raised to be a farmer and Abel was raised to be a shepherd. During this time, men began to make offerings to God. The Bible does not go into detail about why men began to make offerings to God at this time, but we know that the rite was established and clearly understood by the first generation born on earth because Cain and Abel made offerings to God (Gen. 4:3–5). Because of their occupations, Cain made offerings from the field and Abel made offerings from the flock to God.

Gen. 4:3 And in the process of time it came to pass that Cain brought an offering of the fruit of the ground to the Lord.

4 Abel also brought of the firstborn of his flock and of their fat. And the Lord respected Abel and his offering,

5 but He did not respect Cain and his offering. And Cain was very angry, and his countenance fell.

I have read and heard many opinions about why God rejected Cain's offering. Some ministers go as far as saying this was because Cain was Satan's son, but Eve thanked God in Genesis 4:1 after her husband, Adam, had known her in the biblical sense of the word. This disproves any speculation about Cain's physical lineage.

God's rejection is no doubt based on the attitude of the giver and the quality of the gift. Abel gave the first born of his flock, while Cain's gift is not described as his first fruits. The fact that God had respect for Abel's offering and rejected Cain's should give some insight into the character of each man because God would not just single Cain out to pick on him, as verses 6 and 7 clearly point out.

Gen. 4:6 So the Lord said to Cain, "Why are you angry? And Why has your countenance fallen?

7 If you do well, will you not be accepted? And if you do not do well, sin lies at the door. And its desire is for you, but you should rule over it."

The attitude of Cain is shown through his obvious sullen, angry demeanor. All he had to do to be accepted was the right thing. The fact that God told Cain that he did not do well proves that either the gift or the giver, or both, has some serious flaws. Cain clearly is in control here—do well or not do well; he had a choice.

The original sin of Adam and Eve may have seemed like a small thing, but it certainly was not. The first child born with the knowledge of good and evil is about to show how dangerous it is when you have the awareness of something in your mind that can create a temptation in your physical body. The knowledge of good and evil is about to become an act of pure evil in the hands of a man who cannot control it. Then he becomes a spiritual child of Satan by choice.

The fact that Satan is in the world and can use his supernatural powers to enhance the temptation is evident in Genesis 4:7. God tells Cain if he does not do well, sin (also described as "the fruit of the devil") desires to work through him or to have him. The strength of verse 7 is revealed when God tells Cain that he can rule over evil, temptation and the Devil himself, if he does not give in to them.

The same principals are in action today if all people could do well and rule over the desire to do wrong. The righteous actions of a minority of people would ease a lot of confusion between individuals, groups, or nations. James speaks of the human's way out of situations similar to Cain's situation. Please read James 1:12–24 and James 4:1–10 (NKJV). In James 4:7, James goes to the bottom line: "Therefore submit to God. Resist the devil and he will flee from you."

The truth for us is the same as it was for Cain. Satan's mission is to exploit every human weakness we have, use whatever ammunition he can obtain, appeal to the weakness in our flesh, and use every act of deception available to turn us away from our Creator. Human beings here appear to be pawns in a battle that began before our creation, but that does not diminish a human's responsibility to obey his Creator.

Cain could not overcome his emotions. Not doing well led to Cain's offerings not being accepted. Not being accepted by God led to Cain's jealousy and hatred of Abel because God accepted Abel's actions and offerings, not because of something Abel did to Cain. The jealousy and hatred raging uncontrollably in Cain's soul and mind comes out in anger directed at Abel. Cain takes on the physical act of violence toward him and kills the innocent brother.

Cain has no defense for his actions. God's question about Abel's whereabouts in verse 9 brings the type of response we have learned to expect from Cain: "I don't know." Of course, he knew. Then Cain said, "Am I my brother's keeper?" The sarcasm in that question after what Cain had just done is amazing. Cain's punishment is laid out in verses 11 and 12.

> Gen. 4:11 So now you are cursed from the earth, which has opened its mouth to receive your brother's blood from your hand.

12 When you till the ground, it shall no longer yield its strength to you. A fugitive and a vagabond you shall be on the earth."

In verse 14, Cain worries about what will happen to him. Cain commits murder, then complains about the exile and worries about being slain—what a nerve. In verse 15, another important point to the story of Cain and Abel is that the mark of Cain was not a curse. It was actually an identifying mark that protected Cain.

Gen. 4:14 Surely you have driven me out this day from the face of the ground; I shall be hidden from your face; I shall be a fugitive and a vagabond on the earth, and it will happen that anyone that finds me will kill me."

15 And the Lord said to him, "Therefore, whoever kills Cain, vengeance shall be taken on him sevenfold." And the Lord set a mark on Cain, lest anyone finding him should kill him.

The Bible and history have recorded many cases where brothers have slain brothers, but there is usually some controversy or confusion surrounding the slaying. In the house of King David, there were two such incidents: Absalom killed Amnon for raping his full sister, and Solomon killed Adonijah for trying to take the King's power and throne in Israel. Ideals and wars have pitted brothers against brothers throughout history. Sometimes the innocent one will win in the here and now, but the righteous ones will be exalted forever in the hereafter.

The identifying mark that God put on Cain to single him out and protect him has been a controversial topic. Some white groups (and even some religions groups) believe that God made Cain a Negro or dark-skinned person, making all Negroes and dark-skinned people the descendants of Cain and inherently evil. On the other hand, some Black, Arab and Oriental groups believe that white-skinned people bear the mark of Cain and some call them blue-eyed devils and so on and so forth.

This label has been applied to various groups over the years by people who have never understood what they read in the Bible. The Bible does not identify the mark of Cain, but it is absolutely ridiculous to slander anyone over it because none of Cain's descendants survived the flood. The Bible says only one line of Adam's descendents, from his son Seth, lived through the flood. The earth was repopulated after the flood, not by Cain's descendents, but by just this one line of descendents of Seth.

One of the first things most people ask when reading Chapter 4 of Genesis is, "Where did Cain find his wife if his parents were the only people and all people came from them?" I will address this in more detail later, but in terms of Chapter 4, the Bible does not give a lot of information about their lives. It only amplifies certain areas. Since all humans came from Adam's blood, instead of asking where Cain's wife came from, the next logical question might be to ask when Cain's wife entered the scene.

The Bible says that in the process of time, Cain and Abel made sacrifices to God. The fact that they were taking the initiative to perform this rite may mean that they were already heads of their families. Cain could have already been married. If so, his wife would have been one of his sisters and she would have been compelled to suffer the same fate as Cain.

On the other hand, Cain may have been a wanderer and vagabond for hundreds of years until the population caught up with him. The world's population could have been well over two billion people by the time Cain's father, Adam, died (Gen. 5:5). You can only speculate about Cain's age when he married. However, if he were Noah's age (500 years old) when he began a family, the population, which was turning away from God at that time, would have given Cain a wide variety of choices.

The author of Genesis simply deals with all he knows of Cain when he wrote about him. He does not deal with the order of the events or tell us Cain's age when he got a wife. In Genesis 4:16–17, the verses could mean that Cain had a wife when he went to dwell in the land of Nod, or that he waited until the population expanded to the area. Neither view is hard to take on faith, but to accept any account suggesting that not all humans came from Adam is a total break from scripture.

We know that Cain had only one wife. Lamech, one of Cain's descendants, is the first man named who had more than one wife (Gen. 4:19). The practice started again at some point after the flood, although the male survivors of the flood, Noah and his sons, had only one wife each.

Cain found prosperity in his lifetime and some of his descendants became founders of various trades and crafts. The Bible does not give any more information on Cain beyond this.

Chapter 4 ends dealing with Adam and Eve again. In Genesis 4:25, Eve sees the birth of Seth as the good person God gave her to replace Abel, her murdered son. The final verse in Chapter 4 gives ample proof that God is still interested in man and some men were being led to seek God as well (Gen. 4:26).

CHAPTER 5

The generations of Adam are covered in Chapter 5 of Genesis. The vital facts revealed should confirm even the weakest believer's faith (Gen. 5:1–3).

> Gen. 5:1 This is the book of the genealogy of Adam. In the day that God created man, He made him in the likeness of God.
>
> 2 He created them male and female, and blessed them and called them Mankind in the day they were created.
>
> 3 And Adam lived one hundred and thirty years, and begot a son in his own likeness, after his image, and named him Seth.

The first three verses of Chapter 5 echo the last two verses of Chapter 4. The fact that Abel offered God his best and was accepted by God leaves no doubt that Abel loved God and tried to serve him. Abel, Seth and repentant Adam and Eve appear to be on the right track with God.

The verses about the generations of Adam are a remarkable blessing. Many casual Bible readers call them boring, but the information in these verses can be very useful when rebutting some of the dangerous theories that are creeping into public schools as facts. The genealogy from Adam to Noah gives the father's age when each son in this line was born. From this, we learn how many years transpired between the time Adam was created and Noah begat Shem, Ham and Japheth—1,556 years.

Only ten sons are recorded, but that would not give an accurate count of a generation. The age of each father varies and there is no evidence to prove the sons named were first-born sons. For example, Noah was 500 years old when he begat Shem, Ham and Japheth (Gen. 5:32). It is not known whether they were triplets, or if the first son was born when Noah was 500 years old.

In any event, that would be 10 generations for the unnamed lines of people if you are using 50 years as a generation instead of the 40 years normally used in the Old Testament. The number of generations from Adam to Noah's sons would be 31 (using 50 years per generation).

The actual names, ages at birth and ages at death of the people named make it clear that the author is not dealing with speculation, guesswork or theory. The words are confirmed by God, then accepted by the author as truth and written as fact.

You may question how I concluded earlier that there were over 2 billion people on earth by the time Adam died. The following population numbers are established from the few figures I could feel safe using in Chapter 5. The following figures are an assumption on my part, but if you study through it with me, you can see how I came to my conclusion. (The statement made earlier about reading in a commentary that Adam and Eve had 56 children will be abandoned here for a figure that I can support from the scriptures.)

According to Genesis 5:4, the original couple, Adam and Eve, had other sons and daughters after Cain, Abel and Seth. I will use three sons and three daughters because the Bible not only names a specific son in Seth's line, but also specifies sons and daughters (plural) born to each person. If each of the three couples produced three couples each, consider the number of offspring that would be produced for 18 generations.

Generation Table

Generation 1:	3 couples produce 3 each = 9 couples
Generation 2:	9 couples produce 3 each = 27 couples
Generation 3:	27 couples produce 3 each = 81 couples
Generation 4:	81 couples produce 3 each = 243 couples
Generation 5:	243 couples produce 3 each = 729 couples
Generation 6:	729 couples produce 3 each = 2,187 couples
Generation 7:	2,187 couples produce 3 each = 6,561 couples
Generation 8:	6,561 couples produce 3 each = 19,683 couples
Generation 9:	19,683 couples produce 3 each = 59,049 couples
Generation 10:	59,049 couples produce 3 each = 177,147 couples
Generation 11:	177,147 couples produce 3 each = 531,441 couples
Generation 12:	531,441 couples produce 3 each = 1,594,323 couples
Generation 13:	1,594,323 couples produce 3 each = 4,782,969 couples
Generation 14:	4,782,969 couples produce 3 each = 14,348,907 couples
Generation 15:	14,348,907 couples produce 3 each = 43,046,721 couples
Generation 16:	43,046,721 couples produce 3 each = 129,222,111 couples
Generation 17:	129,222,111 couples produce 3 each = 387,666,333 couples
Generation 18:	387,666,333 couples produce 3 each = 1,162,998,999 couples

Eighteen generations, multiplied by 50 years per generation, would be 900 years. Adam lived 930 years, so when Adam and Eve passed away, all of the people numbered in generations 1 through 18 could still have been alive and would add up to 1,162,917,048 people. The 18th generation total of 1,162,998,999 couples, multiplied by two people, would be 2,325,997,998 people. The 18th generation, plus the existing people, would make the earth's population 3,488,915,046 people.

The figure previously mentioned as the number of people on earth when Adam died (two billion) is an assumption that allows a full one-third of the population's death through murders, wars, famines, disease—anything except old age, since people lived so much longer then.

Noah would be born 21 generations after Adam through Seth's line. (This line is the only line of people from this multitude that are discussed in any detail, with the exception of the brief biography of Cain.) The fact that Noah is 500 years old when he fathers children gives even more evidence of how long the childbearing years were in those days and could add more credibility to how conservative my figures actually are.

The earth before the flood could have had some very advanced civilizations since the people would have lived long enough to accumulate, analyze and test more information in one lifetime than we ever could, given the shorter lifespan of our times. I would not be surprised if scientists or oceanographers were to find cities or relics under the ocean that remained under water after the flood. For example, if the fabled continent called Atlantis is ever found, it could be some pre-flood society that lived near or below sea level when the flood came and remained under water when the waters receded.

I am not making these statements on the basis of biblical proof. I am advancing some ideas that should let the reader know that a discovery of some society we cannot identify with today should not give us license to doubt scripture. Also, there would be no common sense reason for God to want us to know much about a group that was so bad that he had to destroy all but eight people in it to continue his purpose for creating man.

A question in your mind may be whether God condoned the marriages of brothers and sisters, especially since I previously stated that Cain could have already been married to one of his sisters when he killed Abel. The answer is: YES, HE DID—AT THAT TIME. It was not a sin until God, who is the only being who can make it SIN, made it a sin. He made it a sin in the law of Moses, or correctly stated, the law of God through Moses. This is explained in Leviticus 18:1–30, with an emphasis on verses 6, 9 and 10.

> **Leviticus 18:6 None of you shall approach anyone who is near of kin to him, to uncover his nakedness: I am the Lord.**
>
> **9 The nakedness of your sister, the daughter of your father, or the daughter of your mother, whether born at home or elsewhere, their nakedness you shall not uncover.**
>
> **10 The nakedness of your son's daughter or your daughter's daughter, their nakedness you shall not uncover; for theirs is your own nakedness.**

The relationships identified in Chapter 18 of Leviticus are strictly forbidden. While a lineage distance that determines near kin in Leviticus 18:6 is not clearly stated, the law on inbreeding is clear. The man Abraham, head of the Hebrews, was married to his half-sister Sarah some 500 years before that law. Abraham had one of the best marriages in scripture and it was not a sin (Gen. 20:12).

The Old Testament church nation, Israel, and the New Testament church were then and are now responsible for passing on these laws from the Creator to the world. Israel as an Old Testament church nation had many Satanically inspired internal problems, out-and-out power struggles, problems with understanding the law, problems with assimilating the law and problems passing the law on to the next generations. Israel had some of every kind of problem you can imagine when the people rebelled against God.

The New Testament church has fallen into the same category. These laws, along with many other key laws that have major effects on humanity, are rarely dealt with in churches. When the light of understanding fails to shine through God's appointed bulbs, the end result is that the world in darkness remains in darkness.

The genealogy in Chapter 5 of Genesis is a valuable tool against the many theories about the origin and age of humans on earth. The different dating techniques used today often contradict each other, while some have proven false under testing. The Bible prepares us for these situations as the Apostle Paul passes the torch to the young minister, Timothy, as he warns him not to heed unproven information (1 Tim. 6: 20–21).

> **1 Tim. 6:20 O Timothy! Guard what was committed to your trust, avoiding the profane and idle babblings and contradictions of what is falsely called knowledge—**
>
> **21 by professing it some have strayed concerning the faith. Grace be with you. Amen.**

The statement sounds like it was meant for our times when we look at the way different church denominations shift Bible doctrine around to make it comply with their opinion, or reject scripture altogether if it does not fit into the politics of a given church denomination. The other false knowledge problems Paul warns about would be some of the unproven theories that have gained enough credibility to be accepted as fact.

Chapter 5 details a historical record using names, ages and events that are passed on from human to human without the long unproven, unexplainable time periods between that are common to theories.

CHAPTER 6

The first and second verses of Chapter 6 are recognized by many theologians today as two of the most controversial verses in the Book of Genesis.

> Gen. 6:1 Now it came to pass, when men began to multiply on the face of the earth, and daughters were born to them,
>
> 2 that the sons of God saw the daughters of men, that they were beautiful; and they took wives for themselves of all whom they chose.

I would like to introduce a few of the opinions a person might encounter on the above subject and add the only opinion I can render, an opinion supported by biblical proof and logic compiled from having the Bible and history to work with.

Opinion 1: The terms "sons of God" and "daughters of men" refer to righteous Seth's offspring intermarrying with unrighteous Cain's offspring. I don't know how scripture will support this view, even though some of the males from Seth's line could and may have intermarried with some of the females from Cain's line. The one line of descendents from Seth to Noah is less than one man per generation. On the other hand, Seth and each of the other named descendants up to Noah had other unnamed sons and daughters that were too unrighteous to be saved and could have multiplied into millions of lost people. The righteous line of descendents that stayed with God could not be numbered with the fallen group that did not survive the flood.

Opinion 2: The terms refer to class and society marriages with the wealthy upper-class men identified as sons of God and the females of lower social status identified as daughters of men. The Bible identifies both rich and poor people who are saved, so this view cannot possibly stand up under Bible scrutiny. If wealthy, upper-class men are sons of God, the rich man in Luke 16:19–31 who wanted God to let poor Lazarus touch his tongue with a mere fingertip of water would have been a son of God based on this opinion. Or, King Herod, the rich powerful ruler who tried to murder Christ, would be greater than Christ because Christ does not have Herod's position in life. Nero, the roman emperor who wreaked havoc on the 1st century Christian church, could say his wealth and power made him a son of God and foster the idea that you can buy Godliness with a large bank account and the right social connections.

Opinion 3: The terms mean that, literally, sons of God in Heaven fathered children with women born of men on earth. I believe what the Bible says is literal here and these sons of God are just that. The Bible does not say how long it was before these marriages started, but the sons of God appear to be some of those that made up the heavenly court similar to the ones identified in Job 1:6–7.

> **Job 1:6 Now there was a day when the sons of God came to present themselves before the Lord, and Satan also came among them.**
>
> **7 And the Lord said to Satan, "From where do you come?" So Satan answered the Lord and said, "From going to and fro on the earth, and from walking back and forth on it."**

The distinction is made between the parents in Genesis 6:1–2. The daughters are born to men and the sons (plural) are literal sons of God. Jesus is the only begotten Son of God through human beings and at this time, he was still a promise that had not yet entered the scene. I know it is hard for most of us to accept the fact that we are not the only intelligent beings in the Universe, but it is a strong likelihood that these sons of God were in the group that God refers to when creating man; this would make them superior to man (Gen. 1:26). Verse 4 of Chapter 6 makes sense when you understand who these sons of God were, and even more so, when the evidence proves they had to be in league with Satan.

> **Gen. 6:4 There were giants on the earth in those days, and also afterward, when the sons of God came in to the daughters of men and they bore children to them. Those were the mighty men who were of old, men of renown.**

The fact that many half-angel and half-human offspring were mixed in with the population as renowned individuals who had influence on them would make a very advanced society that followed the flesh. The reality that God created man to serve him on earth renders this self-serving society useless to God.

Myths and legends usually have some basis in fact. The myths and legends of ancient Greece, Rome and other societies that tell about various heroes being sons and daughters of gods may have their basis here, since even a hell-bound fallen angel would appear like a god to men. Verse 3 marks a major change in the average human lifespan.

> **Gen. 6:3 And the Lord said, "My Spirit shall not strive with man forever, for he is indeed flesh; yet his days shall be one hundred and twenty years."**

God is now cutting humanity's average lifespan to 120 years. A person may ask if God can do that—and how did God do that—just by saying it. The answer is: YES, HE CAN–AND HE DID, and he did it just by saying it. The next question may be to ask why God did that. God said his spirit would not always strive with man, for man is flesh. Man in the flesh, under the influence of fallen angels while spiritually dead and knowing good and evil, is capable of doing considerable damage not only to himself, but also to others.

Cain was the living proof of that. Paul explains the war within one's own body (Rom 7; Gal. 5:17) as he explains the contrary relationship created when the flesh lusts against the spirit and the spirit wars against the flesh. The actions attributed to desires of the flesh are listed in Galatians 5:19–21 as adultery, fornication, uncleanness, lewdness, idolatry, sorcery, hatred, contentions, jealousies, outburst of wrath, selfish ambitions, dissensions, heresies, envy, murders, drunkenness, revelries and the like.

The reason God shortened the human lifespan has to do with humanity's unwillingness to do well, as Abel did. In Galatians 5:19–21, the Bible says pursuing any fleshly pursuits summons God's wrath and some type of judgement. In this case, it is the second time man's average lifespan on earth was reduced. The 120-year limit was the last time God reduced man's longevity. The 90th Psalm at verse 10 is often quoted as proof God had declared another cut in man's average lifespan, but that quote is taken out of context.

> **Psalm 90:10 The days of our lives are seventy years; and if by reason of strength they are eighty years, yet their boast is only labor and sorrow; for it is soon cut off, and we fly away.**

In this verse, Moses (who lived 120 years) was praying to God and making a comparison between God's eternal nature and man's short stay on the earth. The statement is in the Bible, but it is not a statement or commandment from God. Most of that particular generation in that group had their lives shortened during the 40 years of wandering in the desert until they died out as punishment for continually sinning against God: Numbers 14:26-33. In modern America, the average lifespan in the 1850s was 39 years; it is nearly twice that much now and could be much higher with modern medicines and proper management of one's life.

The giants referred to in Genesis 6:4 are mentioned before the relationships between the sons of God and daughters of men are mentioned, so it is not clear whether these giants were the offspring of the angel-to-women marriages. The giants were possibly all human and similar to the tall Philistines who produced Goliath, the ten-foot-tall giant David slew, or the Amorites whose size and strength are mentioned in Amos 2:9.

Verse 4 also states that the daughters of men are fair to look at and that seems to be the attraction instead of Godly virtue. The ungodly marriages worked in favor of the wicked. After generations of this behavior, the human race nearly lost all contact with God. The giants and mighty men of renown are no doubt so caught up in their own self-pride and sense of personal greatness that they saw no need to be humble to God.

The societies of that time may have been prosperous and progressive according to their thinking, like the nations that were driven out of Canaan to make a homeland for the obedient Israelites. The anti-Christ will put together a well-ordered, functional society, using a false Messiah and unbeatable military ruler who will look like human perfection to everyone except those who truly serve God, as expressed in Revelation 13.

In Genesis 6:5, the Bible describes the worst condition the human race has ever been in, from God's point of view.

> **Gen. 6:5 Then the Lord saw that the wickedness of man was great in the earth, and that every intent of the thoughts of his heart was only evil continually,**

At that time, everything mankind imagined, thought and ultimately did was continually evil in relation to God. I firmly believe that God created the human race for some long-term service in the Universe and he will reveal it when he, and he alone, is ready. The problems start when the created beings become so corrupt that the Creator cannot trust them to perform the smallest service on his behalf. I think most people who purchase or make specific items to perform certain tasks would be ready to trash them if the items proved useless for that task. God had to look at the human race in the same way. The Bible says in verse 6 that God was grieved at his heart for making man.

> **Gen. 6:6 And the Lord was sorry that he had made man on the earth, and he was grieved in his heart.**

Imagine that—man had followed Satan away from his literal source of life. God's spirit was so tired of striving with man over the nearly 1,000 years of man's existence that he cut the lifespan of future generations to 120 years. The generations of this time appear to be beyond help. Every intent of the thoughts of man's heart continually sought only evil and God was grieved at his heart for creating man. WHAT CHOICE DOES MAN LEAVE GOD? God's decision to destroy all life on earth is stated in verse 7.

> **Gen. 6:7 So the Lord said, "I will destroy man whom I have created from the face of the earth, both man and beast, creeping thing and birds of the air, for I am sorry that I have made them."**

The destruction was to take place on the face of the earth, not in the waters; no sea life was mentioned for destruction. Genesis 7:22 verifies this by saying "All in whose nostrils was the breath of life, of all that was in the dry land died." The other land-based creatures would be made to suffer the same fate as man because of man's extremely poor stewardship.

The only obedient servants in the world at that time were Noah, his wife, their three sons Shem, Ham, Japheth and their wives. The Bible says Noah found grace in the eyes of the Lord. It is obvious that Noah and his family were working hard to live above the violence and corruption described in Genesis 6:11–13. That is the key to God's decision to continue with the human race and use Noah's sons to repopulate the world. In verses 14, 15 and 16, God gives Noah the verbal blueprints for the Ark before he tells him in verse 17 that a global flood would be the instrument for destroying all life.

> **Gen. 6:17 And behold, I Myself am bringing floodwaters on the earth, to destroy from under heaven all flesh in which is the breath of life; everything that is on the earth shall die.**

God makes a covenant with Noah in verse 18. The covenant with Noah is based on God's grace as previously described in verse 8 and the fact that Noah acknowledged God's power and influence in his life and taught this to his family.

God directed Noah how to build the Ark (Gen. 14–16) and told Noah what was to go into the Ark when it was completed (Gen. 19–20). Building the Ark was not a small chore. The size of the Ark, the limited size of the crew doing the work, the tools of that time, the catching and handling of the animals, the food preparation, the fact that they were working alone, and the cost for living while the work was going on—in all of this, Noah and his family were proving their faith by their works. Verse 22 amplifies the character of Noah.

> **Gen. 6:22 Thus Noah did; according to all that God commanded him, so he did.**

God commanded this massive undertaking and Noah never questioned any of it. Noah moved at God's command and proved one fact that the people of his times and all times since seem to have problems with: God is the Creator and man is the created.

CHAPTER 7

Chapter 7 of Genesis sees the Lord calling Noah and his family into the Ark seven days before the forty-day rain begins. The righteousness of Noah in his generations is repeated as God's reason for saving Noah and the other seven people in his house.

The fact that Satan could, and did, entice billions of people to corrupt their way on God's earth must never be overlooked and Satan must never be underestimated or taken lightly. The difference between clean and unclean beasts would later become a part of the law of God through Moses, but it is clear from verses 2 and 3 that God made the distinction long before that law was delivered.

I have read many commentaries on the extent of the biblical flood and how much damage was done to mankind and the animal kingdom. Some commentaries tend to believe the flood was limited to specific areas, destroying only the people and animals in that area, while some put forth other ideas that limit what the Bible says. In verse 4, the Bible clearly states the extent of the biblical flood.

> **Gen. 7:4 For after seven more days I will cause it to rain on the earth forty days and forty nights, and I will destroy from the face of the earth all living things that I have made."**

If the above verse is not convincing enough, then I pray that you will give your undivided attention to the rest of Chapter 7 so you will clearly understand what the Bible says about the flood. Then you will have to decide whether you will complicate your understanding of the

Bible because you choose to ignore what it says, or look at the evidence presented in Chapter 7 and invest your faith in God.

In verse 4, God tells Noah the 40 days of rain would come in seven more days. Everything with life that God made except those living on the Ark and living in the water would die. Think about a forty-day downpour that does not let up until the worldwide cloud system has been emptied. Then think about where you live. Would a 24-hour downpour for 40 consecutive days put you under water? If you still have doubts, keep reading. Verse 11 gives even more evidence of the worldwide flood.

> **Gen. 7:11 In the six hundredth year of Noah's life, in the second month, the seventeenth day of the month, on that day all the fountains of the great deep were broken up, and the windows of heaven were opened.**

The water for the flood described in verse 11 includes the windows of heaven and all the fountains of the great deep. The first source of water is, of course, rain. The second source of water refers to all waters running under the earth, underground rivers, wells, and all sources of underground water that have provided for all uses, for as long as people can remember. This also refers to all other belowground waters, possibly oceans, gushed to the surface when God pulled the plugs and the waters came forth. Genesis 8:22 evidences of a third source of water as well.

> **Gen. 8:22 "While the earth remains, seedtime and harvest, cold and heat, winter and summer, and day and night shall not cease."**

After the flood, God said he would not allow seedtime and harvest, cold and heat, summer and winter, or day and night to cease. If he allowed those climate changes to cease around the world, continents of great snow and ice mountains at the North and South Poles would melt and become water that adds to the rain. Readers who lean to their own opinion might doubt this. But the reader who studies the Bible would know that before God prepared the atmosphere and fitted the earth for the current occupants, it was covered with water. During the flood, God removed the powers he established to hold the waters. Then, after the flood, he promised Noah that he would not remove the powers again, making the third source of water obvious.

The question for you is whether you believe it or not. If you do not believe it, then study the world you live in. Is there evidence that great underground caverns and tunnels exist now and show evidence of massive upward flows of water? Are there underground rivers and is there well water? Are there great areas of snow mountains at the two Poles? Is water in the clouds? The study should conclude with a "YES" for anyone who diligently seeks the truth.

The water that covered the earth before and during the flood is still in, above and upon the earth right now. The Bible means what it says. The flood covered the whole earth and killed every land-based creature on earth except those in the Ark. The Holy Spirit did not authorize and inspire the writing of the Bible so people could reduce it to their level. The truths of the Bible are designed to equip humanity with the knowledge that brings us up to God's level. I accept it as the truth. I pray for each reader's acceptance of these truths because without them, there will be problems with believing and accepting the rest.

The latter part of Genesis 7:16 says the Lord shut Noah in after the Ark was loaded. Noah's faith and works were instrumental in his group's survival and they stand as an example of how each servant of God must learn to trust the Creator in all situations, even if they must stand alone against the world. God can and will deliver his own. The Bible does not refer to any steering or motoring devices on the Ark. They were drifting around in the biggest storm in the history of the world, but they were the most secure group in history because of whom they served.

CHAPTER 8

Chapter 8 marks the end of the flooding. The first two verses detail how God made a wind pass over the earth and the waters subsided. The fountains of the deep (underground waters) and windows of heaven (rains) were stopped. The things that we take for granted—the weather, the climate, winds and so on—that are so common to us, yet so completely beyond our control, should make us think and know that we should always acknowledge the one who can send or refuse them.

In Genesis 8:3, the verse says the water returned from off the earth continually, and after 150 days, the waters were decreased. On the other hand, Genesis 7:24 says the waters prevailed upon the earth 150 days. The two ways this is written might make the reader think there is a controversy, but there is not.

The start of the flood is recorded as the 2nd month and 17th day (Gen. 7:11). The Ark stopped floating and came to rest on Mount Ararat in the 7th month on the 17th day—five months later (Gen. 8:4). The calendar we currently use records exactly 150 days from February 17 to July 17, the 2nd month to the 7th month. The waters were prevailing where Noah was, but the waters were steadily decreasing until the 150th day when the Ark touched the ground again, so the waters had given way and decreased enough for the Ark to touch the earth again the same day. This dispels the controversy.

At this time, the Ark was resting on land on top of a mountain, but the world still looked like a giant ocean as the waters continued to recede. In Genesis 8:5, Noah can see the other mountain tops that are no doubt lower than the one he is on, but he sees the other mountain tops on the first day of the 10th month (October).

Another 40 days pass before Noah would send out first the raven, then the dove, to seek dry land in the lower areas. The dove came back with no evidence of dry land (Gen. 8:6–8). The 13th verse records the 1st day of a new year when Noah could see enough ground to feel safe enough to remove the covering from the Ark. The Bible says that on the 27th day of the 2nd month, or 1 year and 10 days after the flood started, the earth was dried (Gen. 8:14). That is when God allowed Noah to leave the Ark and remove every living land-based creature from the Ark.

Building an altar and preparing a sacrifice unto the Lord was the first order of business for Noah. When the altar was built, the Bible says Noah "took of every clean animal and of every clean bird, and offered burnt offerings on the altar," according to verse 20. At verse 21, God expresses that he is pleased with Noah's sacrifice.

> Gen. 8:21 And the Lord smelled a soothing aroma. Then the Lord said in his heart, "I will never again curse the ground for man's sake, although the imagination of man's heart is evil from his youth; nor will I again destroy every living thing as I have done.

God's promise to maintain the order of the seasons of the earth (Genesis 8:22) should stand as our guarantee from God that the whole earth will never be flooded again. God said in his heart that he would not curse the ground again for man's sake, but he still acknowledged the devastating effects sin has had on the human race.

The sin of Adam and Eve not only changed them, but also had a negative affect on all people born after them. Before sin, it was natural for Adam and Eve to obey God. After sin, the normal actions of people, especially children, usually involve doing what the flesh dictates with no thought about doing right or doing wrong. It takes training and preparation, and sometimes rigorous preparation, to do what is right.

CHAPTER 9

The 9th Chapter opens with Noah and his family being blessed by God with the ability to be fruitful and the order to replenish the earth—the whole earth (Gen. 9:1). Noah did not father any more children according to the Bible, but his three sons would be empowered to repopulate the earth. Noah would not see as many generations as Adam did, but Noah would live 950 years. The second populating of the earth would be much faster this time because three couples would make families, where only one couple (Adam and Eve) brought forth offspring in the first generation of humanity.

The second and third verses of Chapter 9 re-establish man as the dominant creature on earth. This is underscored when God explains the food that man could now eat, which includes every moving thing that liveth and the green herb (Gen. 9:3). Compare this to the original diet for man, as stated in verse 29 of Chapter 1:

> **Gen. 1:29 And God said, "See, I have given you every herb that yields seed which is on the face of all the earth, and every tree whose fruit yields seed; to you it shall be for food.**

Although humans could now eat flesh, God commands humans to drain blood from a butchered animal out of respect for its life, which is represented by the blood (Gen. 9:4). The command is clarified in several places in the Bible and firmly established in the law of God through Moses (Lev. 17:10–14).

> **Lev. 17:10 And whatever man of the house of Israel, or of the**

strangers who dwell among you, who eats any blood, I will set my face against that person who eats blood, and will cut him off from among his people.

11 For the life of the flesh is in the blood, and I have given it to you upon the altar to make atonement for your souls; for it is the blood that makes atonement for the soul.

12 Therefore I said to the children of Israel, "No one among you shall eat blood, nor shall any stranger who dwells among you eat blood."

13 "Whatever man of the children of Israel, or of the strangers who dwell among you, who hunts and catches any animal or bird that may be eaten, he shall pour out its blood and cover it with dust;

14 For it is the life of all flesh. Its blood sustains its life. Therefore I said to the children of Israel, "You shall not eat the blood of any flesh, for the life of all flesh is its blood. Whoever eats it shall be cut off."

The statement made in Leviticus 17:11 sums up the reason for respecting the blood: "For it is the blood that maketh an atonement for the soul." As first commanded in Genesis 9:4, it is imperative that mankind learn to respect blood because the blood of Christ would be the reality of true atonement for the soul and salvation of all who accept his blood's saving power.

God requires that both humans and animals take responsibility as it relates to shedding the blood of others (Gen. 9:5). Verse 6 leaves no doubt about God's commandment concerning capital punishment.

Gen. 9:6 Whoever sheds man's blood, by man his blood shall be shed; for in the image of God He made man.

The term "shedding of blood" here refers to killing another person without justification. The authority to shed the blood of a murderer is given to whatever legal authorities are in power in a given country and the law is established before any nations exist, so it should be the norm for all of humanity. The law through Moses would make distinctions between accidental deaths and establish degrees of homicides based on the actual circumstances surrounding the homicide. The law through Moses also establishes man's responsibility in controlling his animals (Ex. 21:28–36).

Chapter 6 of Genesis also speaks to the corruption and violence of the pre-flood world. In Genesis 6:11, there is no mention of a legal system to contain or control these actions by people. God appears to be establishing human controls over the worst human crimes up front. Killing a person without justification would be first degree murder that is punishable by lawful execution of the murderer. The modern debate over the constitutionality of capital punishment can be resolved in a heartbeat if people accept God's law as law.

The next thing God did was to establish a covenant with man and beast never to flood the world again. The evidence, or token, of the covenant would be the bow that appears with the clouds and rain—what we call a rainbow (Gen. 9:13–17).

Prior to this, God issued his blessing and the commandment to be fruitful and multiply in the earth (Gen. 9:7). Taken with the first verse of Chapter 9, there is no doubt that God is commanding man to spread out over the whole earth. In verses 18 and 19, God called Noah's sons by name as the three men who would repopulate the whole earth in accordance with God's Word.

> **Gen. 9:18 Now the sons of Noah who went out of the Ark were Shem, Ham, and Japheth. And Ham was the father of Canaan.**
>
> **19 These three were the sons of Noah, and from these the whole earth was populated.**

Some ministers claim that Noah's sons fathered what they call the Adamic race, which excludes all non-Caucasian races. This implies that other races apparently survived the flood, or the flood had to be limited to a specific area and all non-Caucasians had to live beyond those specific areas. If that was true, it means only Caucasians earned God's judgement, but it's unproven.

The view of these ministers challenges what the Bible says and forces people to decide whether they will follow the precepts of men, or accept what the Bible says in Genesis 9:19, "...and from these the whole earth was populated." The question is, what part of the word WHOLE didn't they understand?

Wisdom compels us to stay with what can be proven from scripture. The scripture clearly says the whole earth was flooded, the whole population drowned, Noah's family was the only exception and the whole earth was repopulated by Noah's three sons and daughters-in-law. The Bible said it, so we can take it or leave it, but we cannot change it.

Genesis 9:20–29 deals with an incident that will confirm some things that are important to further study and understanding of the Bible. Apparently, the knowledge of and use of grapes to make wine was well-known to Noah (Gen. 9:20).

Wine is identified in the Bible as (1) fresh, unfermented grape juice, (2) fermented wine with the ability to intoxicate its users and (3) various mixtures of grape juice, water and spices. Wine was used in sacrificial offerings, Lev. 23:13, for one, and used in establishing the Lord's supper, Matt. 26:27-29, in the New Testament.

The Bible does not say that it is a sin to make or drink wine. In fact, Jesus Christ, the sinless man, was called a winebibber by the scribes and Pharisees of his day for drinking wine. To say it is a sin to drink wine makes Jesus a sinner and that's not possible, as reported in Matthew 11: 19 and John 2:1–12.

The second type of wine described in the Bible, fermented wine, can intoxicate its users if they drink too much at one time. There is a biblical warning about over-indulging; the writer of Proverbs warns about the dangers of over-indulging in both food and drink (Prov. 23:20–21).

Noah made wine from the grapes in his vineyard and drank way too much (Gen. 9:21). I don't know why Noah got drunk. He may have been depressed because all of humanity was dead, but the incident could have been avoided if he had used more self-control and stopped drinking before he passed out.

The idea that a parent must be perfect to be worthy of respect is put away here. The whole human race is imperfect; no one except Jesus would pass a test like that. The command to honor your father and mother is without strings (Ex. 20:12). The job could be very hard for a child with abusive, unsaved parents, but the rule says honor them—if not for their worthiness, then for yours.

The wise child learns from their parents one way or the other. The child with good parents should be thankful and still follow the rules of respect, then seek to follow or improve on that blessed upbringing. A child with uninvolved parents should work at being careful to follow the rules of respect, while improving on their own views of what good parenting should be and living it when they are parents. I know the idea of any child being in that situation sounds bad, but too many children are in just that situation and a word of wisdom may be the only thing they can build on until their change comes.

Noah was an excellent father. The fact that he drank too much that day does not speak against him. It only speaks to his humanity. Verses 22 and 23 say that after Noah overindulged, the younger son, Ham, came in the tent and looked on his father's nakedness. The Bible does not spell out whether he saw his father as humorous, disgusting, or what he thought. The Bible says only that Ham went outside and told his brothers, without detailing what Ham said to them, and describes the brother's reaction.

> **Gen. 9:22 And Ham, the father of Canaan, saw the nakedness of his father, and told his two brothers outside.**
>
> **23 But Shem and Japheth took a garment, laid it on both their shoulders, and went backward and covered the nakedness of their father. Their faces were turned away, and they did not see their father's nakedness.**

The question I would ask is, why not discretely cover your father and not mention it to anyone? The fact that Shem and Japheth knew in advance that they should enter the tent backwards with a cover proves Ham told them a lot of details about his father's condition.

I have read and heard a lot of wild stories about Ham's actions here. One story claims Ham uncovered his father's nakedness and applies the terminology Moses used in Chapter 18 of Leviticus concerning the laws of sexual morality. That would mean Ham had a sexual relationship with his mother; there is absolutely no biblical basis for that idea. Genesis 9:21 says only that Noah got drunk and literally became uncovered.

There is no evidence that Ham was anywhere in sight when all of this happened and their mother is never mentioned at all, so Ham did not uncover his father.

Another wild story says he sodomized his father while he was asleep, a story that makes even less sense than the first one. To understand what the Bible says, you must first read the Bible. Don't assume that God needs you to fill in the blanks because there are no blanks. Noah got drunk and removed his clothing for some reason, passed out and was later seen by Ham who committed the disrespectful act of speaking of his father's nakedness.

Genesis 9:24 does not say how Noah found out what his younger son had done, but it is apparent that he found it disrespectful and cursed him. Ham was not the physical recipient of the curse right then. The curse was passed to Ham's son, Canaan.

The nations that would follow Canaan came to be known as Canaan's Land. These nations would see the curse come to fruition when God later delivered their lands and possessions to the Israelites and allowed Canaan's Land to be known as Israel's Promised Land. The land's exact boundaries are given in Deuteronomy 17:24, Josh. 1:3–4 and several other scriptures. These boundaries are currently being contested by modern day Israelites who claim a divine right to possess that very land, which, by the way, is not in Africa.

Because Ham is the father of the African nations as well as the Canaanites (Gen. 10:5–20), it has not been clearly understood that the curse was specifically placed on Canaan and none of the other descendents in Ham's line. In light of this, Genesis 9:25–27 has been misunderstood and demonstrates yet another incidence of the Bible being misquoted, in this case, to justify the enslavement of millions of Africans over the last 500 years.

> Gen. 9:25 Then he said: "Cursed be Canaan; a servant of servants he shall be to his brethren."
>
> 26 And he said: "Blessed be the Lord, the God of Shem, and may Canaan be his servant.
>
> 27 May God enlarge Japheth, and may he dwell in the tents of Shem; And may Canaan be his servant."

Ham is the father of the African nations as well as the Canaanites. (Gen. 10:6-20). The curse was clearly placed on Canaan and none of the others in Ham's line. The reason for disinheriting the Canaanites is so plain that a child should be able to read the passage and get the message (Deut. 18:9–14). Ham disrespected his father. Canaan may even have had the same disrespectful attitude, but even if he did not, the cluster of nations that would carry his name were overtly disrespectful of authority and would earn their fate, as explained in Deuteronomy 18:9–14.

> Deut. 18:9 When you come into the land which the Lord your God is giving you, you shall not learn to follow the abominations of those nations.
>
> 10 There shall not be found among you anyone who makes his son or his daughter pass through the fire, or one who practices witchcraft, or a soothsayer, or one who interprets omens, or a sorcerer,
>
> 11 or one who conjures spells, or a medium, or a spiritist, or one who calls up the dead.
>
> 12 For all who do these things are an abomination to the Lord, and because of these abominations the Lord your God drives them out from before you.
>
> 13 You shall be blameless before the Lord your God,
>
> 14 For these nations which you will dispossess listened to soothsayers and diviners, but as for you, the Lord your God has not appointed such for you.

The cursings and blessings that would characterize the future of the descendants of these nations would be determined by the character these men exhibited. They were told not to adopt the sins practiced by the people who already lived in the land God would give them. We should know how to reject the bearer of these sins, even if he is an intelligent, young sorcerer, knowing that these sins will sow the seeds of destruction among our most vulnerable group—THE CHILDREN. Children who do not learn to take God at his Word become the ones who bring the wrath of God down on a whole nation when they become adults.

The curse on Canaan came from Noah's mouth, but God is no doubt speaking through him. The Canaanites were pushed out of the specified area when the Hebrews arrived and that satisfied the curse. The reason for their failure is clearly laid out in Deuteronomy 18:9–14 and would stand as a warning for any other nation that claims to love God.

Noah lived 950 years, 350 years after the flood. Noah was alive during the construction of the Tower of Babel and lived until Abraham was almost 60 years old.

CHAPTER 10

Chapter 10 of Genesis starts with the generations and names of the sons of Japheth, Ham and Shem. Grandsons, great-grandsons and others were named as well, although not all of the descendents are named. Five sons of Shem are mentioned in Chapter 10, although Chapter 1 of I Chronicles says Shem had nine sons. The different numbers do not mean there is a controversy. This points to an earlier statement that not all of Shem's sons are mentioned in Chapter 10 of Genesis.

The statements in verses 5, 20 and 31 would give the impression that these men could have been heads of nations or leaders. Although they may have been named for that purpose, this did not mean they were the only ones born. The fact that no women were named follows the customs of the time, but it is safe to say that each of these men fathered female children.

The final verse in Chapter 10 concludes that the offspring of the sons of Noah populated the nations of earth after the flood.

> **Gen. 10:32 These were the families of the sons of Noah, according to their generations, in their nations; and from these the nations were divided on the earth after the flood.**

The nations were divided by these families when the earth was repopulated. Every human alive today can be traced back to one of these groups, even if the blood lines have crossed over the centuries.

Nimrod, the grandson of Ham, is mentioned in Genesis 10:8–12 and is referred to in a negative way by some theologians and writers of our times. The Bible, however, has never referred to Nimrod in a negative way. The fact that he was a mighty hunter before the Lord, one of the earliest nation builders and probably the first leader to build walled cities would lean more toward his being a chosen man of God and protector of people. Genesis 10:10 identifies that Nimrod's kingdom began in Babel, Erech, Acad and Calneh in the land of Shinar. The Tower of Babel, as identified in Chapter 11 of Genesis, is in the land of Shinar also.

The brief biography of Nimrod's life must have taken place after the rebellion at the Tower of Babel, because the people were as one nation before the rebellion. Nimrod's kingdoms appear to have started there and then extended to the other lands later (Gen. 10:11–12). The Bible does not identify any movers and shakers in the building of the Tower of Babel, but verse 25 might give us an approximate timeframe.

> **Gen. 10:25 To Eber were born two sons: the name of one was Peleg, for in his days the earth was divided; and his brother's name was Joktan.**

Eber, the great-grandson of Shem, fathered two sons. The name of one son was Peleg. The Bible says that, in his time, the earth divided. The division of the earth most likely means the scattering of the people after they tried to build the Tower of Babel. Since Peleg was the great-great-grandson of Shem, we can assume an approximate timeline for the Tower of Babel from Chapter 11 of Genesis. However, we cannot determine a more exact date unless we know Peleg's exact age during the rise and fall of the Tower of Babel.

CHAPTER 11

Chapter 11 of Genesis covers the Tower of Babel. In verse 1, the world's existing population is functioning as one nation and one family, speaking the one language that God had given them. The picture is one of cooperation and harmony. That might raise some questions about why God confused their language. The questions will be answered as you begin to clearly understand this issue. Verse 2 pictures a nation of nomads traveling from the east until they selected a plain in the land of Shinar and settled there.

Verses 3 and 4 explain the unity, cooperation, and resolve of these people. Their form of government is unknown, but Genesis 11:3–4 seems to show they have full agreement on the actions they chose to take. In verse 3, they said one to another, "Let us make brick." Then, in verse 4, they said, "Let us build a city, let us make a name for ourselves, lest we be scattered abroad over the face of the whole earth."

The idea of working together to accomplish greatness for ourselves does not sound that bad. The desire not to be scattered abroad upon the face of the whole earth sounds reasonable as well. But when God blessed Noah's descendants with a multitude of children, God commanded Noah and his sons to replenish and fill up the whole earth, not stay bunched together for their own selfish reasons (Gen. 9:1; Gen. 9:7).

Yet Noah and all of his sons were in the group that decided they did not want to be scattered abroad across the face of the earth. The same God who told Adam and Eve not to eat forbidden fruit told Noah and his sons to fill up the whole earth. Once again—WHAT GOD COMMANDED THEM TO DO WAS FLAGRANTLY DISOBEYED.

I do not know why God's will and words were not communicated to each generation as they came along. Because all the people spoke the same language, God's command could have been communicated, and should have been kept, by everyone. If they had obeyed God and scattered naturally as the population grew, the world could have experienced a lot less confusion and bloodshed. It was clear that Noah, his sons and their wives knew that God does not take disobedience lightly. They had been the only human survivors of a flood that covered the whole earth and killed everyone except them.

Verses 5 and 6 show how dangerous their unity was.

> **Gen. 11:5 But the Lord came down to see the city and the tower, which the sons of men had built.**
>
> **6 And the Lord said, "Indeed the people are one and they all have one language, and this is what they begin to do; now nothing that they propose to do will be withheld from them.**

The entire population was working together, as one, to do just the opposite of what the Creator told them to do. Genesis 6:5 comes to mind again when you consider what is going on here.

> **Gen. 6:5 Then the Lord saw that the wickedness of man was great in the earth, and that every intent of the thoughts of his heart was only evil continually.**

The people of this time were doing something similar to what the pre-flood people did 300 years earlier and caused their own destruction. Genesis 11:6 presents God's thoughts: Man is communicating well with other men, but they are not working within the context of God's will.

The world before the flood was a one-language society that successfully communicated evil continually. Building a tower tall enough to reach into heaven is yet another attempt by man to be his own God and ignore his Creator. Man, left to his own imagination and the inspiration of Lucifer, will think he can do anything on his own and God's reason for creating mankind will not be acknowledged or accepted. Failure to communicate and failure to do God's will puts all mankind at risk with

God, in spite of mankind's idea that he is making great progress. According to verse 6, God knows that man is just beginning another trip down the road of self-destruction. God is pushed into a corner again by man's disobedience and is forced to take action.

The ability to communicate is a useful tool if it is used for the right reasons. Genesis 11:7–8 tells how God accomplished the job of making man do what God commanded him to do.

> **Gen. 11:7 Come, let Us go down and there confuse their language, that they may not understand one another's speech."**
>
> **8 So the Lord scattered them abroad from there over the face of all the earth, and they ceased building the city.**

The various theories of mankind's origin have never come up with a workable theory to explain the different languages. The only thing that can explain the past and current language differences is the Bible. God, who created man with vocal chords and gave him language, was forced by man's disobedience to alter their language to continue his purpose for man's existence—it is as simple as that.

God confused the language of the whole population so they would scatter over the earth and collect in groups of people who spoke the same language. Verse 8 bears witness to a scathing indictment against mankind. God had to put them in a position where they could not communicate and cooperate before they would obey his command. Genesis 11:9 says Babel was the name given to the area after the attempted tower construction.

The scattered groups appeared to carry some of the knowledge of God with them, but it is not known how much or how well it was passed on. The centuries that follow would see the different nation's views of God branch out in several different directions. I do not know how far God went with any of the other groups, but it is plain that there was some communication, as will be discussed later.

The remainder of Chapter 11 deals with the lineage from Shem to Abram. The father of Abram was Terah and he was 70 years old when he began to father children. That would make him more than twice as old as his forefathers were when they fathered their first named children. Genesis 11:26–32 tells the genealogy of Terah.

Gen. 11:26 Now Terah lived seventy years, and begot Abram, Nahor, and Haran.

27 This is the genealogy of Terah: Terah begot Abram, Nahor, and Haran. Haran begot Lot.

28 And Haran died before his father Terah in his native land, in Ur of the Chaldeans.

29 Then Abram and Nahor took wives: the name of Abram's wife was Sarai, and the name of Nahor's wife, Milcah, the daughter of Haran the father of Milcah and the father of Iscah.

30 But Sarai was barren; she had no child.

31 And Terah took his son Abram and his grandson Lot, the son of Haran, and his daughter-in-law Sarai, his son Abram's wife, and they went out with them from Ur of the Chaldeans to go to the land of Canaan; and they came to Haran and dwelt there.

32 So the days of Terah were two hundred and five years, and Terah died in Haran.

I do not know if the fact that Terah was much older when he fathered Abram caused some hereditary reason why Abram and his half-sister, Sarai, were slow to reproduce. The Bible does not say. However, it appears that God allowed the issue to take over and used it to make childbirth and lineage very important; it provided a test of their faith as well. Whatever the case, God's hand was on them for a reason.

Terah initiated the move from Ur. Terah and his family were going to Canaan, but stopped at Haran and dwelt there (Gen. 11:31). The Bible does not say whether Terah had a divine call to go to Canaan, why he stopped at Haran, how long the group lived there before Abram and Lot left, or if the city of Haran had any connection to his dead son named Haran. Terah settled in Haran and was nearly 145 years old when Abram and Lot left. Terah lived 60 more years and died at the age of 205.

CHAPTER 12

The 12th Chapter of Genesis covers the call of Abram. In verse 1, the Lord tells Abram to leave the country and his family and go to a land where God would lead him. The Bible says the Lord said this unto Abram, but does not say when the Lord said this. The fact that Abram was told by God to leave his father's house meant he left his father's house in Haran. Genesis 15:7 probably bears witness to an even earlier call.

> **Gen. 15:7 Then He said to him, "I am the Lord, who brought you out of Ur of the Chaldeans, to give you this land to inherit it."**

This verse may raise some questions about the involvement of Terah in the call to Abram, but the life of Terah is a natural place to start in order to understand the call of Abram.

The 205-year lifespan of Terah is covered in eight verses of the Bible. This is not a full biography of his life; his part only fills spaces in the narrative. There is no evidence that Terah was acting under a divine call when he moved the family toward Canaan, only that he was the elder and identified as head of the group that moved (Gen. 11:31). As the head of the family, it was custom that he be given preeminence in any dialogue of the time.

Genesis 15:7 is a direct quote from God and it overrides all unstated assumptions. God said he called Abram from Ur of the Chaldeans. The Bible did not record the actual call, but God confirmed it himself, so that is where Abram's call originated. The fact that Abram took Lot, his dead brother's son, with him after his father settled in Haran may bear witness to his leadership, but his father's headship was always identified in an important decision as a family move. The important thing to realize here is that a direct quote from God always overrides the conclusions we might reach on our own.

It is unclear whether Terah was acting with his son when they all left Ur together and Terah settled in Haran, apparently Abram got a second call from Haran. Since Abram's answer to God's call was, "Yes Lord, I'll go," the question is irrelevant at this point.

The call and promise to Abram was a two-step process. First, God made promises to Abram that he would fulfill only if Abram would believe or have faith. He would then have to confirm that faith by acting on God's words. The promise, as stated first in Gen. 12:2–3, was to make childless Abram into the father of a great nation. Abram, himself, would be blessed, his name would be great as it has been throughout the ages and he shall be a blessing. The Bible goes on to say in verse 3 that God will bless or curse others based on their relationship to Abram. Last, but certainly not least, all the families of the earth shall be blessed in the man, Abram.

The faith needed by individuals and nations throughout the ages to get into God's graces would be demonstrated through the life of Abram. Verses 4 through 6 show how Abram responded to God's call.

> **Gen. 12:4 So Abram departed as the Lord had spoken to him and Lot went with him. And Abram was seventy-five years old when he departed from Haran.**
>
> **5 Then Abram took Sarai his wife and Lot his brother's son, and all their possessions that they had gathered, and the people whom they had acquired in Haran, and they departed to go to the land of Canaan. So they came to the land of Canaan.**
>
> **6 Abram passed through the land to the place of Shechem, as far as the terebinth tree of Moreh. And the Canaanites were then in the land.**

When Abram was 75 years old, he left his father in Haran and journeyed toward the land that God had promised him. Abram might seem very old to us with our 70- to 80-year life expectancy, but that was not very old for people in Abram's generation. Abram lived 175 years; his father lived 205 years. The fact that Abram obeyed God and left his family, comfort, and security at any age shows remarkable faith on his part.

In verse 5, Abram, Sarai, and Lot travel into Canaan. Abram took all his wealth—livestock, servants, silver, gold and other material things—and left like a man burning all bridges behind him, stepping out on nothing but faith.

God appeared to Abram again after he arrived in Canaan. In verse 7, God identified Canaan as the land he promised to show him and confirmed Canaan as the land he would give to his seed. Abram's seed would make the nation of Israel, the same nation that is currently struggling to regain and hold that very land. The basis for their claim is God's promise to Abram, plus the fact that they took it the same way all other conquests are made—by force of arms. In their case, God's arm provided the force.

In verse 8, Abram takes the initiative in honoring God on a mountain near Bethel. He builds an altar unto the Lord and calls upon his name, or prays to God. The fact that Abram followed God's promise away from everything he held dear to receive a blessing that he would not see come to fruition shows faith and character that was then, and still is, very rare.

The famine in Canaan drove Abram into Egypt (Gen. 12:10–20). The spiritual faith and obedience that Abram had just shown is about to be tested by this same man of flesh who fears for his life in Egypt. The land and seed of God's promise was put on the back burner when Abram thought the men of Egypt might kill him to take his wife, Sarai (also his half-sister), whom the Bible said was a very beautiful woman. Abram devised a scheme to tell the Egyptians Sarai was his sister to save his own life.

In verse 16, the actions of the Pharaoh prove he does not think that way at all, nor is he that type of person.

> **Genesis 12:16 He treated Abram well for her sake. He had sheep, oxen, male donkeys, male and female servants, female donkeys, and camels.**

Pharaoh gave many gifts to Abram for Sarai, apparently thinking he was gaining a brother-in-law. If the Pharaoh had been the type of person who would have killed Abram to take his wife, he certainly would have killed Abram to take his sister. He would not have given him the gifts and he would have taken all of his wealth and provisions.

Pharaoh was victimized by Abram's lie. Abram's lie was a human attempt to save himself from an imagined threat. Abram did not realize that God's promise had him so well protected that the only thing that could hurt him was his own lapse in faith. The plagues that God put on Pharaoh were to protect Abram and the sanctity of Abram's house by keeping his wife from being with another man, even though Abram had created the situation. Genesis 12:18–20 show a rightfully indignant Pharaoh after he realized he was being deceived.

> Gen. 12:18 And Pharaoh called Abram and said, "What is this you have done to me? Why did you not tell me that she was your wife?
>
> 19 Why did you say, "She is my sister?" I might have taken her as my wife. Now therefore, here is your wife; take her and go your way."
>
> 20 So Pharaoh commanded his men concerning him; and they sent him away, with his wife and all that he had.

The statements and actions of Pharaoh after the event do not reveal a person that Abram should have feared. The same God who had made him promises and protected him, even after he lied, would certainly have protected him more for telling the truth. The man Abram was just that—a man who could exhibit a great deal of faith on the one hand and, on the other hand, give in to human fears and rely on his own understanding and the works of his hands when he perceived danger, even if it was unsubstantiated.

The same holds true for us, the modern-day followers of God, even though we have Abram and the rest of the Bible to show us how and why we should do God's will in all situations. The God who protects and loves us in spite of our human frailties took excellent care of Abram in this situation.

CHAPTER 13

Chapter 13 of Genesis opens with Abram, Sarai and Lot leaving Egypt and going south. They returned to the place between Bethel and Ai where Abram had camped earlier and called on God from the altar he built to honor the Lord. The altar was still there because verse 4 says Abram prayed to the Lord from that same altar upon his return.

It appears Abram left Egypt with all of his goods and there is no evidence that he returned the gifts given to him for Sarai. You can safely say he left with some of Pharaoh's wealth and he would have left Egypt with more weath than he took there.

> **Gen. 13:2 Abram was very rich in livestock, in silver, and in gold.**

The wealth of Abram was tempered by his obedience, humility, and thankfulness to God. This is in contrast to the rich young ruler in Matthew 19:16–26; many Christians who read that passage assume that God does not want them to be well off. The comparison between these two scriptures must be made and the differences must be understood before such an unwise decision is made. The most important difference is that Abram heeded the call of God—the rich young ruler did not.

The statement Christ made about how difficult it is for the rich of this world to go to heaven has created questions about wealth since he said it. Peter was the first to ask Christ what the reward was for following him if it is hard for a rich man to be saved (Matt. 19:23–30). The other Apostles questioned that also because they all gave up whatever wealth they had acquired from their trades and professions to follow him (Matt. 19:25). The answer in Matthew 19:28–30 leaves no doubt that they would be amply rewarded, but it specifies a time that goes beyond the temporary lives we live on this earth. The reward would be based on how they would invest their faith, whether in temporary wealth that you lose when you die, or the permanent wealth of traveling with Christ to the next level.

Wealth, in and of itself, is neither good nor bad; it's value to you is based on how far you are willing to go to obtain it. The children of Israel were promised complete wealth and security for following God in Chapter 26 of Leviticus and a reversal of the same if they rejected him.

The people in this world who will stop at nothing to be rich are selling their souls cheap. The people who invest their time and efforts in a Godly way to obtain riches are just as blessed as the rich young ruler, but they must realize a direct offer from the giver of those things must be accepted, or they could lose them, and eternal life, as well. The bottom line is not as complicated as one may think: CAN YOU LOVE GOD AND CONTROL WEALTH, OR DO YOU LOVE WEALTH AND ALLOW THE LURE OF IT TO CONTROL YOU?

Verse 5 says Lot was also quite well off. Abram and Lot were so blessed with wealth, provisions, people, tents and so forth, that their caravans probably would have looked like good-sized cities when they set up camp. The wealth of both men created a problem that would require some adjustments.

Genesis 13:6–7 says that there was not enough land, grazing and watering area to support both men's livestock and their herdsmen were having problems over it. The Canaanites and Perizzites were in the land at that time also. It is not known whether they figured into the grazing rights confusion, or if this was simply being noted again because the descendants of Canaan (Noah's grandson) would eventually lose this same land to Abram's future heirs. Verses 8 through 12 record the split between Abram and Lot.

> **Gen. 13:8 So Abram said to Lot, "Please let there be no strife between you and me, and between my herdsmen and your herdsmen; for we are brethren.**

> 9 Is not; the whole land before you? Please separate from me. If you take the left, then I will go to the right; or, if you go to the right, then I will go to the left."
>
> 10 And Lot lifted his eyes and saw all the plain of Jordan, that it was well watered everywhere (before the Lord destroyed Sodom and Gomorrah) like the garden of the Lord, like the land of Egypt as you go toward Zoar.
>
> 11 Then Lot chose for himself all the plain of Jordan, and Lot journeyed east. And they separated from each other.
>
> 12 Abram dwelt in the land of Canaan, and Lot dwelt in the cities of the plain and pitched his tent even as far as Sodom.

The reason for this separation is obvious; some action had to be taken. The wisdom and character of Abram comes through at this point. Abram would not allow strife over grazing and water rights to escalate into a feud or range war between them. From Abram's standpoint, the relationship was more significant than who could get the upper hand in a contest to increase one's wealth. Since Abram was Lot's blood kin and father figure, he would have had first choice of the best grazing lands. Instead, he gave Lot the choice. Would the rich young ruler of Matthew 19 be so generous under the same circumstances?

Verses 10 and 11 identify Lot's choice, the plain of Jordan—plenty of water, green and excellent for livestock. The choice Lot made was logical and there is no proof that he knew how wicked his future neighbors in Sodom were until he settled there (Gen. 13:12–13). Verse 13 says the men of Sodom were exceedingly wicked and sinful against the Lord. The full depth of their wickedness will be explored in later Chapters.

Abram lived in Canaan according to verse 12 and the Lord communicated the promise again in Genesis 13:14–17. The focus in these scriptures seems to be on the physical boundaries of the future nation of Israel and the Jewish people. Chapter 13 closes with Abram moving to the plain of Mamre in Hebron and there he built an altar unto the Lord. The altar seemed to be a pattern with Abram when he lived somewhere for any length of time.

Abram's actions convey faith, respect, and love toward God, in spite of his weak moment when he thought Egypt presented danger. His actions in other areas so far were proving that Abram operated from a pure heart and kept a good conscience.

CHAPTER 14

Chapter 14 of Genesis provides the first look at military science in the Bible. The pre-flood account says the world that had to be destroyed was filled with violence. However, it does not explain how the violent acts were carried out on the large scale, nor does it detail the causes other than sin. The cause-and-effect here seems plain enough, as Genesis 14:1–11 explains.

The four Kings and their armies were superior in strength to the five Kings and their armies. The 12 years of service noted in verse 4 meant that because the four Kings were stronger, they took what they wanted by way of tribute services and anything they desired to make life better for their nations. The weaker groups were the victims of the stronger groups' greed.

If you try to find the reason for war by reading history books, or if you study war from the perspective of an invading nation, you might think one nation has every right to invade the other because they are bad, mean, evil, ungodly, unfriendly, or worse, if yours is a Christian nation (Romans 12:18 should guide your attitude toward war. Unless you are attacked or invaded, peace should be your objective). The Book of James covers the subject in chapter 4 and the truth revealed there covers war for all times (James 4:1–3).

> James 4:1 Where do wars and fights come from among you? Do they not come from your desires for pleasure that war in your members?

2 You lust and do not have. You murder and covet and cannot obtain. You fight and war. Yet you do not have because you do not ask.

3 You ask and do not receive, because you ask amiss, that you may spend it on your pleasures.

The facts hold true in the case of small groups, large groups, or whole nations. The desire to have more may lead one to buy, trade, steal, or kill if that evil desire is not controlled, as James 4:1–3 points out. The speeches men deliver to motivate soldiers to go forth and kill or die in this endeavor can sound patriotic and noble, but the bottom line is still the same: The stronger take advantage of the weaker if they do not have the spiritual force of God to guide them.

Before the rise and fall of the Tower of Babel, the population of Babel communicated with one language. They might have exhibited the same evil desires, but because they spoke the same language, fair trade could have been more desirable than domination. After serving the four stronger Kings for 13 years, they no longer wanted to serve them and that brought an army into the area the 14th year. The four Kings were determined to continue their domination, even if it meant war.

The Bible says they were successful in their endeavor until they took Lot hostage, even though he was not a member of the coalition that rebelled against the four Kings (Gen. 14:12). The Bible does not say how long Lot had been in the area, but the approximate timeframe does not support him being there for 14 years prior to this time. The fact that Lot happened to be among the nations at war, had a great deal of wealth and did not have enough soldiers to protect it was reason enough for the four Kings to capture him and take everything he owned.

The emotion they operated under was greed, so Lot was taken for what he had, not for anything he did. Genesis 14:13 tells us that one of the people who escaped told Abram of Lot's fate. Three leaders who lived in his immediate area made an alliance with Abram. They were no doubt friends because their alliance was not made to fight off an invasion—they were pursuers.

Abram armed 318 of his trained servants for the pursuit, but neither the number of fighting men provided by his allies, nor the number of soldiers serving the four Kings, are mentioned. Verse 15 says Abram's forces divided and struck at night. This gave them the advantage and they defeated the four Kings. Abram's forces chased them as far as Hobah and recovered goods and hostages.

The King of Sodom met Abram after his victory. Genesis 14:18 says Melchizedek, King of Salem and priest of the Most High God, was there also. Melchizedek has been called mysterious, and possibly controversial, because of how he comes onto the scene and then exits without any mention of an ancestry, lineage or future actions as a King and priest of the Most High God. Yet, the 110th Psalm prophecy refers to the coming Messiah as a priest forever, after the order of Melchizedek.

The author of the Book of Hebrews draws a distinction between the temporary nature of the Aaronic priesthood and the permanent nature of Christ's priesthood using Melchizedek as an example. The author of Hebrews makes the point that Melchizedek received tithes of Abram before the Israelites or Aaronic priesthood ever existed. He also points out that since the receiver of the tithe is preeminent; the Aaronic priesthood is not the last word on salvation or the greatest and only priesthood.

The coming of Christ's priesthood was prophesied before Aaron's and will continue forever, long after the priesthood of Aaron has served its purpose.

The phrase "after the order of Melchizedek" does not mean Melchizedek is a rival of Christ. The coming and going without dealing with his past or future is a figurative way of showing an eternal nature, which is only designed to show an example of the true eternal nature of Christ's priesthood.

The other important fact about Melchizedek is that his position with God proves that other individuals, and possibly nations, were calling on God around 600 years before Israel left Egypt as a nation. The reason why none of them emerged as the chosen people is not known, but later evidence suggests that they sold out to the adversary at some point in their history.

In Genesis 14:19–20, the authority of Melchizedek is confirmed by his actions and statements.

Gen. 14:19 And he blessed him and said: "Blessed be Abram of God Most High, Possessor of heaven and earth:

20 And blessed be God Most High, Who has delivered your enemies into your hand." And he gave him a tithe of all.

He serves a newer servant of the same Most High God. In verse 19, he blessed Abram and identified him as the recipient of God's blessing and favor in the war to liberate Lot. The tithe was no doubt paid from all of the recovered goods and loot captured from the opposing army before they were allowed to reclaim any of it. Verses 21 through 24 deal with the redistribution of goods and captives.

Gen. 14:21 Now the King of Sodom said to Abram, "Give me the persons, and take the goods for yourself."

22 But Abram said to the King of Sodom, "I have raised my hand to the Lord, God Most High, the possessor of heaven and earth,

23 that I will take nothing, from a thread to a sandal strap, and that I will not take anything that is yours, lest you should say, "I have made Abram rich"—

24 except only what the young men have eaten, and the portion of the men who went with me: Aner, Eshcol and Mamre; let them take their portion."

Verse 21 may reflect a grateful and humble image of the King of Sodom, or it may reflect an acceptance of the fact that Abram's forces were stronger. Regardless of the King's motives, the fact that the King of Sodom offered to let Abram keep the recovered items shows us that he had a degree of decency in his offer. All he wanted in return for the goods was to have the hostages returned to him.

The character of Abram is on display again. Genesis 13:13 says the men of Sodom were wicked and sinners before the Lord exceedingly. Abram, being a servant of God, would and should not want to associate with men who were exceedingly wicked and sinners before the Lord. Because Abram was rich through the blessing of God, he refused the goods on spiritual, ethical and personal grounds. His position is very plain in the statement he made in Genesis 14:23b: "I will not take anything that is yours, lest you should say, "I have made Abram rich."

The wicked Sodomites would not get any of the credit for Abram's wealth or success. The only thing Abram chose to accept was food for his men and a portion for his allies, Aner, Eshcol and Mamre. Abram's primary objective was to free his nephew Lot and return his goods. God blessed him to meet that objective and that was enough for Abram. The lesson of not associating with the wicked unless there is an evangelical objective is conveyed by a man who did not have the Bible, as we do today, for moral and ethical training.

CHAPTER 15

Chapter 15 of Genesis begins with God appearing to Abram in a vision. I am not sure whether Chapter 15 is entirely about the vision, but the evidence leans this way.

Verse 1 says that God's promise came in a vision, so the conversation and visual images were just as real as Abram and the covenants and commitments that were made to him. We also learn that the vision occurred after the rescue of Lot, but we are not told how long after Lot's rescue. The events of the next Chapter establish Abram's age, so it's safe to assume Abram had been away from his father nearly 10 years, making him around 85 years old when he had the vision.

The statement God makes to Abram in verse 1, "Do not be afraid Abram. I am your shield, your exceedingly great reward," must have been a comfort to Abram since God had proven most of this by his wealth and successful military campaign. However, Abram's question in verse 2 and statement in verse 3 shows his needs went beyond wealth and power.

> **Gen. 15:2 But Abram said, Lord God, what will You give me, seeing I go childless, and the heir of my house is Eliezer of Damascus?"**
>
> **3 Then Abram said, "Look, You have given me no offspring; indeed one born in my house is my heir!"**

The Bible says Abram called upon the name of the Lord on other occasions, but this time he asked God to give him something. In other words, he expresses a specific need in his petition to God. Abram wanted a child and heir from his own body.

Genesis 11:10–26 records the lineage of Abram from Shem and shows that his ancestors ranged from 29 to 35 years old when they fathered the children named in these verses. The only exception to this was Terah, Abram's father, who was 70 years old when he fathered Abram. Abram was around 85 years old now and he was worried about a natural heir. God addresses his worries in verse 4.

> **Gen. 15:4 And behold, the word of the Lord came to him, saying, "This one shall not be your heir, but one who will come from your own body shall be your heir."**

God's word came to Abram. He told Abram that Eliezer of Damascus would not be his heir because he would father a child of his own to be his heir. The promise of a natural heir is clearly made by God without a shred of doubt or hesitation, nearly 10 years after Abram answered God's call to leave his father's home. God then shows childless Abram the success, longevity and multitude of his seed in verse 5.

The question for Abram is the same one that is put to each of us when we are in crises or have a justifiable need that we cannot satisfy. Does Abram, or do you and I, for that matter, believe God? Gen. 15:6, the faith verse, says, "And he believed in the Lord, and he (meaning God) accounted it to him for righteousness."

Jesus would ask one important question before healing the sick: "Do you believe?" In other words, he was asking, "Do you have faith?" Faith is defined in Hebrews 11:1.

> **Hebrews 11:1 Now faith is the substance of things hoped for, the evidence of things not seen.**

The evidence or proof of things not seen moves the man of flesh into the spiritual realm where God operates (2 Cor. 4:18).

> **2 Cor. 4:18 while we do not look at the things which are seen, but at the things which are not seen. For the things which are seen are temporary, but the things which are not seen are eternal.**

The entire Chapter 11 of Hebrews, known as the "roll call of the faithful," is must reading for Bible students who want to understand what motivated Abram and others who moved toward God on nothing but faith. As stated in Genesis 15:6, "And he believed in the Lord, and He accounted it to him for righteousness." Believing in the Lord is the most important part of the salvation formula and God accounted it to Abram for righteousness.

A faithless man's service to God must be without even one sin for the curse of death to have no hold on him. Since no one born from Adam has done this, the challenge for God's gift to the world, God's Messiah, or Christ, is to do what Adam could not do: Live a sinless life and offer that perfect life—the life that earned Christ the right to not die—as an acceptable sacrifice to cover the sins of the world.

Eternal salvation is the prize for all who believe in this unseen reality and act on the unseen in a positive way, as Abram did. Abram believed God. God accounted his belief as righteousness and Abram established his faith by his works of obedience. The formula is established and functional for all who apply it to their life.

Verse 7 marks another time God communicates the promise of this particular land to Abram as an inheritance. The recipient of an inheritance is usually someone who earns the inheritance with some degree of service or family connection. Even though God promised Abram the inheritance, Abram asked for some evidence or document that proved he would inherit the land (Gen. 15:8).

The land has to be God's for him to give it as an inheritance to anyone. The Lord is not a lawyer or realtor who needs to provide deeds or legal transactions to transfer the land. The Lord is God and Creator of the land who can blot out anyone on the land who does not earn some degree of favor from him. We know this because Deuteronomy 18:9–19 describes how the descendants of Canaan fell so far from God that he deemed them unworthy of the land he gave to them.

The evidence God would give Abram is contained in Genesis 15: 9–17. In verses 12 through 14, God showed Abram the horror of the enslavement of the Israelites in Egypt. From verse 18 onward, God states the covenant, identifies some of the land's boundaries, and names the nations that would lose it.

God has spoken. Abram's questions about his lineage, his lifespan, and his offspring's future have been answered. The only thing he needs to do is enjoy all of God's blessings and continue to be faithful, patient and obedient to God's promises.

CHAPTER 16

Chapter 16 of Genesis opens with Sarai, Abram's wife, coming up with her own plan after God had informed Abram, and he no doubt informed her, that his heir would come from his own body. Sarai, who is around 75 years old at this point, must have had some serious doubts about being the physical mother of this promised heir. In fact, Genesis 11:30 tells us before this that Sarai was barren; she had no child.

Sarai's plan, as stated in verse 2, reflects basic human thinking.

> **Gen. 16:2 So Sarai said to Abram, "See now, the Lord has restrained me from bearing children. Please, go in to my maid; perhaps I shall obtain children by her." And Abram heeded the voice of Sarai.**

Verse 1 mentions the Egyptian handmaid by name—Hagar. Hagar may have been given to Sarai by the Egyptian Pharaoh at Genesis 12:16 when he thought she was Abram's sister and hoped to make her his wife. The Bible does not confirm that Hagar was a gift from the Pharaoh, although Chapter 12 records this as the first time Abram went to Egypt. It is entirely possible that a man with his wealth and entourage of soldiers, workers and servants could have had people from many lands seeking him out for employment.

Sarai clearly recognizes God as the only one who grants life. She believed Abram's claim that he would be allowed to father his own heir and she recognized the fact that she had not yet been named as the natural mother. She leaned to her own understanding and took matters into her hands. Wisdom would have demanded that Abram go back to God in prayer for guidance on such a delicate matter since God had supplied everything else they needed.

By custom at that time, a child born to a servant or slave became the property of the owner, even more so if the slave owner's husband was the father. The statement Sarai made in verse 2, "Perhaps I shall obtain children by her," shows that she is not sure of God's will, but she is willing to invest the lives of other people in a speculative venture.

The idea is only talk when Sarai said it. The fact that Abram acted before consulting the Lord made it a reality with unfavorable consequences. Verses 3 and 4 record the marriage between Abram and Hagar when Abram is around 85 years old. Hagar conceives soon after and Sarai quickly sees the downside of her actions (Gen. 16:3–4).

> Gen. 16:3 Then Sarai, Abram's wife, took Hagar her maid, the Egyptian, and gave her to her husband Abram to be his wife, after Abram had dwelt ten years in the land of Canaan.
>
> 4 So he went in to Hagar, and she conceived. And when she saw that she had conceived, her mistress became despised in her eyes.

The maid understood that she was providing the husband with something her mistress could not—a child. Her status as the maid was upgraded to the position of a wife with child and she held at least a moral claim on some of the husband's time and affection. The knowledge that she was pregnant must have made Hagar feel very secure about her position because she became hostile toward her mistress, despising her, possibly flaunting her youth and anything else that would strengthen her position. The situation was becoming unbearable, as demonstrated by Sarai's statement in verse 5.

> Gen. 16:5 Then Sarai said to Abram, "My wrong be upon you! I gave my maid into your embrace; and when she saw that she had conceived, I became despised in her eyes. The Lord judge between you and me."

The plan Sarai instigated put her at odds with her husband and, if there was any fellowship between Sarai and Hagar before the plan, it was over after Hagar's conception. When Sarai says, "The Lord judge between you and me," she is making a plea for justice and looking to lay the blame for this unbearable situation at the responsible party's feet. The ancient Nuzu law of their time gave Sarai the legal right to give her maid to her husband so she could bear children in Sarai's name, but there was no law that said the maid had a right to despise or disrespect her mistress. That was the root of the problem.

Sarai is saying, "My wrong," no doubt meaning, "the wrong this girl is doing to me." Sarai says, "be upon you," meaning it is her husband's fault. Why? The husband is the head of the household and he must oversee the well-being of everyone in the household. The maid should not be allowed to act as his wife's adversary and it was Abram's job to keep confusion out of the house. Sarai's claim is that she gave Abram the maid to embrace and, now that the maid is pregnant, she despises Sarai and Abram does nothing about it. Abram, who knew and acted on those same Nuzu laws of their time, had to acknowledge Sarai's claim. In verse 6, the statement made by Abram clearly shows that his heart is with Sarai.

> **Gen. 16:6 So Abram said to Sarai, "Indeed your maid is in your hand; do to her as you please." And when Sarai dealt harshly with her, she fled from her presence.**

Abram should have dealt with this situation before it became a problem—as we, the people of today, with 20/20 hindsight and the benefit of the entire Bible, usually say. Because he did not seek the guidance of God before acting on his wife's request and did not keep the peace after granting his wife's request, many people suffered—and one is about to suffer a whole lot more. Hagar would learn that she is not Abram's favorite just because she conceived a child. Abram put her at the mercy of Sarai and Sarai did not have any mercy on her at all.

In Genesis 16:6, the Bible says the harsh treatment that Hagar received at the hand of Sarai caused her to run away. The Bible does not say whether the harsh treatment was physical, mental or both, but it must have been quite severe for her to leave in her condition.

The guiding hand of God is still with Abram in spite of his actions. The proper way to deal with Sarai's plea for justice in verse 5 would have been to restrain Hagar, not put her in Sarai's hands for revenge, as verse 6 seems to imply. Sarai's accusation of favoritism toward Hagar might have been why Abram told Sarai, "She is your maid and in your hand."

But she was no longer a maid; Abram had accepted Hagar as a legal wife. I would think that keeps Abram on the hook to be the peacemaker.

The woman carrying Abram's child is taken care of by God for her sake, and for the sake of the child, because she did not have any control over her situation. The Angel of the Lord found Hagar and advised her on her future actions, according to Genesis 16:7–9. Hagar is the first woman in the Bible God communicated with other than Eve, who only heard God pronounce the curse on her. God spoke through the angel who instructed Hagar to return and submit to her mistress.

The command to submit should have taken care of Hagar's attitude toward Sarai. The fact that there seemed to be peace for the time being suggests that Sarai toned down as well. Genesis 16:10–13 reveals a blessed future for Abram and Hagar's son.

> Gen. 16:10 Then the Angel of the Lord said to her, "I will multiply your descendants exceedingly, so that they shall not be counted for multitude."
>
> 11 And the Angel of the Lord said to her: "Behold, you are with child, And you shall bear a son. You shall call his name Ishmael, Because the Lord has heard your affliction.
>
> 12 He shall be a wild man; His hand shall be against every man, And every man's hand against him. And he shall dwell in the presence of all his brethren."
>
> 13 Then she called the name of the Lord who spoke to her, You-Are-the-God-Who-Sees; for she said, "Have I also here seen Him who sees me?"

Abram and Hagar's son fulfilled part of God's promise to multiply Abram's descendents exceedingly. Eventually, this son would become the head of the Ishmaelites, who would later be called Arabians. In verse 11, the Angel of God told Hagar that the child would be given the name Ishmael. This name indicated that God had heard Hagar's cry of affliction. The angel also related to Hagar that God knew the character of Ishmael before he was born.

The Bible does not say how Abram knew what to name his first-born son (Gen. 16:15), but no doubt Hagar related her encounter with the angel to him and he accepted her word on the matter. The encounter with God's angel is significant in that it proves God is the only true God and Hagar is just as important to God as Abram, or everyone else, for that matter.

The special attention afforded Abram had a divine purpose designed to serve all of humanity. Abram was 86 years old when Ishmael was born.

CHAPTER 17

The Abrahamic covenant's promises, signs, requirements and rules are discussed in Chapter 17 of Genesis. Abram is 99 years old when the Lord appears to him again. The words God speaks to Abram in verse 1 literally carry the weight of the Universe.

> **Gen. 17:1 When Abram was ninety-nine years old, the Lord appeared to Abram and said to him, "I am Almighty God; walk before me and be blameless.**

He is the Almighty God, the ultimate reality, Creator of the whole Universe, our particular solar system, planet earth and man, who is the earth's appointed caretaker. The same God is now establishing a covenant with one little man here on earth.

The covenant God makes with Abram has caused varying effects on individuals and nations throughout history. The most prevalent opinion is that God played favorites with Abram and the nation of Israel. This has caused many nations of the world to be jealous of and hateful toward Israel throughout history. The truth is that God had been fine-tuning the qualities of Abram's character for more than 24 years, grooming him to be the head of a nation that would communicate his message to the rest of the world. God chose Abram because Abram believed and obeyed God and it was counted to him as righteousness (Gen. 15:6). In verse 1b, God asked Abram to "walk before me and be blameless." This request comes with a promised reward, as told in verses 2 through 8.

Gen. 17:2 "And I will make My covenant between Me and you, and will multiply you exceedingly."

3 Then Abram fell on his face, and God talked with him, saying:

4 "As for Me, behold, My covenant is with you, and you shall be a father of many nations.

5 No longer shall your name be called Abram, but your name shall be Abraham; for I have made you a father of many nations.

6 I will make you exceedingly fruitful: and I will make nations of you, and kings shall come from you.

7 And I will establish My covenant between Me and you and your descendants after you in their generations, for an everlasting covenant, to be God to you and your descendants after you.

8 Also I give to you and your descendants after you the land in which you are a stranger, all the land of Canaan, as an everlasting possession; and I will be their God."

The covenant's promise is based on the above-named conditions. In verse 3, Abram is on his face in the position of humility as God continues to communicate with him. In verse 4, God promises that Abram would be the physical father of many nations. Ishmael was already prophesied to establish a great nation; that nation still exists today. Israel would be promised through Isaac. Abram would father other children after Sarai's death whose descendents would become leaders of great nations also.

The promises of God are absolute guarantees. If any promise from God to man is conditionally based on the actions of men, then it is the men who do not meet those conditions. God cannot fail on his end. In the latter part of verse 5, God tells Abram, "For I have made you a father of many nations." Notice that God uses the past tense, "MADE YOU," not "want to make you" or "need to make you." God's words are reality when he says them.

The name of Abram is changed to Abraham in verse 5. The name itself relates to the change in his parenting status. Abram means high or exalted father, while Abraham means father of a multitude.

Verse 6 continues God's part of the covenant to this 99-year-old man who currently has only one son, but is now being told how he would be exceedingly fruitful, producing whole nations and great Kings. Verse 7 extends the Abrahamic covenant to Abraham's descendants from generation to generation and establishes a tie that puts God first in their lives.

The seeds of Abraham, the Israelites in particular, are born into a relationship with God before they even exist and, to this day, God is not dropping his end of that relationship. God still has plans, not only for Israel, but also for all of Abraham's physical seeds when certain conditions have been met by the humans involved. God restates that Canaan is the land promised in verse 8 and identifies himself as Israel's only God.

In Genesis 17:9–10, we see where God ties the responsibility for keeping the conditions of the covenant to Abraham and his seed in their generations.

> Gen. 17:9 And God said to Abraham: "As for you, you shall keep My covenant, you and your descendants after you throughout their generations.
>
> 10 "This is My covenant which you shall keep, between Me and you and your descendants after you: Every male child among you shall be circumcised;

The nation of Israel came out of Egypt after 400 years of unfair slavery. As God's covenant people, they would vote unanimously to keep the existing covenant and accept the rest of his words as the law they would live by (Ex. 19:1–8). The laws they would receive at that time through Moses would be in addition to laws that had already been established through Abraham: Believe God and it will count as righteousness—FAITH. Walk before God and be blameless—WORKS. These laws are more important than the law whose purpose is to set boundaries and establish guidelines. Faith and works get the job done.

The importance of thoroughly teaching all of the Abrahamic covenant and the law of Moses to each generation is clear when Christ and Paul have to show the Judaizers, who controlled religion, the necessity of both doctrines and the New Testament. The passages at Matthew 5: 17–20 give a small sample of what the New Testament offers to prove this point.

Matt. 5:17 "Do not think that I came to destroy the Law or the Prophets, I did not come to destroy, but to fulfill.

18 For assuredly, I say to you, till heaven and earth pass away, one jot or one tittle will by no means pass from the law till all is fulfilled.

19 Whoever therefore breaks one of the least of these commandments, and teaches men so, shall be called least in the kingdom of heaven; but whoever does and teaches them, he shall be called great in the kingdom of heaven.

20 For I say to you, that unless your righteousness exceeds the righteousness of the scribes and Pharisees, you will by no means enter the kingdom of heaven.

Paul makes a point of teaching that the Bible is one Book and both Testaments are tied to Abraham. References can be found throughout the New Testament, such as Chapter 3 of Galatians, which verifies the actions established by Abraham. In Chapter 28 of Acts, verses 22 through 24 describe Paul teaching Jews that Christianity is the conclusion of what God started with Abraham's covenant.

Acts 28:22 But we desire to hear from you what you think; for concerning this sect, we know that it is spoken against everywhere."

23 So when they had appointed him a day, many came to him at his lodging, to whom he explained and solemnly testified of the kingdom of God, persuading them concerning Jesus from both the Law of Moses and the Prophets, from morning till evening:

24 And some were persuaded by the things which were spoken, and some disbelieved.

In his time, James settled some of the controversy concerning which quality is greater, works or faith (James 2:14–20).

James 2:14 What does it profit, my brethren, if someone says he has faith, but does not have works? Can faith save him?

15 If a brother or sister is naked and destitute of daily food,

> 16 and one of you says to them, "Depart in peace, be warmed and filled," but you do not give them the things which are needed for the body, what does it profit?
>
> 17 Thus also faith by itself, if it does not have works, is dead.
>
> 18 But someone will say, "You have faith, and I have works." Show me your faith without your works, and I will show you my faith by my works.
>
> 19 You believe that there is one God. You do well. Even the demons believe and tremble!
>
> 20 But do you want to know, O foolish man, that faith without works is dead?

The point James is making has already proved to be true through the actions of Abraham—faith without works is dead. Abraham believed God, but if he had refused to put his beliefs to work and had not left his comfortable home, he would have been like the demons that believe only, and tremble from the fear of knowing there is a living God that they choose not to obey.

The principles taught in the New Testament would have been easier for the Jews of the first century to grasp if they had read and understood the Old Testament. The same is true for people today.

Verse 10 introduces circumcision as the covenant in a confusing way at first, but verse 11 clarifies the issue.

> Gen. 17:11 and you shall be circumcised in the flesh of your foreskins, and it shall be a sign of the covenant between Me and you.

The circumcision is a sign or token that proves a person is legally bound to the group and covered by the covenant's promises as long as that person abides by the conditions of the covenant. The age, conditions, qualified people and penalties regarding the command to circumcise are spelled out in Genesis 17:12–14.

In verses 15 and 16, Sarai's name is changed to Sarah (Princess) and God blesses her with motherhood. Her son shall make her a mother of nations and Kings of peoples shall be from her. The promise of Sarah's motherhood comes roughly 14 years after her plan to have children through Hagar, her maid, because she doubted the possibility of motherhood at her age.

Her doubts were even greater now, compounded by Abraham's reaction in verse 17 to the thought of Sarah conceiving a child: "Abraham fell upon his face and laughed." Abraham said in his heart (maybe he thought God could not see the thoughts of his heart), "Shall a child be born to a 100-year-old man and a 90-year-old woman?" The doubts he had about parenting children at both his and Sarah's ages are quite obvious here but the scriptures at Genesis 17:21-22 leave no doubt that Sarah would be the mother and leave no question about God's intentions for Abraham and Sarah's child.

In verse 18, Abraham put Ishmael before God in the hope that God would make him the key person for the covenant.

> **Gen. 17:18 And Abraham said to God, "Oh, that Ishmael might live before you!"**

The fact that Abraham had doubts about Sarah's promised conception, and the fact that he obviously adored Ishmael, made the request natural from the human standpoint, but God had already planned his course of action.

Verse 19 says God had already named this promised child Isaac and identified his natural mother as Sarah, whose age is not a problem for God. Isaac was already established as the father of Jacob, who would later become the nation of Israel. Jacob would father the 12 sons whose descendents would become the heads of the 12 tribes that make up the Israelite nation. In verse 20, Ishmael would have a rough road to travel after he is put out of the family circle, but his safety and future is guaranteed by God.

> **Gen. 17:20 And as for Ishmael, I have heard you. Behold, I have blessed him, and will make him fruitful, and will multiply him exceedingly. He shall beget twelve princes, and I will make him a great nation.**

The petition by Abraham on Ishmael's behalf did not go unheeded by God. "I have heard you in regard to Ishmael," God told Abraham.

Would this mean that Ishmael would be blessed the same as his half-brother Isaac? Yes, but they do not have the same mission in life.

Isaac would be the covenant carrier. The covenant carrier would develop a very close relationship with God in order to be better equipped to deliver the message that would be carried to the world. This means God will not break his commitment to Ishmael or his descendants, the Arabic people. If a break comes, it will be the result of the people falling away from God, not God falling away from them.

The Bible does not say how many different groups were in Abraham's company, but all the men, including Abraham at 99 and Ishmael at 13, were circumcised (Genesis 17:23–27).

CHAPTER 18

In Chapter 18 of Genesis, the Lord appeared to Abraham again in the plains of Mamre, near the terebinth trees. According to verses 2 and 3, the Lord was in the person of one of the three men who stood near the tent door.

> **Gen. 18:2 So he lifted his eyes and looked, and behold, three men were standing by him; and when he saw them, he ran from the tent door to meet them, and bowed himself to the ground,**
>
> **3 and said, "My Lord, if I have now found favor in Your sight, do not pass on by Your servant.**

The verses that follow show the humility, hospitality and willingness to serve that may have been the norm for Abraham, even though he was a rich powerful man. The statement and reference in verse 3 to one of the men as "my lord" proves humility and respect. Later, Lot would refer to the angels who visited him at Genesis 19:2 in Sodom as lords.

Verse 8 says these heavenly visitors ate the food prepared by Abraham. The question was asked in Genesis 18:9, "Where is Sarah your wife?" Abraham answered, "Here, in the tent." In verse 10, the all-important promise that Sarah would give birth was made by one of the men who said he would return at the appointed time and, in effect, make an impossibility a reality.

> **Gen. 18:10 And He said, "I will certainly return to you according**

to the time of life, and behold, Sarah your wife shall have a son." (Sarah was listening in the tent door which was behind him.)

11 Now Abraham and Sarah were old, well advanced in age, and Sarah had passed the age of childbearing.

12 Therefore Sarah laughed within herself, saying, "After I have grown old, shall I have pleasure, my lord being old also?"

Verse 10 shows Sarah eavesdropping behind the tent door and hearing the promise for what might have been the first time. The scene should not be hard to establish in your mind. Sarah was a 90-year-old woman who had passed the age of childbearing (Gen. 11:30; Gen. 18:11). The monthly preparation cycle for women might have passed her already and, in her mind and according to human knowledge, it would be impossible for her to have a child. Taking into account the age of her husband, Sarah did what her husband did—Sarah laughed within herself. Any of us would do the same or some similar thing.

In verse 12, Sarah refers to Abraham as "lord." The way she refers to her husband by calling him her lord after so many years of marriage speaks volumes about Sarah's dignity and character as a wife, in spite of her doubts in this particular situation.

In verse 13, the Lord asked why Sarah laughed and said, "Shall I surely bear a child, since I am old?" It must have come as quite a surprise to her since she thought no one knew of or heard her private laughter. The Lord not only knew she laughed, he also knew her thoughts.

The private laughter and doubts concerning this child would soon be known to the public. Abraham fell on his face and laughed in Genesis 17:17, then God named their son in Genesis 17:19. Sarah laughed shortly thereafter, and then according to the time of life, she would give birth to the child Isaac.

The name God gave the child, Isaac, means laughter. I don't think God meant for this name to be a joke, even though most of us might think it was funny. I think this most precious child of this rich father and mother of the faithful was named "laughter" in accordance with their lack of faith in God's promise here. Verse 14 bears this out and it would be in keeping with God's pattern of raising them to a point of obedience and spiritual maturity.

Gen. 18:14 Is anything too hard for the Lord? At the appointed time I will return to you, according to the time of life, and Sarah shall have a son."

Is anything too hard for the Lord? The Lord does not fail in his endeavors, but how does he get a busted jug to hold what he pours into it, patch it up, build it up and reinforce it until it becomes useful? Abraham, Sarah and the rest of us with our limited capabilities need to understand that trust is the bridge that brings us to the unlimited grace and power of God. Abraham and Sarah's faith should have been reinforced as they watched the fruit of their love grow up in front of them and remembered their laughter, lapse in faith and failure to accept and understand God's divine power.

In Genesis 18:15, Sarah denied that she laughed. Sarah's denial was the basic human response to being caught in a lie, but the Lord understands and accepts our humanity and the promise goes forward as made.

The remainder of Chapter 18 covers God's preparation to deal with the total destruction of some disobedient nations. Verse 16 says Abraham went with the men to send them on the way. They looked toward Sodom, then began to journey there. Abraham did not know why they were going there, but in verses 17 through 19, we see that God's plan for Abraham continues to develop and we learn something about why the Lord called Abraham to be the father of the faithful.

Gen. 18:17 And the Lord said, "Shall I hide from Abraham what I am doing,

18 since Abraham shall surely become a great and mighty nation, and all nations of the earth shall be blessed in him?

19 For I have known him, in order that he may command his children and his household after him, that they keep the way of the Lord, to do righteousness and justice, that the Lord may bring to Abraham what he has spoken to him."

First, the Lord had known Abraham even before we see the faith, obedience and character unfold in his spiritual upbringing. Second, the fact that he went so long without children appears to be God's design to make Abraham and Sarah take parenthood more seriously. Being older and wiser, they would naturally use more wisdom and care in raising children. The Lord is training Abraham to train his children and his household after him to keep the way of the Lord, do justice and judgement, which were already proven attributes of Abraham to some extent. The third reason is that the Lord wanted to satisfy the promises made to Abraham.

Abraham, the father of nations, is still a work-in-progress at this point. He would face other situations where he would have to step out on nothing but faith, so any knowledge or life experience that strengthened his faith would be helpful.

The things Abraham is being taught in order to be a teacher of nations are just as useful and relevant today as they were then. The people of nations and nations of the world could exist with more peace and tranquility today if the lessons of Abraham were accepted by the world, especially considering the reasons for the demise of Sodom and Gomorrah to come.

Verse 20 deals with God's reason for destroying Sodom and Gomorrah.

> Gen. 18:20 And the Lord said, "Because the outcry against Sodom and Gomorrah is great, and because their sin is very grave,
>
> 21 I will go down now and see whether they have done altogether according to the outcry against it that has come to Me; and if not, I will know."

It is unclear who is making these outcries, but it is quite clear that the sins of the people of Sodom and Gomorrah are very grave or grievous. The citizens of those cities may have argued the same arguments as every other pride- and lust-driven, destruction-earning city—we can make our own laws, we can say what we do behind closed doors is our own business and so on—but it will not change the facts.

> **FACT:** God holds the only patent on the Universe and because there is no patent office that can register his claim, he must register it with himself and hold it with his ability to stop whoever comes against it.

FACT: God planned, then created the Universe, so he is the owner.

FACT: God can—and does—command a degree of obedience from his creation.

FACT: God can—and will—destroy parts of his creation for disobedience of his words and will.

In verse 21, the Lord is going to decide if Sodom and Gomorrah are as bad as the outcry he has heard against the cities. If he finds this to be true, God as Creator, owner, potter, judge, jury and executioner has the authority and responsibility to remove the people of these cities if they do not repent. It is a vital lesson for Abraham to learn that man is controlled by a higher power that will not allow him to continue forever outside of God's will.

Verse 22 explains the parting of the three men. Two set out for Sodom and, according to Genesis 19:1, they are angels. The Lord remained and Abraham stood there before the Lord.

The fate of Sodom and Gomorrah was determined by the actions of the people of Sodom and Gomorrah. Lot, the nephew of Abraham, was living in Sodom. Abraham must have been concerned about him although he does not mention his name during this conversation with the Lord.

Genesis 18:23–33 shows Abraham making an appeal for mercy on behalf of the cities. The concepts of judgement against unrighteousness must have been clear to him because his only basis for mercy to these cities was the hope of finding a few righteous people there.

God first offers clemency if the angels can find 50 righteous people in the cities. It would appear as if Abraham's personal knowledge of the wickedness of these cities caused him to doubt that they could find fifty righteous people, so he bargained down to the number of righteous people he thought they could find to ten. Ironically, that is the approximate size of Lot's family, including Lot, Lot's wife, two unmarried daughters, two married daughters and two sons-in-law.

The Lord left after this conversation and Abraham went back to his home. Sodom and Gomorrah did not earn God's favor, but if only ten righteous people could be found there, they could all escape the judgement of God.

CHAPTER 19

Chapter 19 of Genesis continues the story of Sodom and Gomorrah as the two men who left the Lord and Abraham are heading toward Sodom and Gomorrah. They are referred to as angels in verse 1 as they approach the gate into the city of Sodom.

> Gen. 19:1 Now the two angels came to Sodom in the evening, and Lot was sitting in the gate of Sodom. When Lot saw them, he rose to meet them, and he bowed himself with his face toward the ground.
>
> 2 And he said, "Here now, my lords, please turn in to your servant's house and spend the night, and wash your feet; then you may rise early and go on your way." And they said, "No, but we will spend the night in the open square."
>
> 3 But he insisted strongly; so they turned in to him and entered his house. Then he made them a feast, and baked unleavened bread, and they ate.

Lot was sitting at the gate when the angels approached. He showed them hospitality and welcomed them by rising to meet them and bowing before them. The Bible refers to these visitors as angels after the facts involved, but at their first meeting, there is no proof that Lot or Abraham saw them as anything other than weary travelers that they chose to serve (Gen. 18:1–4). Abraham certainly did not inform Lot that angels were about to visit him because Genesis 18:33 says he went home after he appealed for mercy on behalf of the cities, and Abraham lived some 18 to 20 miles away from Lot.

Lot and Abraham treated these men with hospitality and humility from the time they first met them. It would appear to be the way they treated all people. Hebrews 13:2, which reads, "Do not forget to entertain strangers, for by so doing some have unwittingly entertained angels," appears to be the way these men were raised, long before it was advised in the New Testament.

The choice of Abraham's descendents to carry God's covenant as stated at Genesis 18:17–19 is based on what is important to God, including peace, love, respect for others, Godly parenting and many of the traits these men seem to display.

In Genesis 19:2–3, Lot offered the two men his house for the night, but they refused, intending to sleep in the open square. Lot had to know how bad the men of Sodom were, but he could not take the don't-get-involved position that is so common to us in the dangerous areas of our cities today. Lot insisted strongly and they accepted his second invitation.

The men of Sodom would justify God's condemnation of them by their actions in verses 4 and 5.

> **Gen. 19:4 Now before they lay down, the men of the city, the men of Sodom, both old and young, all the people from every quarter, surrounded the house.**
>
> **5 And they called to Lot and said to him, "Where are the men who came to you tonight? Bring them out to us that we may know them carnally."**

Generally, a person traveling in the dangerous areas of an unknown city might encounter thieves, muggers, pick-pockets, drug dealers, prostitutes or others whose objective is to separate that person from his or her money. The activities of these people are both sinful and criminal, but understandable when you know that the love of money is the root of all evil and some people will stoop to any level for money.

The angels traveling in Sodom found an incredibly different situation. Unlike other cities, where you need only fear a certain segment of the population whose objective is greed, the men of Sodom who surrounded Lot's house were from every quarter of the city. All of the men of Sodom were to be feared because their objective was so twisted it makes a common thief look decent.

The statement in Genesis 19:5b, "Bring them out to us that we may know them carnally," means the men of Sodom wanted to know Lot's guest in the biblical sense of the word, meaning men literally wanted to have sex with men. The name we use for that immoral act is sodomy, so-named for the city of Sodom. The attempted act of his neighbors is described as wickedness in verse 7.

Lot, not long a citizen of Sodom, stepped out of his door and shut it behind him in order to convince his neighbors not to sexually assault the two male strangers who had accepted his hospitality. In order to protect the men under his roof, Lot offered his two virgin daughters to the crowd (Gen. 19:6–8). The Sodomites rejected the two young female virgins.

The crowd turned on Lot, accusing him of trying to sit in judgement over them although he was only a newcomer. The husbands of Lot's married daughters were actually in the crowd outside his house, hoping to have sex with men. Thus, the immorality of Sodom had even permeated the family of this righteous man.

A thief might steal because he is hungry or lazy. But a man who lays with another man as with a woman has given himself over to a Satanic appetite that leads to an entirely different level of immorality. Leviticus 18:22 says, "You shall not lie with a male as with a woman. It is an abomination." Paul lays out a detailed account of the unrighteous acts that brings the wrath of God down on a nation at Romans 1:18–32, with a special emphasis on verses 25 through 27.

> Rom. 1:25 who exchanged the truth of God for the lie, and worshipped and served the creature rather than Creator, who is blessed forever. Amen.
>
> 26 For this reason God gave them up to vile passions. For even their women exchanged the natural use for what is against nature.
>
> 27 Likewise also the men, leaving the natural use of the woman, burned in their lust for one another, men with men committing

> what is shameful, and receiving in themselves the penalty of their error which was due.

In Genesis 19:9–10, the crowd around Lot's house first threatened to treat Lot worse than they wanted to treat his guests, then they attempt to do just that. The men outside were trying to break down the door to Lot's house. The men Lot has been protecting must now pull him back into the house and shut the door in order to protect him from his self-destructive neighbors. The angels begin to work in verse 11:

> **Gen. 19:11 And they smote the men that *were* at the door of the house with blindness, both small and great; so that they wearied themselves to find the door.**

The actions of the men outside the house were so reprehensible that the angels had to blind them to repel their attack. The men of Sodom were stumbling around in total darkness and the Bible says they wearied themselves to find the door, even after they were blinded. The scene, which is true, must be hard to comprehend. The Sodomites were so twisted and perverted that blindness did not stop their intentions, even though it reduced their abilities.

In hindsight, Lot may have been wise to think the plush grazing land around Sodom was a little too good to be true and investigated the people before he got too involved with them. The ten righteous people needed to save Sodom had not been found. The angels speak in verses 12 and 13.

> **Gen. 19:12 Then the men said to Lot, "Have you anyone else here? Son-in-law, your sons, your daughters, and whomever you have in the city—take them out of this place!**
>
> **13 For we will destroy this place, because the outcry against them has grown great before the face of the Lord, and the Lord has sent us to destroy it."**

Verse 12 poses the question, "Have you anyone else here?" The Bible does not identify any sons that Lot may have had and neither his wife nor daughters are named, so not much is written that will allow us to identify his family. The Bible does not say how many sons-in-law or married daughters Lot had, but the Bible says daughters (plural), so he had at least two that were married and two that were not, making at least four daughters.

The crux of the message is plain enough though: Get whomever you want to save out of this place. Why? The angels say they are under orders from God to destroy the cities. Why? Because the Lord has to respond to the great outcry against them. They are wicked by God's standard.

The world might produce differing opinions on whether God has the right to enter into judgement against these cities because of their sexual preferences. If Sodom or Gomorrah had a Supreme Court, it might have ruled that homosexuality was not a crime or a sin, merely a lifestyle choice. If they had a legal foundation representing them, anyone who did not readily accept this lifestyle choice might have been sued.

These actions would be a direct assault against God's will, with the elevation of unrighteousness at its core. Questions raised about this issue may be answered in many ways, but this should suffice: "The earth is the Lord's and the fullness thereof." God is Creator and owner of all things. God does not ask for permission to execute judgement on those whose actions merit it. The story of Sodom and Gomorrah has been showing this to the Bible-reading public since the scriptures were written, but Satan can still fix a way to get to individuals as well as nations.

By agreement, Lot should not have been saved because ten righteous people had not been found. By grace and love for Abraham, Lot and his family are given the chance to escape and be saved.

Verse 14 says Lot went outside and spoke to his sons-in-laws about leaving. The appeal to his sons-in-law might have been, "Since women cannot please you, go and get my daughters because this place is about to be destroyed and the Lord has given us a grace ticket out of here."

The Bible says Lot seemed to them like a man who joked (Gen. 19: 14). The blindness had done nothing to soften the Sodomites hearts. I wonder if they ever stopped to question the blindness. Maybe they were accepting it as some strange new sensation. I do know they were about to experience a fatal burning sensation.

Verses 15 and 16 paint an agonizing picture.

Gen. 19:15 When the morning dawned, the angels urged Lot to

hurry, saying, "Arise, take your wife and your two daughters who are here, lest you be consumed in the punishment of the city."

16 And while he lingered, the men took hold of his hand, his wife's hand, and the hands of his two daughters, the Lord being merciful to him, and they brought him out and set him outside the city.

Lot was awakened by the angels and told to take his wife and the two daughters that were still there and leave before they were caught up in Sodom's reward. The family lingered and dragged it out, possibly hoping the other children would come. Finally the angels had to take their hands and drag them out of the city.

When the family is finally outside the city, the angels tell them to leave the plains area altogether and escape into the mountains to avoid being destroyed (Gen. 19:17). Verses 18 through 22 give an interesting look at human nature. The angels, who are in the process of saving Lot's life by literally pulling him and his family out of the city, tell him that the mountains are the safest place to go, but Lot is afraid. He thinks some evil may overtake him in the mountains.

Less than 24 hours earlier, Lot could not have imagined what was now unfolding before his eyes. He is being pulled out of a doomed city while some of his family is still there. The strain he must be under may have dimmed his thinking. The angels would not pull them out of danger just to send them back into danger. Yet Lot, who is being blessed by the opportunity to escape destruction, winds up telling the angles how he wants them to bless him (Gen. 19:20). He wants to escape to a small, nearby city instead of to the mountains.

In Genesis 19:21–22, the angels accepted Lot's pleas and spared the small city that should have been destroyed. Lot is told to hurry up and escape to the city of Zoar because securing the safety of Lot and his family was holding up God's judgement of the plains cities. The destruction of Sodom and Gomorrah takes place that morning, according to verses 23 through 26.

Gen. 19:23 The sun had risen upon the earth when Lot entered Zoar.

24 Then the Lord rained brimstone and fire on Sodom and Gomorrah, from the Lord out of the heavens.

25 So He overthrew those cities, all the plain, all the inhabitants of the cities, and what grew on the ground.

26 But his wife looked back behind him, and she became a pillar of salt.

The Lord rained fire and brimstone on the cities, all the plains, all the people and everything that grew upon the ground. I have read many opinions concerning how or what happened to cause fire to fall on the plains cities. Some say volcanoes erupted, others say oil and tar deposits exploded; they say it in a way that detracts from what God did. The way God implemented this act is not relevant here. The fact that God did it, and he did it for a reason, is relevant. Trying to detract from God's power does not make the people any less dead or hell any cooler.

Lot's wife, for some reason, did not obey the angel's command and she looked back. The Bible doesn't say why. Maybe she was hoping the other children would come running up behind her, maybe she was too nosy not to look back, or maybe she yearned in her heart to return to Sodom. I certainly don't know why she looked back. I just know the Bible says she did and her body became a pillar of salt.

The only survivors were Lot and his two daughters. Abraham returned to the place where he pleaded for the cities and he witnessed smoke rising like a furnace from the area.

Verse 29 shows God's reason for saving Lot.

Gen. 19:29 And it came to pass, when God destroyed the cities of the plain, that God remembered Abraham, and sent Lot out of the midst of the overthrow, when He overthrew the cities in which Lot had dwelt.

Abraham never mentioned Lot by name, as stated earlier, when he was asking God for mercy in relation to these cities. However, given the fact that he would not even take payment when he rescued Lot, you would have to think Lot was his primary concern.

God is quite specific about why he rescued Lot (Gen. 19:29). The petition of Abraham to God, God's desire to train a future father of nations on how to raise children so they will not trap themselves in the same situation and Lot's desire to serve was instrumental in securing God's grace for the three survivors.

Lot escaped to Zoar because he did not want to go into the mountains for fear some evil would overtake and kill him (Gen. 19:17–18). After a time, he changed his mind again and they decided to flee Zoar to dwell in the mountains because the people of Zoar made Lot afraid (Gen. 19:30).

> **Gen. 19:30 Then Lot went up out of Zoar and dwelt in the mountains, and his two daughters were with him; for he was afraid to dwell in Zoar. And he and his two daughters dwelt in a cave.**
>
> **Gen. 19:31 Now the firstborn said to the younger, "Our father is old, and there is no man on the earth to come in to us as is the custom of all the earth.**

Perhaps Lot and his family were not treated well and were made to be afraid because they were the only three survivors of Sodom and Gomorrah and were strangers to the people of Zoar. The Bible doesn't say what the people of Zoar did to them, but if Zoar was slated for destruction with the plains cities, you can safely assume they were just as bad.

The oldest daughter's statement in Genesis 19:31, "There is no man on earth to come in to us in the custom of all the earth," may prove that the men of Zoar preferred sex with other men instead of women. Lot, as a follower of God, would not have participated with the locals in the practice of abominations, probably giving him an uneasy feeling at the very least. This may have influenced him to leave. Also in verse 31, the oldest daughter seems to think that, except for the people of Zoar, she and her family were all alone. She is also concerned that she and her sister will not be able to preserve the lineage of their father.

Lot and his daughters were living alone in a cave and the situation was not good: Everything was gone—the fertile grazing lands, all of the livestock and wealth, their mother was dead, at least two sisters were dead, at least two brothers-in-law were dead and, if there were any brothers, they were dead as well.

This may be why the oldest daughter was concerned about preserving the lineage of their father. Their method of doing this, which appears to be one of desperation, is to get father drunk so he does not know what is happening and lie with him. The girls must have known their father would not do this if he were sober. They might have thought that they could lie to him after the fact and say they were pregnant before leaving Zoar. Their apparent exposure to the wickedness of Sodom would make this act of treachery a minor chore. A lie would be second nature, for even the good children, coming from a place as far from God as Sodom allowed its people to go.

Their error was in thinking they had to take this matter into their own hands. The daughters should have talked to their father before they acted. He might have told them what the angels told him in verses 12 and 13 so they would know that the destruction was only in a limited area. He also could have assured them that they would rejoin his Uncle Abraham who had an army of young men ready to be married. That would have meant that the daughters, the last existing seeds of Lot, could find husbands to help them preserve their father's lineage.

The daughters followed through on their plan. The actions of Lot's daughters cannot be classified as what the law of Moses would later call "the duty of a husband's brother," since Lot was their father and they never had husbands.

Lot unknowingly became the father of two nations—the Moabite nation through Moab, son of the first-born daughter, and the Ammonite nation through BenAmmi, son of the younger daughter. Ruth, the Moabite great-grandmother of King David, would come from Lot's lineage.

The Bible does not say how many other sins or types of sin the Sodomites practiced. The Bible just says they were very wicked and their ungodly sexual perversion appears to be their undoing. The question is, how did this sinful act succeed in saturating their whole society? They did not have the mass media advantage that could show a homosexual man dying such a brave death that anybody who said he was dying because of the dangerous way he lived would be considered a bad person. Perhaps a group of rich, well-meaning idealists whose desire to help the underdog could have encouraged the Sodomites' actions, especially if they didn't seek God's will before acting.

The way it happened is not answered here, but the end result should leave no doubt about how God feels about it. The warning to any person, group of persons or nation is that perversion is a sin and God will not bless anyone who persists in this activity.

CHAPTER 20

Chapter 20 of Genesis focuses on Abraham again. Abraham and his entourage are moving toward the south country. They stayed in Gerar, between Kadesh and Shur. The Bible does not say whether or not the destruction of Sodom, all the plains cities except Zoar, inhabitants and what grew on the ground had anything to do with the move (Gen. 19: 25). The waters could have been poisoned and the ecosystem for miles around could have been damaged. The Bible does not confirm this, so the author only raises this point to explain why they might have moved from a comfortable place.

Abraham's group is so large that he cannot enter a new area unnoticed. The livestock alone may require enough water and grazing lands to cause concern among the inhabitants of the land, so Abraham is always concerned about how he will be received by the kings he encounters in new lands.

Verse 2 shows Abraham again passing off his Sarah, who is also his half-sister, as his sister instead of his wife. King Abimelech does not know that Sarah is also Abraham's wife. The King tried to separate her from Abraham the same way the Pharaoh of Egypt did in Chapter 12.

The Bible says Sarah was a very beautiful woman. I certainly accept what the Bible says. I must admit, I am awed at the thought of how beautiful she must have been at 90 years old to cause this King and the Egyptian Pharaoh, over 20 years earlier, to be so driven for her company. Like the Egyptian Pharaoh, the King and his household were plagued by God over Abraham's wife. The King was warned in a dream from God before there was any type of relationship between him and Sarah (Gen. 20:6–7).

The Bible says the King reported the events of the dream to his servants early the next morning and they were very much afraid. King Abimelech's obedience to God and his honest defense of his innocence saved him and household (Gen. 20:8). The fear of God is manifested more through the King, at this point than through Abraham.

In verses 9 and 10, King Abimelech asks Abraham why he engaged in a deceptive act that could endanger him as well as his household. Abraham explains his actions in verses 11 through 13.

> Gen. 20:9 And Abimelech called Abraham and said to him, "What have you done to us? How have I offended you, that you have brought on me and on my Kingdom a great sin? You have done deeds to me that ought not to be done."
>
> 10 Then Abimelech said to Abraham, "What did you have in view, that you have done this thing?"
>
> 11 And Abraham said, "Because I thought, surely the fear of God is not in this place; and they will kill me on account of my wife.
>
> 12 But indeed she is truly my sister. She is the daughter of my father, but not the daughter of my mother; and she became my wife.
>
> 13 And it came to pass, when God caused me to wander from my father's house, that I said to her, "This is your kindness that you should do for me: in every place, wherever we go, say of me, "He is my brother."

Abraham's answer exposes more of this faithful man's fears, human frailties, lack of total trust, and reflects again on how dangerous his calling was from the human point of view. Abraham's answer to the King in verse 11 reveals Abraham's fears, but it also shows a man who went in spite of his fears. The fact that he had personal knowledge of Sodom and Gomorrah's utter lack of respect for anything that pleased God could have been his reason for jumping to that conclusion.

The half-truth was his way of tilting the scales in his favor. The thing Abraham should have learned then, and we could still learn today, is that when God is weighing things in your favor, all you need to do is concentrate on obedience to him. Asking his wife to say she was his sister, while concealing the fact that she was also his wife, reveals his human frailty.

Verse 13 reveals how the plan to preserve his life while being obedient to God's call took shape from the very beginning. A reflection of Abraham's walk with God up to this point reveals his blessings.

> **Abraham traveled in and out of Egypt during a famine at home and prospered, acquiring more wealth for his troubles.**
>
> **He executed a successful military campaign to save Lot.**
>
> **He became a parent for the first time in his old age, with the promise of fathering more children at an even older age.**
>
> **Abraham asked for God's mercy before the downfall of Sodom and Gomorrah and God acknowledged his petition.**
>
> **Lot was saved from destruction as a gift to Abraham even though the ten righteous people had not been found.**

To read how God had continually blessed Abraham through every situation would make us think he should have had enough confidence in God not to pull this trick from his survival bag again. The flip side of that is that we are not the ones in a strange land, thinking we could get killed—Abraham was and his faith had not matured enough for him to give up his efforts and give it over to God. Abraham made himself look bad to some degree, but he did not have the story of his life to give him the answers that we have. He was still living the story and every facet of it was life or death, not only him, but from his standpoint, for his entire entourage as well.

God's favorable dealings with King Abimelech should not go unnoticed, as it proves God is fair and just and he respects integrity in everyone. Genesis 20:6 says, "For I also withheld you from sinning against Me; therefore I did not let you touch her." The choice and purpose of God concerning Abraham and Sarah could not be clearer. God sees any act against this couple as a sin against him because God knows what he is planning through Abraham's bloodlines by Sarah.

Abimelech's integrity establishes him, but Abraham is favored again and he is enriched by the gifts mentioned—the return of his wife and an open invitation to live anywhere in Abimelech's kingdom. Abraham, whom God called a prophet with a direct prayer line to him in verse 7, did not lose favor with God here. In fact, it appears he gained another step on which to build his stairway of faith. The accumulation of more wealth and a new place to spread out his vast holdings is a reality and his prayers prove to be a fulfillment of God's promise of Genesis 12:3, in that Abimelech's home was blessed and healed (Gen. 20:17).

CHAPTER 21

In Chapter 21 of Genesis, Isaac is born right on the schedule set by the angels (Gen. 17:21; Gen. 18:10). The visitation came after the incident in Gerar with Abimelech. If the narrative is in sequence with the facts, that would mean it was only a few months from the time Abraham got the message of Isaac's birth (Gen. 17:1) until the conception at Genesis 21:2.

The actual birth takes place when Abraham is 100 years old according to verse 5. That would mean that the visits from the Lord, the fall of Sodom and the situation in Gerar take place in a relatively short time. Lot is not mentioned again as an active character, so it would seem that he and Abraham never made contact again.

The fact that Abraham found a new place to spread out his vast holdings instead of going back might still raise questions about how much damage the destruction of the plains cities had done to the area. However, it is not an issue for Sarah and Abraham now because they are about the business of being proud parents.

In verses 3 and 4, Abraham follows the angel's directive by naming his son Isaac, meaning laughter. In accordance with the covenant, he circumcises him. In verses 6 and 7, Sarah laughs again, but it is not the laughter of scorn or mockery as indicated by the Hebrew text and context of Sarah's earlier laughter.

> Gen. 21:6 And Sarah said, "God has made me laugh, and all who hear will laugh with me."

> 7 She also said, "Who would have said to Abraham that Sarah would nurse children? For I have borne him a son in his old age."

The laughter this time, by definition and context, is of pure pleasure and happiness. The parents are elated. A feast on the day Isaac was weaned would start out as a gala event. It would turn into a heart-wrenching affair when Sarah saw Abraham and Hagar's son, Ishmael, scoffing (Gen. 21:8–9).

The word scoffer in Hebrew and Greek means to mock or deride, along with other negative terms. The text does not say whom, how or what Ishmael was scoffing. Ishmael was a teenager and could have been involved in any number of youthful stunts. The teenager probably could have been brought under control, but there was no way to control Sarah's desire to oust this woman she had brought into the intimate circle of their lives, verse 10.

> Gen. 21:10 Therefore she said to Abraham, "Cast out this bondswoman and her son; for the son of this bondswoman shall not be heir with my son, namely with Isaac."
>
> 11 And the matter was very displeasing in Abraham's sight because of his son.

Verse 11 deals with Abraham's sorrow because of his wife's request. Sarah could still be harboring a grudge toward Hagar for despising her when she conceived Ishmael. The Bible does not say whether there was some underlying animosity between the women that continued even after Hagar returned from running away. The Bible does not tell us what type of relationship developed between Sarah and her legal son Ishmael, but her feelings toward him are openly hostile after she gives birth to a natural son.

The young man, Ishmael, is Abraham's first-born natural son and all communications show that he loved Ishmael dearly. Abraham had God's word that he would father children in Chapter 15. Abraham took his wife Sarah's opinion of how he should father children, and whom he should father children with (Chapter 16), when he should have taken direction from God. The end result is pain, suffering, and confusion for all involved.

The lesson they had to learn the hard way should teach us to scrutinize the information and beware of making the same mistake. Abraham appears to have sought God's council this time after Sarah's request to have Hagar and Ishmael removed from the group. The answer that comes from God in verses 12 and 13 gives Sarah her way in the matter.

> **Gen. 21:12 But God said to Abraham. "Do not let it be displeasing in your sight because of the lad or because of your bondwoman. Whatever Sarah has said to you, listen to her voice; for in Isaac your seed shall be called.**
>
> **13 Yet I will also make a nation of the son of the bondwoman, because he is your seed."**

The first consideration is God's plan for the nation that would carry the knowledge of him to the world for all times. When God said, "In Isaac your seed shall be called," he verified whose line would provide that nation. The grief that Abraham had to be suffering over Ishmael's immediate future was eased by God's promise in verse 13 to make a nation from Ishmael's offspring, too. Ishmael gained God's favor because he is Abraham's seed and, according to Genesis 16:6–13, neither he nor his mother had any control of how they came into this situation that Genesis 16:11 calls an affliction. God is still carrying all parties involved through their human weaknesses, to the point where they can come to know and trust him.

Abraham performed one of the hardest jobs a good father could in verse 14. He sent his son away.

> **Gen. 21:14 So Abraham rose early in the morning, and took bread and a skin of water; and putting it on her shoulder, he gave it and the boy to Hagar, and sent her away. Then she departed and wandered in the wilderness of Beersheba.**

God had promised to protect him, so Abraham knew the boy would be taken care of, but seeing him leave his presence and knowing he might never see him again had to be heart-wrenching. The trials and tribulations that Ishmael and his mother encounter are covered in verses 15 through 21. The fact that God is true to his promise to take care of them can be observed here, too. The water ran out as they wandered in the wilderness of Beersheba and she left Ishmael under a shrub and moved the distance of a bowshot away from him because she did not want to see him die.

The promise from God to Hagar in Genesis 16:9–15 to make Ishmael a man is the farthest thing from Hagar's mind as she prepares to lose him as a boy. Hagar was reacting to her crisis the same way that most of us would, looking at WHAT IS while forgetting what God said WILL BE. God had to open her eyes so Hagar could see how close she was to the life-giving water (verses 17, 18 and 19).

God was with Ishmael, even though he did live up to or down to the prophecy of Genesis 16:12. A wild man, his hand against every man and every man's hand against him, sounds like a ruthless individual who asked no quarter and gave no quarter. Verse 21 says Ishmael's wife was from Egypt, which was one of the major African nations at that time. Hagar, his mother, was Egyptian and his father was becoming the head of the Jewish nation. Ishmael would eventually become the father of Arabia.

Verses 22 through 34 deal with King Abimelech and his top general, Phichol, who seek an agreement with Abraham to guarantee honesty between them that would extend to future generations.

> **Gen. 21:23 Now therefore, swear to me by God that you will not deal falsely with me, with my offspring, or with my posterity: but that according to the kindness that I have done to you, you will do to me and to the land in which you have dwelt."**
>
> **24 And Abraham said, "I will swear."**

The key element in Abimelech's desire for this agreement was the fact that Abraham had dealt falsely with him on their earlier meeting. God was clearly Abraham's protector and wouldn't allow him to be harmed. Abimelech could truthfully say that he had dealt kindly with Abraham and kindness was due. In verses 25 through 27, they settle some confusion over a well that Abimelech knew nothing about. They parted company with a covenant intact.

CHAPTER 22

The first three verses in Chapter 22 of Genesis reveal God's command to have Abraham offer Isaac as a sacrifice on one of the mountains in the land of Moriah. Abraham's response is immediate and without questions, according to verse 3.

> Gen. 22:1 Now it came to pass after these things that God tested Abraham, and said to him, "Abraham!" And he said, "Here I am."
>
> 2 Then He said, "Take now your son, your only son Isaac, whom you love, and go to the land of Moriah, and offer him there as a burnt offering on one of the mountains of which I shall tell you."
>
> 3 So Abraham rose early in the morning and saddled his donkey, and took two of his young men with him, and Isaac his son; and he split the wood for the burnt offering, and arose and went to the place of which God had told him.

Isaac's age is not disclosed here, but verse 6 says he was old enough to carry the wood for the sacrifice. Abraham was 75 years old when he left his father in Haran to answer God's call. He was 100 years old when Isaac was born and, if Isaac were in his teens now, Abraham would have been with the Lord at least 37 years when this event takes place.

Abraham had grown from a man who misrepresented his true relationship with Sarah twice out of fear and into a man who can, and will, put total trust in God. Human sacrifices are a common practice in the areas all around them, but since God had never required that of any person before, it must have been a most difficult thing for Abraham.

Isaac had been tagged as the promised child with seed coming through him, but now his father is on the way to a mountain where he will sacrifice him before he ever reproduces. The author of Hebrews describes what Abraham was thinking (Heb. 11:17–19). The author of Hebrews is being inspired by the Holy Spirit to explain Abraham's faith in God's ability to raise Isaac from the dead.

> **Heb. 11:17 By faith Abraham, when he was tested, offered up Isaac, and he who had received the promises offered up his only begotten son,**
>
> **18 of whom it was said, "In Isaac your seed shall be called,"**
>
> **19 concluding that God was able to raise him up, even from the dead, from which he also received him in a figurative sense.**

When the group arrives at the mountain, Abraham tells the two young men with him to stay with the donkey while he and Isaac go and worship, and then they would come back down (Gen. 22:5). Abraham was intent on doing exactly what God told him to do, but he seemed just as certain that Isaac would come down off of that mountain with him—alive. The only thing he could believe was that God would raise Isaac from the dead after he killed him in the sacrificial rite.

At verse 7, Isaac noticed that everything was present for the burnt offering except the lamb. Abraham explained that God would provide himself a lamb for a burnt offering in verse 8. The altar was built at the appointed place, the wood was placed in order, and Isaac was bound and laid on the altar. In verse 9, Isaac must know now that he is about to be the sacrificial lamb, but he was obedient to his father and didn't question what had happened so far. Genesis 22:10–12 describes the events.

> **Gen. 22:10 And Abraham stretched out his hand and took the knife to slay his son.**
>
> **11 But the Angel of the Lord called to him from heaven and said, "Abraham, Abraham!" So he said, '"Here I am."**
>
> **12 And He said, "Do not lay your hand on the lad, or do anything**

> to him; for now I know that you fear God, since you have not withheld your son, your only son, from Me."

The scriptures clearly show that God was testing Abraham. I pointed out some scriptures earlier in this Chapter that suggest Abraham believed God would raise Isaac from the dead before he took him upon the mountain. I know theologians who raised the following question: If Abraham knew God would raise Isaac from the dead, then the test is rigged. What is the point of the exercise?

Knowing and believing that God, whom Abraham has never seen, can and will raise the dead is the point. Developing his faith so strongly that Abraham can give up the life of a child that is much more important to him than his own life, and trust God to return it, is the point. Abraham is being taken into areas that all Christian believers will have to travel in order to be saved. Christ teaches on this in several places in the New Testament, the following may be one of the clearest passages (Mark 8:35–37).

> **Mark 8:35 For whoever desires to save his life will lose it, but whoever loses his life for My sake and the gospel's will save it.**
>
> **36 For what will it profit a man if he gains the whole world, and loses his own soul?**
>
> **37 Or what will a man give in exchange for his soul?**

Christ is teaching his followers that this life (which is passing anyway, because in Adam, all die) is not as important as the life based on enough faith that God will return a life lived in his service, for eternity, when he rules the earth as King of Kings and Lord of Lords.

Every person who trusts in God must be able to go all the way to the grave believing that life has been established on the other side of it by Christ—that is the point. Verse 12 reveals the crux of the matter: "For now I know that you fear God, since you have not withheld your son, your only son, from Me."

The man Abraham is there. He has grown into that area of faith that all followers of God should be growing toward: Fear God enough to be obedient even to death. Fear God enough to give up all things for him and the future kingdom if this passing world makes it necessary. Fear

God enough to move at his command, regardless of what that command is.

Abraham is using his key to unlock the kingdom of Heaven and enter it on the basis of his faith in the same way Christ taught (Luke 17: 20–21).

> **Luke 17:20 Now when He was asked by the Pharisees when the kingdom of God would come, He answered them and said, "The kingdom of God does not come with observation;**
>
> **21 nor will they say, "See here!" or "See there!" For indeed, the kingdom of God is within you."**

The kingdom of Heaven will come physically at some point as the Lord taught in his prayer, "Thy kingdom come, thy will be done on earth as it is in heaven," but citizenship is obtained by the actions in the heart of the individual. Abraham is a functioning citizen in this world, but he is not of this world. The certainty of God's ability to deliver on his promises has been established in Abraham's heart and that is where the kingdom is for him.

The same holds true for you and I. Living and leaving this present world with the internal certainty that God's eternal kingdom is coming means that we have met the same faith requirements that establishes the kingdom of God in us as well.

The above-mentioned Pharisees did not get the point. They were thinking of another temporary kingdom whose powers were limited by the lifespan and abilities of the men who established it. A person who accepts God's terms for service, and believes God is able to deliver on both sides of the grave, has met all citizenship requirements in their heart. The rest is just a matter of time.

Abraham was gravely serious about his intentions and would have given his and Sarah's only son back to God. A person may ask if God condones human sacrifices in light of his testing of Abraham: ABSOLUTELY NOT. The only one who would give up his son as an acceptable sacrifice would be God.

The Lamb of God was promised before Adam and Eve were expelled from the Garden of Eden. The Lamb would be the only physically begotten son of God on earth, through Adam's seed. The Lamb's mission on earth would be to satisfy God's sentence of death on all who sin by living a sinless life and dying for all who accept and continue in the coming Kingdom's standards.

Abraham can almost know how God would feel about sacrificing his son to satisfy the punishment that mankind earned. One difference is that no one would step in and save Jesus. The sacrifice of Christ would have to go forward for the possibility of salvation to exist. God would provide Abraham with a suitable sacrifice (Gen. 22:13). A ram caught in a thicket by his horns was substituted for Isaac. At verse 14, Abraham named the place where all this transpired.

> **Gen. 22:14 And Abraham called the name of the place, The Lord-Will-Provide; as it is said to this day, "In the Mount of the Lord it shall be provided."**

Abraham named the place, "The Lord Will Provide." The Hebrew rendering is (YHWH Yireh) in this text and Jehovah Jireh is the rendering in earlier King James Version translations. The same angel that had stopped Abraham from sacrificing Isaac has something to give him that comes from the Lord. The gift and the reason for this gift is clearly stated in Genesis 22:16–18.

> **Gen. 22:16 and said: "By Myself I have sworn, says the Lord, because you have done this thing, and have not withheld your son, your only son—**
>
> **17 blessing I will bless you, and multiplying I will multiply your descendants as the stars of the heaven and as the sand which is on the seashore; and your descendants shall possess the gate of their enemies.**
>
> **18 In your seed all the nations of the earth shall be blessed, because you have obeyed My voice."**

If the gift identified in verses 17 and 18 sounds a lot like the same gift that God offered Abraham at Genesis 12:1–3, that is because it is the same gift. The 37 or so years since God first offered this gift did not alter God's desire to give the gift, but it would not belong to Abraham until he had met certain criteria. God would fulfill the promises to Abraham only if he would believe or have faith, and then confirm that faith by acting on God's words.

Abraham's faith is no longer a work-in-progress; it is a finished product now. It does not mean that Abraham is incapable of human error since the possibility of error exists as long as we are in the flesh. It does mean that he can put total trust in a God that he cannot see. He fears God more than he fears the King and Pharaoh that he lied to about Sarah. The faith he demonstrated is the connection point between fallen man and Infallible God.

The angel appears to be elated at Abraham's victory, as he says in verse 12, "Now I know that you fear God since you have not withheld your only son from Me." The angel focuses on the act again in verse 16. The angel knows that if Abraham had failed God, the covenant, gift and blessings would be null and void.

God saw and accepted Abraham's act as real, then repeated the promise that would confirm Abraham's place in history as the father of the faithful. His seed would be multiplied beyond measure, they would prevail against their enemies and his descendants through Isaac would produce the sacred communication—THE BIBLE—that would make God real and reachable to all the nations of the earth. And Jesus would come through Isaac's line of Abraham's seed. The reason is because Abraham obeyed the voice of God in verse 18.

I don't know if God had approached other Holy men like Melchizedek to test them and see if they would qualify for this blessing. I do know that Abraham passed the test by believing, acting, serving, sacrificing, and praying with his whole heart to obtain a promise that some men may not have valued.

Verse 19 tells us that Abraham collected the young men who came there with him and they all went to Beersheba where Abraham dwelt. Verse 20 does not say how long it was after Isaac's situation when Abraham got reliable news that his brother Nahor had fathered several children. Bethuel, Nahor's youngest son by Milcah, fathered a daughter named Rebekah, who would be Isaac's second cousin and future wife.

CHAPTER 23

In verses 1 and 2 of Chapter 23 of Genesis, we learn that Sarah lived 127 years and died in Kirjath Arba, also known as Hebron, in the land of Canaan.

> **Gen. 23:1 Sarah lived one hundred and twenty-seven years; these were the years of the life of Sarah.**
>
> **2 So Sarah died in Kirjath Arba (that is, Hebron) in the land of Canaan, and Abraham came to mourn for Sarah and to weep for her.**

Verse 2 says Abraham came to mourn for Sarah; it does not say from where. Genesis 22:19 says Abraham dwelt in Beersheba after the events of the sacrifice of Isaac. Beersheba was some 20 to 30 miles from Hebron. It is impossible to establish how much time passed between the sacrifice and Sarah's death because, although we know Isaac was 37 years old when Sarah died, the Bible does not say how old Isaac was at the sacrifice.

The trained student of the Bible would certainly ask this question, and also would ask if they were together when Sarah died. The Bible does not give any occasion to question their relationship from start to finish. Abraham had so much livestock, servants and herdsmen shortly after leaving Haran that he and Lot had to part company because the land would not support them. The 60 years or more since then only saw him multiply that wealth over and over, so he could have been holding grazing lands in both places.

While we don't know where Abraham came from to mourn for Sarah, Genesis 24:62 says Isaac came from the way of Beer Lahai Roi, where he dwelt in the south when he first met Rebekah. The exact area cannot be located now, but the fact that it must have been near his mother's tent may suggest that Abraham, Sarah, and Isaac were living in and holding down three different areas for business purposes (Gen. 24:67).

Abraham is referred to by the sons of Heth as "a mighty prince among us" in verse 6. Abraham's saying he is a foreigner and visitor in verse 4 only means that he was not born there. It is clearly shown, however, that he is well known in that area.

My reason for advancing this discussion is that I have been asked why Abraham came to mourn his wife and where he came from. Someone had suggested that they broke up over the sacrificing of Isaac, but there is absolutely no biblical evidence of that and it is not wise to speculate on such a theory.

Verses 3 through 20 cover Abraham's negotiations with Ephron the Hitite who dwelt among the sons of Heth. The negotiations were for the cave of Machpelah located at the end of Ephron's field. Abraham wanted to buy it for a burying place for Sarah and it would become a family cemetery.

The offer from the children of Heth to give Abraham any area he wanted as a burying place was rejected. The offer of Ephron to give him the area he wanted was also rejected, as Abraham insisted on paying for it. He finally closed the deal in front of witnesses at the cities gate for 400 shekels of silver.

Verses 19 and 20 say Abraham buried Sarah in the cave on the field of Machpelah. The sons of Heth respected and accepted the cemetery as Abraham's permanent burying place.

CHAPTER 24

Chapter 24 of Genesis tells us that Abraham had been in and around Canaan's land about 65 years when he sent back to Mesopotamia to get a wife for Isaac. Abraham insisted on selecting a daughter-in-law from among his people. Genesis 24:1–4 reflects the detailed motions Abraham made his servant go through to swear he would definitely not take one of the daughters of the Canaanites as a wife for Isaac.

Sodom and Gomorrah fell because of how sinful the people were. Men had sex with men and women probably had sex with women. Abraham knew this and did not want Isaac to marry a woman raised around those societies, even if they had escaped God's wrath for the moment.

> Gen. 24:1 Now Abraham was old, well advanced in age; and the Lord had blessed Abraham in all things.
>
> 2 So Abraham said to the oldest servant of his house, who ruled over all that he had, "Please, put your hand under my thigh,
>
> 3 and I will make you swear by the Lord, the God of heaven and the God of the earth, that you will not take a wife for my son from the daughters of the Canaanites, among whom I dwell;
>
> 4 but you shall go to my country and to my family, and take a wife for my son Isaac."

The flood would have been over for about 450 years. The groups separated from each other by distance and language after the Tower of Babel would have been scattered for as much as 300 years before this time. The knowledge of and respect for God was obviously very important to Abraham's people, while the Canaanites and others rejected God and chose the way of the flesh.

Abraham is living the reason for the future law of Moses that forbids marriages outside of your belief in God for fear the unbeliever will turn the believer away from God and salvation (Deut. 7:3–4). The people of the world then, and most people now, errantly think of proper marriages as a racial issue rather than a matter of faith.

In verse 5, the servant has questions about Abraham's request. He wonders, "What if the woman does not want to come here and marry a man she does not know? Should I take your son to her?"

In verses 6 and 7, Abraham is confident that God will establish him in the land he is in. He is certain that God has an angel that can go before his servant and handle the arrangements. In verse 8, Abraham insisting that Isaac not be taken back is no doubt seen by him as a breach of the covenant he just told to the servant.

> **Gen. 24:8 "And if the woman is not willing to follow you, then you will be released from this oath; only do not take my son back there."**
>
> **9 So the servant put his hand under the thigh of Abraham his master, and swore to him concerning this matter.**

The servant will not be held to the oath he made to Abraham if he finds the woman and she chooses not to return with him. Rebekah may be the targeted wife since Genesis 22:23 proves he is aware of her existence and she is the only female listed among his relatives, but Rebekah is not referred to directly.

The oath is executed and confirmed on these conditions in verse 8 and 9. The servant, as his oldest and most trusted, may have come from Mesopotamia with him and shared his knowledge of and faith in God. Whether he did or not, verses 10 through 28 show his faith, ability to pray, and willingness to act on that faith, when you follow his trip and see his interaction with Rebekah.

The servant refers to God in verse 12 as the God of his master, Abraham. The oral traditions and communications about God that had been handed down certainly got jumbled and confused over the years. People being people, adding and subtracting things along with everything Satan put in the mix, created a situation where the different groups adopted their own idea about God—hence, different Gods.

The servant of Abraham clearly called on Abraham's God and he is the real God who made man, not a god that man made up. Abraham is the man from which God is building a nation that will deliver the truth and knowledge of one God and how to be saved by him. A believing wife from a believing clan is a necessary link in this believing chain.

Rebekah emerges as the first step of the answer to the servant's prayers. The second and final step would be her acceptance of the servant's proposal. Laban, the notorious brother of Rebekah, is introduced in verses 29 through 31. Much of his character seems to be exposed by his actions after seeing the material things that Abraham's servant gave to Rebekah.

> Gen. 24:29 Now Rebekah had a brother whose name was Laban, and Laban ran out to the man by the well.
>
> 30 So it came to pass, when he saw the nose ring, and the bracelets on his sister's wrists, and when he heard the words of his sister Rebekah, saying, "Thus the man spoke to me," that he went to the man. And there he stood by the camels at the well.
>
> 31 And he said, "Come in, O blessed of the Lord! Why do you stand outside? For I have prepared the house, and a place for the camels."

Abraham's servant takes Laban's offer of hospitality, but will not take time to eat the meat that is set before him until he has told his errand (Gen. 24:33). The events of the servant's errand were explained to Bethuel and Laban in verses 34 through 48, with all emphasis on the Lord's workings in the whole affair.

Verse 49 covers the servants unwavering desire for an immediate answer.

> Gen. 24:49 "Now if you will deal kindly and truly with my master, tell me. And if not, tell me, that I may turn to the right hand or to the left."

Bethuel, the father of Laban and Rebekah, was also the nephew of Abraham, so the Lord had directed the servant of Abraham to the right place. The faith Abraham put in the Lord's ability to send an angel ahead of his servant at verse 8 paid blessed dividends, according to verses 50 and 51.

> Gen. 24:50 Then Laban and Bethuel answered and said, "The thing comes from the Lord; we cannot speak to you either bad or good.
>
> 51 Here is Rebekah before you; take her and go, and let her be your master's son's wife, as the Lord has spoken."
>
> 52 And it came to pass, when Abraham's servant heard their words, that he worshipped the Lord, bowing himself to the earth.

Faith and obedience went seeking faith and obedience and they came together at Bethuel's home. The father and brother of Rebekah would gladly comply with God's will and agree to the marriage to Isaac.

The servant put first things first: He bowed and worshipped the Lord for the success of the mission and the joy he must have had at being able to fulfill the oath to his master in a positive way. Abraham's servant presented Rebekah and her family with an array of precious gifts, as described in verse 53. The servant and his men were fed, slept for the night, and arose the next day wanting to be on their way with Rebekah.

Both Rebekah's brother Laban and her mother wanted Rebekah to stay for at least ten more days so they could get used to the idea of probably never seeing her again (Gen. 24:54–55). The request is understandable when you see that 24 hours earlier their sister and daughter was safe in their midst. The young lady was going about her daily routine with no known matrimonial prospects and all of a sudden everything had changed in an urgent way.

The servant, noting how God had prospered his trip and how smoothly things had gone so far may be thinking, "Let's go now before someone changes their mind." He does not want to be held up (Gen. 24: 54–56). If you have ever been involved in arrangements for a wedding, you know how quickly a slight ripple can become a tidal wave. The situation here does not seem critical yet and a wise decision in verses 57 and 58 settles the issue quickly.

> **Gen. 24:57 So they said, "We will call the young woman and ask her personally."**
>
> **58 Then they called Rebekah and said to her. "Will you go with this man?" And she said, "I will go."**

The customs of that time gave the parents the authority to arrange a marriage. Abraham's making the decision about where Isaac's wife should come from, and Rebekah's parents approving the union that God had certified without asking her, proves it.

You might ask how the two principals in the marriage feel about marrying someone they have never seen. Verses 57 and 58 reveal Rebekah's attitude about leaving. Upon being asked if she wanted to stay for an additional ten days or if she wanted to go with this man that she had met a day earlier to marry a man she had not met yet, her words, "I will go," speak volumes about how she felt.

Rebekah had a nurse and an unspecified number of maids accompanying her, so it is obvious that her family is well off also (Gen. 24:59, 61). Isaac and Rebekah were married and verse 67 says that Isaac loved Rebekah. Her presence was obviously a great comfort to him after his mother's death.

CHAPTER 25

Chapter 25 of Genesis does not give Abraham's age when he marries Ketorah, as stated in verse 1.

> **Gen. 25:1 Abraham again took a wife, and her name was Keturah. And she bore him Zimran, Jokshan, Medan, Midian, Ishbak, and Shuah.**

There is not a shred of evidence to suggest that Abraham married her while Sarah lived, so he was over 137 years old when he remarried. The Bible does not give Keturah's age or lineage when they married either, but Abraham was at least 37 years older than the remarkable Abraham who fathered Isaac in his old age. Even still, he fathered six more sons with Keturah.

Abraham left the bulk of his considerable estate to Isaac, gave gifts to his other sons and sent them away while he was still alive. The six other sons who were sent east would have lasting nations in northern Arabia and in parts of the current Middle East. The Bible does not give a specific reason for sending them away, but verse 6 says that he "sent them eastward, away from Isaac his son, to the country of the east."

The gifts could have been enormous and still left plenty for Isaac. The reason for the separation while he lived might have been a precaution to guarantee Isaac's safety and security. Isaac, the carrier of the promised seed, could be in danger if the six younger half-brothers chose to contend for Isaac's share of the inheritance. The important thing to Abraham was obviously God's promise concerning Sarah's son Isaac and keeping him healthy, wealthy and powerful in that area, which is the promised land.

The Bible does not give any evidence that Abraham loved any of his sons any more or any less than the other. The fact that they had different mothers created a potentially volatile situation because each mother was seeking more for her child. Isaac would have been old enough to be their father, so any problems would probably surface when Keturah's children were older and Abraham was dead. This may also have been on Abraham's mind when he sent them away (Gen. 25:1–6).

Abraham lived 175 years. His grandsons, Esau and Jacob, would have been around 15 years old when he died, so they got a chance to know him. At Genesis 25:7–11, the two oldest sons, Ishmael and Isaac, came together to bury him with Sarah, in the same cave of the field of Machpelah that he had purchased 38 years earlier.

> Gen. 25:7 This is the sum of the years of Abraham's life which he lived: one hundred and seventy-five years.
>
> 8 Then Abraham breathed his last and died in a good old age, an old man and full of years, and was gathered to his people.
>
> 9 And his sons Isaac and Ishmael buried him in the cave of Machpelah, which is before Mamre, in the field of Ephron the son of Zohar the Hittite,
>
> 10 the field which Abraham purchased from the sons of Heth. There Abraham was buried, and Sarah his wife.
>
> 11 And it came to pass, after the death of Abraham, that God blessed his son Isaac. And Isaac dwelt at Beer Lahai Roi.

Verse 11 tells us that God blessed Isaac and he dwelt at Beer Lahai Roi. The blessing is no doubt the second leg of the perpetual promised seed and promised land blessing, along with his continued wealth. The genealogy, age, lands and the death of the rugged, contentious and tough man, Ishmael, are discussed in verses 12 through 18.

I like to think of Ishmael, the wild man, as the little boy who had to survive the confusion created and cast on him by others. The boy had to grow into manhood the hard way, facing challenge after challenge to survive and live to a good age of 137 years. The 12 princes he fathered stand as a testimony of God's love and blessing to him because they would go on to become the great Arabian nation.

The fertility issues that plagued Sarah and Abraham are plaguing Rebekah and Isaac now. After nearly 20 years of marriage, they are still childless (Gen. 25:20–28).

> Gen. 25:20 Isaac was forty years old when he took Rebekah as wife, the daughter of Bethuel the Syrian of Padan Aram, the sister of Laban the Syrian.
>
> 21 Now Isaac pleaded with the Lord for his wife, because she was barren: and the Lord granted his plea, and Rebekah his wife conceived.
>
> 22 But the children struggled together within her; and she said, "If all is well, why am I like this?" So she went to inquire of the Lord.
>
> 23 And the Lord said to her: "Two nations are in your womb, Two peoples shall be separated from your body: One people shall be stronger than the other. And the older shall serve the younger."
>
> 24 So when her days were fulfilled for her to give birth, indeed there were twins in her womb.
>
> 25 And the first came out red. He was like a hairy garment all over; so they called his name Esau.
>
> 26 Afterward his brother came out, and his hand took hold of Esau's heel; so his name was called Jacob. Isaac was sixty years old when she bare them.
>
> 27 So the boys grew. And Esau was a skillful hunter, a man of the field; but Jacob was a mild man, dwelling in tents.
>
> 28 And Isaac loved Esau because he ate of his game, but Rebekah loved Jacob.

Verse 21 says Isaac pleaded with the Lord on Rebekah's behalf and she conceived. The pregnancy was apparently hard on Rebekah. It was her first and only known pregnancy and it was two babies instead of one.

Verse 22 says the children struggled together within her and she went to inquire of the Lord.

The Lord answered her inquiry with the famous, often-quoted, verse 23. The breakdown of this verse should not be misunderstood if you want a clear picture of Jacob and Esau.

"Two nations are in your womb." This means each son would be strong enough to found his own nation. The news should have been music to Rebecca's ears and would have been exhilarating news to anyone else.

"Two peoples shall be separated from your body." The men would be twins, but distinctly different in character and the nations they would found would take on the characteristics of their founders, making the nations very different.

"And the one people shall be stronger than the other people." This makes a clear distinction between groups and individuals. The two nations would come into their own and Israel, Jacob's nation, would be stronger than Edom, Esau's nation. The prophecy would not have an immediate impact on either man in their lifetime because Israel was over 500 years away from coming out of Egypt as a free nation.

"And the elder shall serve the younger." This statement is still referring to the nations that would come from each man. The Edomites, the elder son's nation, would serve the younger son's nation, the Israelites. The verse does not imply that Esau would be Jacob's flunky in his lifetime. The reference can be clarified by the act of King David after a great victory over the Syrians in the Valley of Salt (2 Sam. 8:13–14).

> **2 Sam. 8:13 And David made himself a name when he returned from killing eighteen thousand Syrians in the Valley of Salt.**
>
> **14 He also put garrisons in Edom; throughout all Edom he got garrisons, and all the Edomites became David's servants. And the Lord preserved David wherever he went.**

The prophecy at Genesis 25:23 is from God and it has nothing to do with the existing birthright system that was like a seniority system in a family that carried both privileges and responsibilities. That same basic idea would become a working part of the law of Moses, but there would be exceptions to it (Deut. 21:15–17; 1 Chron. 5:2). Rebekah's misunderstanding of what God had shown her apparently became a convenient highway that Satan used to drive her to an obsession that would shame both her and Jacob.

The statement God made in verse 23 was about which man would become the nation that would carry on the Abrahamic covenant and be the nation that would be God's tool for blessing all of the families on earth. The birthright gave a double portion of the inheritance to the oldest son. It also gave him the responsibility to provide for all survivors in his father's absence, incapacity or death. The duty could make the first son poorer than the others if he had to use his double share to provide for the family. The duty could mean near slavery in a poor family.

The stolen birthright blessing in Genesis 27:27–29 and the Abrahamic covenant blessing in Genesis 28:3–4 are different in scope, destination and intent. Verse 23 clearly explains God's choice for the Abrahamic covenant in the same way God chose Isaac, the younger, over Abraham's desire for Ishmael, the older, to be heir to the Abrahamic covenant. God chose Isaac, then Jacob, for the Abrahamic covenant. He revealed it to Rebekah to ease her mind and pain and never asked her to help him steal anything. He had made the choice before they were born.

The actions of Rebekah and Jacob forced God to train Jacob in the school of hard knocks. The mother did not have to do anything except thank God and work at being the best mother she could be to both sons and the most dutiful wife she could be to her husband. Instead, she got busy trying to steal something for Jacob that Jacob already owned.

Verses 24 through 27 contrast the birth, different appearances and different characters of the twins. I have read and heard many scholars and ministers write and preach about how the twins fought in the womb and Jacob was born clutching the heel of Esau, as if he was holding onto Esau while they were in the womb and fought all through the delivery. The Bible simply does not bear that out. Verse 25 says the first came out red, hairy, and alone. Then verse 26 says afterward his brother came out, and his hand took hold of Esau's heel.

The Bible's version may not give a charismatic speaker the drama base he needs to excite a crowd. The Bible's version, however, is the truth and truth is what the crowd needs. Satan can take the smallest deviation from the truth and form the same kind of weapon against you and I that he formed against Adam and Eve.

Verse 28 reveals an atmosphere of contention. Isaac loved or favored Esau because of something as simple as the taste of wild game. Rebekah loved and favored Jacob. The Bible does not say why here, but all evidence points toward her misunderstood ideas about the two blessings, and possibly because he was a gentler person than his brother. The poor parenting skills of both parents probably made home life for this rich family a chore.

Verses 29 through 34 deal with the birthright and the apparent knowledge Jacob had about it already. Jacob was focused on the birthright and willing to use any means at his disposal to get his brother to relinquish his claim on it.

> Gen. 25:29 Now Jacob cooked a stew; and Esau came in from the field, and he was weary.
>
> 30 And Esau said to Jacob, "Please feed me with that same red stew, for I am weary." Therefore his name was called Edom.
>
> 31 But Jacob said, "Sell me your birthright as of this day."
>
> 32 And Esau said, "Look, I am about to die; so what is this birthright to me?"
>
> 33 Then Jacob said, "Swear to me as of this day. So he swore to him, and sold his birthright to Jacob.
>
> 34 And Jacob gave Esau bread and stew of lentils; then he ate and drank, arose, and went his way. Thus Esau despised his birthright.

The rest of the story will prove Rebekah's efforts were helping to drive this deceitful vehicle. God's blessings cannot be bargained-off or transferred by agreements between men. God's blessing has to be bestowed by God in order for it to be God's blessing and it cannot be stolen from God.

Jacob already had this. The birthright blessing dealt with a material inheritance and was to be bestowed by the father to the first-born. Esau came home from the field hungry, not starving, to a rich mans home where there was plenty of food but none was cooked. He was apparently too trifling to take time to prepare his own food, so he asked Jacob for some of the stew he had cooked. Jacob was focused on the birthright blessing already and used Esau's request as an opportunity to entice him into trading it for something as insignificant as a bowl of stew.

I doubt that Esau was actually at the edge of starvation, as he said in verse 32. His actions afterwards would bear that out. He ate and got up and left; a starving man needs rest and attention. Esau may have not considered a deal of this type binding or serious, or he may have said anything Jacob wanted to hear to get what he wanted right then. Whatever the case, he swore Jacob could have the birthright for the bowl of stew.

Esau may have had a flippant attitude about it then thinking, as he was his father's favorite, his father would not honor such an agreement. The text would bear this out later. Jacob and his mother were obsessed with this blessing and her misinterpretation of the vision would lead them into even more deceptive practices that would not stop with Esau.

Verse 34 says Esau despised his birthright. Regardless of what Esau was thinking, the fact that he would even consider trading the responsibility of the birthright for such a small thing also reflected on his overall character and attitude toward serious things.

CHAPTER 26

Chapter 26 of Genesis deals with another famine that is clearly not the same famine that occurred in Abraham's time (Chapter 20) and caused them to move to Gerar.

> Gen. 26:1 There was a famine in the land, besides the first famine that was in the days of Abraham. And Isaac went to Abimelech King of the Philistines, in Gerar.
>
> 2 Then the Lord appeared to him and said: "Do not go down to Egypt; live in the land of which I shall tell you.
>
> 3 Dwell in this land, and I will be with you and bless you; for to you and your descendants I give all these lands, and I will perform the oath which I swore to Abraham your father.
>
> 4 And I will make your descendants multiply as the stars of heaven; I will give to your descendants all these lands; and in your seed all the nations of the earth shall be blessed;
>
> 5 because Abraham obeyed My voice and kept My charge, My commandments, My statutes, and My laws."
>
> 6 So Isaac dwelt in Gerar.

A lot of theologians doubt that this is the same Abimelech encountered by Abraham in Chapter 20. Abraham encountered him when he was 100 years old, shortly before Isaac was born. Isaac is somewhere between 75 and 100 years old. How do I know this? Abraham died 75 years after Isaac's birth. If Esau married at 40 years old after these events, and Isaac was 60 years old when he was born, this would have happened before Esau's marriage. The Bible gives no clue as to how long it was before Esau married, but the event with Abimelech is within a 100-year window. The question we are trying to answer is this: Is this the same Abimelech that Abraham dealt with, or is Abimelech a dynastic name used by many Philistine kings?

I don't know the answer to that, but men certainly lived longer in those days. It would depend on when the Abimelech known to Abraham took the throne and how long he reigned. The only references to Abimelech in Genesis are in these two meetings with Abraham and Isaac. If Abimelech is a dynastic name and this is not the same King Abimelech that Abraham dealt with, then Phichol must be the permanent name for the commander of the army.

Phichol is named as the commander of Abimelech's army shortly after Isaac is weaned and Ishmael and his mother are cast out (Gen. 21:22). Phichol is named as the commander of Abimelech's army again at Genesis 26:26 when he is dealing with Isaac, the 75- to 100-year-old man. This is not vital to scripture, but it might raise or help answer some questions as you work through this Chapter. The first verse says that Isaac went to Abimelech, but it does not reveal what they talked about.

Verse 2 says the Lord appeared to Isaac and told him not to go to Egypt. Isaac must have been leaving Gerar and heading for Egypt when the Lord stopped him, so it would stand to reason that Abimelech did not welcome him with open arms. The Lord instructs Isaac to live in the land God would choose. Gerar is apparently where he told Isaac to live, so Isaac stayed there.

Verse 3 reveals the Lord's reasons for having Isaac stay in Gerar: "Dwell here, I will be with you and bless you." Fear of any man should not be an issue for Isaac now. God explains that he wanted Isaac to live in the lands that would eventually belong to Isaac and his descendants. This shows the divine hand of God directing Isaac's path. To perform the oath sworn to Abraham, God is simply following through on his end of the covenant.

The alert reader is asking if God is fair for giving Isaac's future nation the lands of this nation. The alert reader, and all other readers as well, should always know that God is the primary owner of this land and planet and the whole Universe. The secondary, temporary ownership of any person or group is based on how they respond to the primary owner's directives.

The Sodomites and plains cities were evicted by God in one sudden, fiery cleansing of his land because they utterly rejected him. The group on this land seem to be tempting the same fate for the same reasons, even though Abimelech responded to direct threats from God, as it related to Abraham.

Genesis 20:18 says God closed the wombs of all women in the house of Abimelech for Sarah's sake, and Abraham found out that God can bring fear on anyone (Gen. 20:11). The fact that God came to King Abimelech in a dream, at Genesis 20:3, and offered to kill him over Abraham's wife may have something to do with the fact that Isaac's group had been there a long time and no one had touched his wife (Gen. 26:8).

The land would be transferred because, at verse 5, Abraham obeyed God's voice. God didn't have to threaten or force him to obey. For God, Abraham obeyed "... My charge, My commandments, My statutes and My laws." Abraham learned to trust God to take him beyond the grave and that made him an excellent representative for God's kingdom that is coming.

The prophecy of Noah against Canaan and his descendants is also fulfilled with the future conquest of Canaan. Isaac heard the word of the Lord. Obviously, he obeyed God because verse 6 says he dwelt in Gerar, but he succumbed to fear when the men of the area inquired about his beautiful wife.

A situation similar to the one his father was in, at the same place, brought the same results. He passed his wife off as his sister because of fear they may kill him and take her, and also all of his goods, for that matter. The human fears of Abraham and Isaac are understandable under the circumstances, but Abraham grew to a point where his love of God was greater than his fear of men. Isaac is not there yet, as verse 7 points out.

> Gen. 26:7 And the men of the place asked about his wife. And he said, "She is my sister"; for he was afraid to say, "She is my

wife," because he thought, "lest the men of the place kill me for Rebekah, because she is beautiful to behold."

8 Now it came to pass, when he had been there a long time, that Abimelech King of the Philistines looked through a window, and saw, and there was Isaac, showing endearment to Rebekah his wife.

9 Then Abimelech called Isaac and said, "Quite obviously she is your wife; so how could you say, She is my sister?" Isaac said to him, "Because I said, Lest I die on account of her."

10 And Abimelech said, "What is this you have done to us? One of the people might soon have lain with your wife, and you would have brought guilt on us."

11 So Abimelech charged all his people, saying, "He who touches this man or his wife shall surely be put to death."

I mentioned the opinions of theologians who did not believe Abimelech of Chapter 20 was the same as Abimelech of Chapter 26. I can only point out some facts and raise a few questions about what is written here.

The men of the area were quite taken with Rebekah's beauty and thinking she was Isaac's sister should have been a green light for potential suitors. Why had none of the men approached her? Verse 8 says they had been there a long time before Abimelech saw Isaac showing endearment in a way that made him know Rebekah was his wife. Was Abimelech casually looking out of that particular window when he saw them, or was he cautiously spying on them? Did Abimelech seem like he had been victimized in verse 10? Was he afraid of what might have happened if one of the people might have lain with her?

If this is not the same Abimelech Abraham encountered, then he would not be the one that God offered to kill then shut the wombs of the women in his house. If he is the same Abimelech, then he would certainly remember it. That would explain his fear and caution, because Chapter 26 does not record a communication from God to this Abimelech.

Again, if this is the son of the king that Abraham encountered, then you must say that his father taught him to be very afraid of Hebrews passing beautiful women off as their sisters. That would explain why, according to verse 11, he pronounced an unconditional death sentence on anyone in his kingdom that touched Isaac or his family. The Lord is taking much better care of Isaac than he could possibly take of himself.

Verse 12 says Isaac sowed and reaped a hundred-fold crop that year in a land where he was out numbered, feared and disliked. Isaac's blessings would continue, but would cause envy from his neighbors (Gen. 26: 13–14). Verses 15 through 33 cover some of the water rights problems that Isaac had. The Philistines had filled-in some of the wells that Abraham dug when he was there. The Philistines were giving Isaac many problems over that, among other things. God blessed Isaac wherever he went and eventually Abimelech sought and negotiated a covenant of peace between their peoples. Isaac would settle in the city he named Beersheba.

At verses 34 and 35, Esau married two Canaanite women when he was 40 years old and brought grief to his parents.

> **Gen. 26:34 When Esau was forty years old, he took as wives Judith the daughter of Beeri the Hittite, and Basemath the daughter of Elon the Hittite.**
>
> **35 And they were a grief of mind to Isaac and Rebekah.**

The land of the Canaanites was promised to the Israelites by God. He spoke the curse of losing it on Ham's son, Canaan, through Noah because of the disrespect Ham showed in viewing his father Noah's nakedness. God could foresee what Ham's disrespect for his elders and authority would do to his children before they ever became the Canaanite nations. The evil, immoral sexual practices of Sodom and Gomorrah, idolatry, sorcery, witchcraft, human sacrifices and any other sinful act you may think of were common practices for the Canaanites.

The wives of Esau would have been a part of this environment, while Abraham, Sarah, Isaac, Rebekah, Esau and Jacob would have been full-blooded descendants of a group that honored and accepted what they knew about God. The above-named people certainly were not sinless, but they sought a higher moral way of life in spite of their many failures.

The bottom line is that Esau took wives from this intentionally wicked group and created even more confusion in their dysfunctional family. The question is, why didn't the parents send to Mesopotamia to get wives for both Esau and Jacob? Did the favoritism games both parents were playing hamper this wise idea? Was the birthright issue making the home such a battle ground that competition and stumbling blocks took precedence over careful family planning? I don't know the answer, but nothing is said about matrimonial planning prior to Esau's marriages. Rebekah's future desire to send Jacob to Mesopotamia for a wife would be more of a smoke screen to get him out of Esau's range after the theft of the birthright.

CHAPTER 27

Chapter 27 of Genesis deals with the actual deception of Isaac, the father of Jacob and Esau. The way Jacob deceived Esau into trading his birthright for a bowl of stew opens a window into the character of each man, but it was not legal or binding within their legal circles. The father was the only one that could make this legal, with his word as bond; he did not need a signed paper to convey it.

The age of Isaac is not given when he called to Esau and asked a favor of him before passing the blessing on at Genesis 27:1–7.

> Gen. 27:1 Now it came to pass, when Isaac was old and his eyes were so dim that he could not see, that he called Esau his older son and said to him, "My son." And he answered him, "Here I am."
>
> 2 Then he said, "Behold now, I am old. I do not know the day of my death.
>
> 3 Now therefore, please take your weapons, your quiver and your bow, and go out to the field and hunt game for me.
>
> 4 And make me savory food, such as I love, and bring it to me that I may eat, that my soul may bless you before I die."
>
> 5 Now Rebekah was listening when Isaac spoke to Esau his son. And Esau went to the field to hunt game and to bring it.

6 So Rebekah spoke to Jacob her son, saying, "Indeed I heard your father speak to Esau your brother, saying,

7 "Bring me game and make savory food for me, that I may eat it and bless you in the presence of the Lord before my death."

Isaac was 60 years old when the twins were born and Esau was 40 years old when he married the Canaanite women. The Bible does not say how much time passed between Esau's marriage and the time of the blessing. The Bible says Isaac lived 180 years so the twins would be 120 years old when he died and they were not close to that yet. The pain that is about to be created here would have been over for many years when they came together to bury their father (Gen. 35:27–29).

Verses 1 and 2 do not say that Isaac was sick. The Bible says his eyesight was gone and he was an old man. The Bible does not say how he was blinded, or if whatever caused the blindness caused him to think he was about to die. If, in fact, he was sick, he recovered and lived a long time afterward. It is obvious however, that Isaac took the duty of passing on the customary birthright blessing very seriously.

Isaac's reasons for having Esau prepare for the birthright blessing is plainly stated in verses 1 through 4. He is over 100 years old, blind and unsure of how much longer he may live. The savory way Esau prepared the wild game was just something Isaac enjoyed. It had nothing to do with the birthright, but it would become a tool for deception.

Rebekah was listening. The question is whether she just happened to be passing by at that time, or if she was eavesdropping. The next verses will have you and I making that decision and rightly dividing the words of truth, as stated in 2 Timothy 2:15.

2 Tim. 2:15: "Be diligent to present yourself approved to God, a worker who does not need to be ashamed, rightly dividing the word of truth."

The mother hears instructions from the father to the elder son and she uses this information to deceive her blind husband. The mother speaks to Jacob, the younger son, to pass on what she heard. Since she relayed the entire conversation, it leaves no doubt that she was eavesdropping instead of just passing by. Verses 5 and 6 refer to Esau as his son and Jacob as her son, when in fact they are twins, born the same day from the same womb. Was this a family divided over the birthright issue? Verse 8 removes any doubts about Rebekah's role in this deception.

> Gen. 27:8 Now therefore, my son, obey my voice according to what I command you.
>
> 9 Go now to the flock and bring me from there two choice kids of the goats, and I will make savory food from them for your father, such as he loves.
>
> 10 Then you shall take it to your father, that he may eat it, and that he may bless you before his death."
>
> 11 And Jacob said to Rebekah his mother, "Look, Esau my brother is a hairy man, and I am a smooth skinned man.
>
> 12 Perhaps my father will feel me, and I shall seem to be a deceiver to him; and I shall bring a curse on myself and not a blessing."
>
> 13 But his mother said to him, "Let your curse be on me, my son; only obey my voice, and go, get them for me."

Verses 11 and 12 show that Jacob's only fear was that his father would catch him at his deception and curse him. Lying, cheating, stealing and showing the utmost disrespect for his father never troubled him. The principals of love, respect, obedience and honor were not a part of what is going on here from both Jacob and Rebekah's standpoint. Their actions prove that they believe Isaac may be nearing death as he stated. The wife who is clear on her job description as a wife should be more involved in her husband's comfort and well-being at this point. Rebekah calms Jacob's fear of being cursed in verse 13 by speaking the curse upon herself, or claiming responsibility for the act.

The fact is, they are both adults and responsible for their actions. The futility of the act is incredible. The Abrahamic covenant blessing that was given by God to Jacob took precedence over the birthright custom, but Rebekah may not have known there was a difference. The Bible does not show any evidence that she ever told her husband about what God revealed to her about the elder's nation serving the younger's nation at Genesis 25:23. If the parents were not communicating their revelations then it is easy to see how Lucifer got into their house.

Isaac had an Abrahamic covenant revelation at Genesis 26:3–5. If he knew and understood his wife's revelation, they might have been able to make the distinction between the birthright custom and Abrahamic covenant. The bottom line is that God can handle his end of any agreement he makes with people without any help from people, especially the dishonest, deceitful actions being taken now.

Verses 14 through 19 show how well Rebekah orchestrated the deception. The food preparation: Verse 14. The use of some of Esau's clothing: Verse 15. The use of the animal skins: Verse 16. The way she either knew or learned to prepare the food in the same savory way that Esau would: Verse 17. These verses show how quickly this mother of both sons, and the wife of this husband, responded.

Verses 19 through 26 present a sort of cat-and-mouse game where Isaac raises questions about who he is dealing with.

> Gen. 27:19 Jacob said to his father, "I am Esau your firstborn; I have done just as you told me; please arise, sit and eat of my game, that your soul may bless me."
>
> 20 But Isaac said to his son, "How is it that you have found it so quickly, my son?" And he said, "Because the Lord your God brought it to me."
>
> 21 Then Isaac said to Jacob, "Please come near, that I may feel you, my son, whether you are really my son Esau or not."
>
> 22 So Jacob went near to Isaac his father, and he felt him and said, "The voice is Jacob's voice, but the hands are the hands of Esau."
>
> 23 And he did not recognize him, because his hands were hairy like his brother Esau's hands; so he blessed him.
>
> 24 Then he said, "Are you really my son Esau?" He said, "I am."
>
> 25 He said, "Bring it near to me, and I will eat of my son's game, so that my soul may bless you." So he brought it near to him, and he ate; and he brought him wine, and he drank.
>
> 26 Then his father Isaac said to him, "Come near now and kiss me, my son."

The question about the speed of the hunt and preparation of the food brings a lie on God from the mouth of Jacob. The trick with the animal hair was well thought out by Rebekah because her husband, being blind, used his sense of touch to feel what he thought was the hairy-bodied older son, in verses 21 through 23. When Isaac asked Jacob if he was really Esau, Jacob answered with an absolute lie, a lie told by the future father of the 12 tribes of Israel.

I have heard many sermons and opinions on the actions of Rebekah and Jacob. The ministers and speakers are always trying to find a way to justify their actions and present it as a part of God's master plan. The idea is beyond the pale of common sense—there is absolutely no right way to do what is wrong. No matter how excited we were when Abraham's servant found Isaac the right woman in the person of beautiful Rebekah, we cannot put enough positive spin on this to make it right. The actions of Rebekah and Jacob were wrong from start to finish and they would pay the price for their bad decisions in the very near future.

God would bring Jacob closer to a point of spiritual maturity in time, but Jacob's actions would be the biggest obstacle between him and that point. The blessing Jacob coveted, then stole, is the older son's customary blessing (Gen. 27:27–29). It does not contain the Abrahamic covenant's responsibility to bless all of the families of the earth.

> Gen. 27:27 And he came near and kissed him; and he smelled the smell of his clothing and blessed him and said: "Surely, the smell of my son is like the smell of a field, Which the Lord has blessed.
>
> 28 Therefore may God give you of the dew of heaven, Of the fatness of the earth, And plenty of grain and wine.
>
> 29 Let peoples serve you, And nations bow down to you, Be master over your brethren, And let your mother's sons bow down to you. Cursed be everyone who curses you, And blessed be those who bless you."

The blessing that Isaac bestows on Esau after they found out about the deception is covered in verses 39 and 40.

> Gen. 27:39 Then Isaac his father answered and said to him: "Be-

hold, your dwelling shall be of the fatness of the earth, And of the dew of heaven from above.

40 By your sword you shall live, And you shall serve your brother; And it shall come to pass, when you become restless, That you shall break his yoke from your neck."

The part about breaking Jacob's yoke from Esau's neck is spoken from a national perspective and would not occur for hundreds of years, as stated in 2 Kings 8:20.

2 Kings 8:20 "In his days Edom revolted against Judah's authority and made a King over themselves."

The days of Edom's revolt are in the reign of Jehoram, who was married to Ahab's daughter and did evil in God's eyes. This prophecy is the reversal of the prophecy that foresaw King David set up garrisons in Edom, as discussed in Chapter 25 and verified by 2 Samuel 8:13–14. During their lifetimes, none of these things ever happened. Jacob, the individual, would never be stronger than Esau, the individual.

Verses 30 through 38 reflect Isaac's feelings of betrayal and justifiable anger over what his wife and younger son had done to him. Verse 33 says Isaac trembled exceedingly and, when explaining the event afterward, declared that he blessed him and affirms the legality of the rite by saying that he shall be blessed indeed.

In verse 34, Esau feels the sting of the act; he cried with a great and exceedingly bitter cry. The fact that this is happening over a misunderstanding between the blessings is not known by them and the under-handed way it happened would not lessen the pain, even if they did know. The private exchange of the birthright between the brothers may have been an off-the-cuff joke on Esau's part, but Jacob was not laughing. He was looking for a way to justify his act and live with himself afterward.

It was the wrong thing for Esau to take lightly and now the reality of his slipshod attitude is causing him severe pain. Verse 41 tells us that Esau is still errantly thinking that his father is at the point of death.

Gen. 27:41 So Esau hated Jacob because of the blessing with which his father blessed him, and Esau said in his heart, "The days of mourning for my father are at hand; then I will kill my brother Jacob."

42 And the words of Esau her older son were told to Rebekah. So she sent and called Jacob her younger son, and said to him, "Surely your brother Esau comforts himself concerning you by intending to kill you.

The hatred he has developed toward Jacob over the theft of the blessing has him saying in his heart that he will kill Jacob after the mourning for their father is over. The death of childless Jacob would certainly return the whole inheritance to Esau. The evidence proved he had taken the idea beyond just saying it in his heart because verse 42 says Rebekah heard from some unnamed person that Esau was in fact planning to kill Jacob.

The lives of these people are in a shambles. The favoritisms, lying, deceit, hatred, envies, plotting and stealing could have been avoided if Rebekah had trusted God to do what he prophesied. The trouble came because she relied on the works of her hands and the reasoning of her mind to accomplish God's will. Verses 43 through 46 are a continuation of the above-named sins.

Gen. 27:43 Now therefore, my son, obey my voice; arise, flee to my brother Laban in Haran.

44 And stay with him a few days, until your brother's fury turns away,

45 "until your brother's anger turns away from you, and he forgets what you have done to him; then I will send and bring you from there. Why should I be bereaved also of you both in one day?"

46 And Rebekah said to Isaac. "I am weary of my life because of the daughters of Heth; if Jacob takes a wife of the daughters of Heth, like these who are the daughters of the land, what good will my life be to me?"

The mother advises her younger son to go to Haran, find her brother and stay with him until her older son's anger turn away. It is no longer, "what I coached and helped you do to him." It is, "you leave until he forgets what you have done to him."

A different reason is given to her husband for Jacob's leaving home (Gen. 27:46). Rebekah wants her husband to believe the primary reason for sending Jacob to her brother in Haran is to find a wife among their kindred. The truth is that he is running from Esau.

The lesson we should learn from rightly dividing the truth here is that God's procedure for building good relationships must be followed to the letter. The ends, no matter what we think of those ends, are never justified by using dishonest means. The lesson to be learned after analyzing this family's life should make every adult with children scrutinize whatever method of parenting they are using in the hope of avoiding this family's situation.

A parent's duty is to distribute their love to their children equally, giving each one whatever they need to grow to responsible adulthood. Children have completely different personalities and have to grow and make their own decisions in life. The last thing a good parent wants to hear is that their children did not find fairness and balance at home and that triggered bad decisions in a child's behavior and life.

Jacob leaves home running for his life. Esau lives in anger with blood in his eyes. Rebekah and Isaac cannot possibly have any joy or happiness left in their relationship and none of this had to happen. God would not quit on his promise and would bring Jacob through the future problems and travels he created to give him the blessing he could have received in the comfort and safety of his rich father's home. Rebekah and Jacob did not need to fix anything because nothing was broken until they tried to fix things.

CHAPTER 28

In Chapter 28 of Genesis, verses 1 and 2, the charge of Isaac telling Jacob not to take a wife from the daughters of Canaan is the first biblical evidence that this was ever discussed with either of their boys.

> Gen. 28:1 Then Isaac called Jacob and blessed him, and charged him, and said to him: "You shall not take a wife from the daughters of Canaan.
>
> 2 Arise, go to Padan Aram, to the house of Bethuel your mother's father; and take yourself a wife from there of the daughters of Laban your mother's brother.

Jacob's destination in Padan Aram was Laban's house and a choice of his daughters, who were Jacob's first cousins on his mother's side and more distant cousins on his father's side. The birthright blessing had already been bestowed on Jacob through a trick. Isaac is asking God to bless Jacob in his own name now with the Abrahamic covenant, which is what God chose to do before he was born.

> Gen. 28:3 "May God Almighty bless you, And make you fruitful and multiply you. That you may be an assembly of peoples;
>
> 4 And give you the blessing of Abraham, To you and your descendants with you, That you may inherit the land in which you are a stranger, Which God gave to Abraham."

"May God Almighty bless you," at verse 3, "and "give you the blessing of Abraham," at verse 4, leaves no doubt that this is the Abrahamic covenant. The careful examination of the blessings will prove they are different. Jacob leaves his wealthy father's home. There is no evidence that he had even one servant or soldier with him for protection (Genesis 28:5).

Rebekah's last recorded words are a deception (Gen. 27:46). She is mentioned four times after that and Genesis 49:31 says she is buried in the family plot. The Bible does not say when she died or if she ever saw her favorite son, Jacob, again. The situation is a tragedy of sorts. While the tendency is to overlook the faults of our heroes, rightly dividing the word of truth demands that we see faults, analyze them and be careful not to make the same mistake. The Bible will teach you by example if you let it. Satan got to Rebekah and made her his tool against her own best interest.

Verses 6 through 9 should be adequate proof that discussions about where to find a wife were not high on this family's agenda. Esau sees that his father is sending Jacob away with a blessing and charge not to take a Canaanite wife. Yet, Esau has two Canaanite wives.

Verse 8 shows that he is just finding out how his father feels about them, even though Genesis 26:35 says they were a grief of mind to Isaac and Rebekah. Esau was no doubt trying to please his father when he married his first cousin Mahalath, Ishmael's daughter, in verse 9.

Verses 10 through 15 cover Jacob's departure and the revealing dream at the place he called Bethel, which was Luz.

> Genesis 28:10 Now Jacob went out from Beersheba and went toward Haran.
>
> 11 So he came to a certain place and stayed there all night, because the sun had set. And he took one of the stones of that place and put it at his head, and he lay down in that place to sleep.
>
> 12 Then he dreamed, and behold a ladder was set up on the earth, and its top reached to heaven; and there the angels of God were ascending and descending on it.
>
> 13 And behold, the Lord stood above it and said: "I am the Lord

God of Abraham your father and the God of Isaac; the land on which you lie I will give to you and your descendants.

14 Also your descendants shall be as the dust of the earth; you shall spread abroad to the west and the east, to the north and the south; and in you and in your seed all the families of the earth shall be blessed.

15 Behold, I am with you and will keep you wherever you go, and will bring you back to this land; for I will not leave you until I have done what I have spoken to you."

This vision confirms Jacob as the recipient of the Abrahamic covenant, the promised land and a divine hand that would see him safely to his destination and back to that land. The grace of God is so marvelous. Jacob, at this point, could not be a member of any organization or group that had any type of honor code, yet here he is receiving the third leg of the most important relay ever run. The unconditional love of God can and will elevate us from the lowest pits to the highest peaks, if we follow his lead. Jacob's ladder in verse 12 is a clear indication of how the Abrahamic covenant would be a blessing to the whole of mankind.

Though some good translators see the ladder as a stairway or staircase, the indication is still the same. The ladder establishes a link or line for communications between Perfect God in heaven and imperfect mankind on earth. God's angels are functioning as messengers who travel up and down the ladder taking and bringing what is needed for the reconnection of man to God.

Jacob is getting his first introduction to that theology in verses 13 through 15. If Jacob ever heard his father or grandfather Abraham talking about their experiences with the God they cannot see, he may have written it off as old-timers' crazy talk. It is being revealed to him in a way that will get his attention.

Jacob is learning that there is a God of his father and grandfather who is saying, "I will give your descendants this land in which you are now strangers." Your descendants shall be multitudes and spread in all four directions and, in you, all the families of the earth shall be blessed. Jacob had no way of knowing then that I would be working from that blessing over three thousand years later. The thought of beguiled Esau seeking vengeance will not allow him to imagine that God is preparing a nation that will produce the most remarkable man of all times, and he is a part of it's foundation.

The ladder would provide passage for the angels who would call, inspire, guide, protect and educate the authors of the Bible. God said to Jacob at verse 15, "I will not leave you until I have done what I have spoken about to you," God is guaranteeing Jacob's unearned protection and showing who is in control. Call it God's grace, love and mercy: He is being faithful to both ends of the covenant.

Jacob awoke from the dream and accepted it as a true visitation. In verse 16, he says, "Surely the Lord is in this place, and I did not know it." The true Godly fear he demonstrates for the first recorded time, and the way he describes the area in verse 17, leaves no doubt about his sincerity. The dream, the acceptance and confession produces positive actions as described in Genesis 28:20–22.

> **Gen. 28:20 Then Jacob made a vow, saying, "If God will be with me, and keep me in this way that I am going, and give me bread to eat and clothing to put on,**
>
> **21 so that I come back to my father's house in peace, then the Lord shall be my God.**
>
> **22 And this stone which I have set as a pillar shall be God's house, and of all that You give me I will surely give a tenth to You."**

Jacob is openly asking for what God had promised him in the dream and he is making definite promises of service, keep me, guide me, feed me and clothe me, bears witness to his needs. He makes a promise to tithe, which is proper, but even more important, he acknowledges God as the grantor of his entire wealth.

The major themes of the Bible, God's grace, love, faith, God's election, power, planning and protection can all be studied here in the lives of the patriarchs before the law or the New Testament existed. Jacob would leave there as a changed man. The return to Bethel, however, would still be a long and difficult journey.

The events described here are the first evidence of a personal relation or visitation from God to Jacob. Jacob was as carnal prior to that as a New Testament-era person who had never been born again. The reader must note and accept this fact before trying to put a righteous spin on his prior actions.

CHAPTER 29

In Chapter 29 of Genesis, Jacob continued on his journey until he reached the land of the people of the east. He came to a well where three flocks of sheep were lying idle, as stated in Genesis 29:2–10.

> Gen. 29:2 And he looked, and saw a well in the field; and behold, there were three flocks of sheep lying by it; for out of that well they watered the flocks. A large stone was on the well's mouth.
>
> 3 Now all the flocks would be gathered there; and they would roll the stone from the well's mouth, water the sheep, and put the stone back in its place on the well's mouth.
>
> 4 And Jacob said to them, "My brethren, where are you from?" And they said, "We are from Haran."
>
> 5 Then he said to them, "Do you know Laban the son of Nahor?" And they said, "We know him."
>
> 6 So he said to them, "Is he well?" And they said, "He is well. And look his daughter Rachel is coming with the sheep."
>
> 7 Then he said, "Look, it is still high day; it is not time for the cattle to be gathered together. Water the sheep, and go and feed them."
>
> 8 But they said, "We cannot until all the flocks are gathered together, and they have rolled the stone from the well's mouth; then we water the sheep."

9 Now while he was still speaking with them, Rachel came with her father's sheep, for she was a shepherdess.

10 And it came to pass, when Jacob saw Rachel the daughter of Laban his mother's brother, and the sheep of Laban his mother's brother, that Jacob went near and rolled the stone from the well's mouth, and watered the flock of Laban his mother's brother.

A well in any area of those times, and even later times, was the lifeblood of the community: Every creature, man or beast would live on the water it provided. According to verse 2, this particular well was used for watering livestock and a great stone covered the mouth of it. The Bible does not say why they had to wait for all of the flocks to be gathered before a stone was removed and the water was released, so I dare not offer an opinion.

Jacob found out that the men at the well were from Haran and that they knew Laban (Gen. 29:4–5). Verse 6 says they pointed out Rachel, Laban's daughter, who was bringing the sheep she was in charge of to be watered. The conversation takes on an odd, yet revealing tone in verses 7 and 8. Jacob, a man who has just walked up to these men, starts telling them how to manage their flocks. It is still high day, not the time for the cattle to gather, so Jacob suggests they water the sheep and feed them. This leaves a question as to whether both flocks of sheep and herds of cattle were waiting to drink.

The advice from Jacob and the way he gives it leads you to believe that he is a man who is familiar with giving orders. The history of his family's wealth in the livestock business and the success his future would provide is also proof that he knew what he was talking about. The fact that he was talking to people he had just met may prove that he was a self-centered rich man who had forgotten that he was not at home anymore.

The men explain that all of the flocks have to gather and they, not saying who, will roll back the stone. Jacob rolled back the stone himself when Rachel's flocks arrived and watered his unseen uncle's stock. The meeting of Rachel and Jacob in verses 11 and 12, and her report of the meeting to Laban, brought Laban running to meet Jacob with an embrace and a non-paying job and lodging for the next month (Gen. 29:

13–14). Then, Laban discusses wages with Jacob in verses 15 through 19.

> Gen. 29:15 Then Laban said to Jacob, "Because you are my relative, should you therefore serve me for nothing? Tell me, what should your wages be?"
>
> 16 Now Laban had two daughters: the name of the elder was Leah, and the name of the younger was Rachel.
>
> 17 Leah's eyes were delicate, but Rachel was beautiful of form and appearance.
>
> 18 Now Jacob loved Rachel; so he said, "I will serve you seven years for Rachel your younger daughter."
>
> 19 And Laban said, "It is better that I give her to you than that I should give her to another man. Stay with me."

Laban brings up the kinship issue as a reason to talk wages when he asks Jacob to name his wages. The description of both daughters is presented in verses 16 and 17. Leah is the oldest and Rachel, the youngest, is described as the most beautiful by far. The stunning younger daughter that Jacob first met at the well, and apparently grew to love during his month there, is what he wants for seven years of service.

Laban was pleased with the deal. I don't know what all these things were that Jacob told Laban at verse 13. But it does not appear like he told the full details of why he, a rich man who could have taken Rachel to wife the same way his father and Rebekah were betrothed, was becoming an indentured slave to get a wife. Jacob's spiritual blessings and security are in place by God's will, but the tab for Jacob's personal actions are still due and payable. Jacob was so in love with Rachel that the seven years he served for her seemed like a few days.

> Gen. 29:20 So Jacob served seven years for Rachel, and they seemed only a few days to him because of the love he had for her.

Afterward, Jacob made the formal request for Rachel. The feast referred to in verse 22 was an all-male affair that was the norm for recognizing a marriage in their time. It was in the evening, or under the cover and power of darkness, when Laban put Leah in the bridal chamber instead of Rachel. The darkness and the possibility of alcoholic beverages at the feast is the likely reason why Jacob consummated a marriage with the wrong woman.

> **Gen. 29:23 Now it came to pass in the evening, that he took Leah his daughter and brought her to Jacob; and he went in to her.**

Laban was not incapacitated; the reason the wrong woman was in Jacob's bed is because Laban tricked him. How ruthless is a man who would pull what Laban pulled on Jacob? He is as ruthless as a man who would pull what Jacob pulled on Isaac and Esau. The morning after must have brought a lot of familiar memories back to Jacob. The tricking of and being tricked by someone you love and should respect—the substituting of one person for another to a person who is incapacitated in order to defraud the incapacitated person—the self-centered greed and reckless disregard for the rights of others, was clearly the driving force behind Laban's actions. Jacob's reaction and Laban's explanation are stated in verses 25 and 26.

> **Gen. 29:25 So it came to pass in the morning, that behold, it was Leah, and he said to Laban. "What is this you have done to me? Was it not for Rachel that I served you? Why then have you deceived me?"**
>
> **26 And Laban said, "It must not be done so in our country, to give the younger before the firstborn.**

Jacob questions Laban in verse 25: "Was it not for Rachel that I served you? Why have you deceived me?" The reason was greed, but the answer was related to the customary birthrights or seniority system that was common to all people of that time (Gen. 29:26).

Laban knew this when he made the agreement for Rachel, so he must have been planning this switch for many years. He could have told Jacob about that custom first, made a marriage for Leah during Jacob's seven years and saw Rachel emerge as the oldest unmarried daughter. That's if his heart was in the right place, but Jacob was a master herdsman and a big profit to Laban, leaving no doubt about where Laban's heart was. Laban was seven years richer because of Jacob. Verses 27 through 30 show his plan unfold for another seven years of wealth at Jacob's expense.

> Gen. 29:27 "Fulfill her week, and we will give you this one also for the service which you will serve with me still another seven years."
>
> 28 Then Jacob did so and fulfilled her week. So he gave him his daughter Rachel as wife also.
>
> 29 And Laban gave his maid Bilhah to his daughter Rachel as a maid.
>
> 30 Then Jacob also went in to Rachel, and he also loved Rachel more than Leah. And he served with Laban still another seven years.

Laban has Jacob over a barrel. He knows he would not have convinced his nephew to serve any time for Leah. The trick made it impossible to take back what had happened between him and Leah the night before, yet his heart was still tied to Rachel. At verse 27, Laban tells Jacob to complete Leah's honeymoon week and he would give Jacob the girl of his heart's desire for seven more years. Jacob followed his heart and took the deal offered by Laban and the unnamed person referred to by the word "we" in verse 27.

I wonder if Jacob gave a thought to Esau or his father during his dealings with Laban. Leah, who appeared to be an obedient daughter and dutiful wife, got in the middle of two people who were in love by custom and her father's greed. God, seeing that Leah was hated in the relationship, allowed her to have children, but Rachel was barren (Gen. 29:31). The Bible does not say how well the sisters got along before, but the competition over the husband has them in opposite camps now. Verses 32 through 35 bear that out when you see the meanings and feelings behind the names of Leah's first four sons.

> Gen. 29:32 So Leah conceived and bore a son, and she called his name Reuben; for she said, "The Lord has surely looked on my affliction. Now therefore, my husband will love me."
>
> 33 Then she conceived again and bore a son, and said, "Because

the Lord has heard that I am unloved, He has therefore given me this son also." And she called his name Simeon.

34 She conceived again and bore a son, and said, "Now this time my husband will become attached to me, because I have borne him three sons." Therefore his name was called Levi.

35 And she conceived again and bore a son, and said, "Now I will praise the Lord." Therefore she called his name Judah. Then she stopped bearing.

Leah is blessed with motherhood and is no doubt earning some degree of respect, but she is still the person who was pushed into Jacob's life through trickery and, unlike Rachel, she will never be the love of his life.

CHAPTER 30

In Chapter 30 of Genesis, the childbearing would become a competition when Rachel gives Jacob her maid, Bilhah, to wife with the hope that she would have children in Rachel's name. The two sons that Bilhah bore Jacob were Dan and Naphtali. Leah countered Rachel's move by giving Jacob her maid, Zilpah, to wife and Zilpah bore Gad and Asher. Verses 14 through 18 show that the competition is still on for Jacob's affections.

Reuben, Leah's oldest son, found some mandrakes and gave them to his mother. The mandrake is a stemless perennial of the nightshade family, having emetic, purgative and narcotic qualities. The plant had many superstitions tied to it, the greatest of which probably was that the mandrake was an aphrodisiac and fertility drug. While fertility drugs exist, it cannot be proven that the mandrake is one.

Rachel wanted to be a natural mother so much that she probably would have believed and accepted anything that could help her achieve that goal. Rachel, still being the favored wife, offered Jacob to Leah that night for her son's mandrakes. The best thing to do would be to have only one wife, according to God's directive for marriage. The reasonable thing to do within the relationship they had might have been to appoint time for all of the women he had accepted as wives.

The reality was that Rachel, the only one that Jacob asked for, had control of his time and she was not giving it away without getting something for it. Leah had not earned Jacob's love with four natural sons and two sons through her maid, but God continued to love her. The bargain got her more time with their husband and God blessed her with three more children.

Issachar and Zebulon were Leah's last two sons. Dinah was her last child and only daughter. The mandrakes may have given Rachel a drug-induced high, but they did not provide any children. After Leah's last three children are born, God remembered Rachel in Genesis 30:22–24.

> **Gen. 30:22 Then God remembered Rachel, and God listened to her and opened her womb.**
>
> **23 And she conceived and bore a son, and said, "God has taken away my reproach."**
>
> **24 So she called his name Joseph, and said, "The Lord shall add to me another son."**

Rachel is vindicated with the birth of Joseph, which must have taken place some time after the second seven years of Jacob's wait had passed, as verse 25 implies. Jacob was ready to go back home after the birth of Joseph. All that we know about Laban would make it a sure bet that he would not even consider releasing Jacob until he had completed the contract. In verses 27 and 28, Laban knows that he is the beneficiary of God's grace through Jacob and letting him go will prove costly to him.

> **Gen. 30:27 And Laban said to him, "Please stay, if I have found favor in your eyes, for I have learned by experience that the Lord has blessed me for your sake."**
>
> **28 Then he said, "Name me your wages, and I will give it."**

The knowledge Jacob exhibited at the well when he came to the area had proven to be extremely beneficial, as Jacob explained it to Laban in verses 29 and 30. Laban's herd had grown large in Jacob's care and the herd was now worth a great deal of wealth. Both men acknowledged God as the source. The experience and advance knowledge he had in the trade was also a great benefit and being a hard worker who would come early and stay late to get the job done didn't hurt either.

Jacob had two wives, two concubines, 12 children and no money. All of the money he tricked his father and brother to obtain will not help him here. The blessings God has given through Jacob is the actual wealth of another man. Jacob, being alienated from his family's wealth by his actions, is still in need of money. In verse 30, Jacob wonders, "And now, when shall I also provide for my own house?" In verse 28 Laban told Jacob to name his wages and he would pay them, so Jacob sets his price in verses 31 through 36.

> Gen. 30:31 So he said, what shall I give you? And Jacob said. "You shall not give me anything. If you will do this thing for me, I will again feed and keep your flocks:
>
> 32 Let me pass through all your flock today, removing from there all the speckled and spotted sheep, and all the brown ones among the lambs, and the spotted and speckled among the goats; and these shall be my wages.
>
> 33 So my righteousness will answer for me in time to come, when the subject of my wages comes before you; every one that is not speckled and spotted among the goats, and brown among the lambs, will be considered stolen, if it is with me."
>
> 34 And Laban said, "Oh, that it were according to your word!"
>
> 35 So he removed that day the male goats that were speckled and spotted, all the female goats that were speckled and spotted, every one that had some white in it, and all the brown ones among the lambs, and gave them into the hand of his sons.
>
> 36 Then he put three days' journey between himself and Jacob, and Jacob fed the rest of Laban's flocks.

The new agreement would allow Jacob to take a share in the existing herds. The guaranteed way to keep their dealings fair was not a specific man-made brand on the animals to identify the owner—it was the whole God-given color of the animal. Jacob's share of the livestock would be the speckled and spotted sheep and goats and the brown lambs that some translate as black. The identification of each one's livestock at the end of the term was as simple as Jacob's proposal and Laban's acceptance (Gen. 30:33–34).

Verse 32 says that Jacob was to pass through the herds that day to remove his agreed upon stock. The agreement was broken by Laban the same day it was made. He took Jacob's stock from the herds, put them in his son's hands and they moved them three days journey from the other herds. Jacob was left starting with nothing as he took charge of Laban's flocks, verses 35 and 36. The fact that Jacob had superior knowledge about breeding and raising livestock is obvious, but the thing he is about to do with livestock is special.

> **Gen. 30:37 Now Jacob took for himself rods of green poplar and of the almond and chestnut trees, peeled white strips in them, and exposed the white which was in the rods.**
>
> **38 And the rods which he had peeled, he set before the flocks in the gutters, in the watering troughs where the flocks came to drink, so that they should conceive when they came to drink.**
>
> **39 So the flocks conceived before the rods, and the flocks brought forth streaked, speckled and spotted.**

Jacob's methods for manipulating the color of livestock have been proven to be credible by modern day scientists. The way Jacob found that out, way back then, is unknown. God may have given him this knowledge as he appears to be explaining to his wives at Genesis 31:7–12. He put forth the physical effort, but gives God the credit and may be saying the dream he mentions at Genesis 31:11–12 was the motivation for his actions. Of course, that depends on when he had the dreams.

Jacob had nothing to start on after Laban had broken the original agreement. Sure, we could say Jacob had a good case in today's courts, but today's courts didn't exist in those days. Jacob's prenatal work with the flocks got him strong seed stock which he selectively bred with the strongest stock and produced superior herds that nobody could deny were his.

> **Gen. 30:42 But when the flocks were feeble, he did not put them in; so the feebler were Laban's and the stronger Jacob's.**
>
> **43 Thus the man became exceedingly prosperous, and had large flocks, female and male servants, and camels and donkeys.**

The weaker herds became Laban's by Jacob's design after Laban cheated him on yet another agreement. Laban was still better off by far, but Jacob grew tremendously in livestock and servants. God had promised Jacob's success and safe return in the dream of Genesis 28:12–16, and the dream is becoming reality in Jacob's life.

CHAPTER 31

In Chapter 31 of Genesis, the tricks Laban used to defraud Jacob failed and created ill feelings within the families.

> **Gen. 31:1 Now Jacob heard the words of Laban's sons, saying, "Jacob has taken away all that was our father's, and from what was our father's he has acquired all this wealth."**
>
> **2 And Jacob saw the countenance of Laban, and indeed, it was not favorable toward him as before.**

The sons of Laban and brothers-in-law of Jacob were angry because the Lord had given Jacob the advantage in the livestock agreement. The same brothers-in-law who had taken Jacob's livestock and moved them three days journey from the other herds so Jacob could not find them were now calling Jacob a thief.

Laban, whose total relationship with Jacob was geared toward material advantages, was turning sour because God was rewarding Jacob with the fruit of his labor. Jacob noticed this and verse 3 says the Lord had advised him to go back home and, from all appearances, he was more than ready to do just that. God said he would be with him, and now all Jacob had to do was sell his plan of departure to Leah and Rachel.

Verses 4 through 13 clear up a few details as Jacob puts his case for leaving before his wives. The wives are called to the field, possibly for privacy, but certainly to get Jacob's side of the story.

Laban is not favorable toward Jacob now. Laban is not using all of

Jacob's skills and blessing to his advantage now, and that was the basis for his favor toward Jacob. Jacob told the truth in verse 6 when he said he gave Laban his best effort. The ten times Laban had changed his wages are not all discussed in detail, but knowing Laban leaves no questions about that number, as stated in verse 7. Jacob reflects on the past by telling his dreams about the livestock and reviewing the rest of the dealings with Laban.

The earlier statement that God could have given Jacob the knowledge to use the rods may have come through some of the dreams to which he is referring. The Bible does not record a specific order concerning the use of the rods, but Jacob certainly does not take any of the credit for it. The selective breeding would be a common thing in Jacob's trade, especially with his skills, but he gives God all of the credit for that, too, in verses 8 through 13. Jacob is growing as he follows God's directives through the dreams and revelations. The wives of Jacob have suffered everything that he suffered at the hands of their father (Gen. 31:13–16).

> **Gen. 31:13 I am the God of Bethel, where you anointed the pillar and where you made a vow to Me. Now arise, get out of this land, and return to the land of your family.'"**
>
> **14 Then Rachel and Leah answered and said to him, "Is there still any portion or inheritance for us in our father's house?**
>
> **15 Are we not considered strangers by him? For he has sold us, and also completely consumed our money.**
>
> **16 For all these riches which God has taken from our father are really ours and our children's; now then, whatever God has said to you, do it.**

In verse 13, the same God that appeared to Jacob at Bethel when he was going away from home, that told him he would keep him and bring him back, was now telling him to come back home. The women are tied to Jacob and they know it. They also know that some of the 14 years of prosperity their father got as Jacob's wages for them should have gone to them. They realize that their father sold them and consumed their money, and that the riches God took from Laban would have belonged to them and their children anyway, if their father had acted honestly.

When Jacob sees that the women are righteously indignant over their father's actions. Jacob is encouraged to follow God's directive to the utmost. The relationship between Jacob and Laban was obviously so strained that Jacob felt a civil exit with his wealth was not possible. They escaped, as covered in verses 17 through 21, while Laban and company were away shearing sheep.

> Gen. 31:17 Then Jacob rose and set his sons and his wives on camels.
>
> 18 And he carried away all his livestock and all his possessions which he had gained, his acquired livestock which he had gained in Padan Aram, to go to his father Isaac in the land of Canaan.
>
> 19 Now Laban had gone to shear his sheep, and Rachel had stolen the household idols that were her father's.
>
> 20 And Jacob stole away, unknown to Laban the Syrian, in that he did not tell him that he intended to flee.
>
> 21 So he fled with all that he had. He arose and crossed the river, and headed toward the mountains of Gilead.

The Lord had given Jacob his order to leave and his destination. The livestock, herdsmen, servants and family members were mobilized to leave with military precision. Before they left, Rachel stole her father's images, or household gods, without Jacob knowing anything about it. The act would give Laban his only legitimate claim against Jacob and would be even worse for Rachel, proving that full disclosure within a family is a necessary tool.

Jacob and company were on the third day of their journey toward the mountains of Gilead when Laban got word that Jacob was gone. At verse 23, Laban and a group overtook them seven days later in the mountains of Gilead. The intentions of Laban were hostile and driven by a sense of financial loss. He dropped his work, formed a posse and chased Jacob for a whole week. The living and true God, not the idol gods that Rachel stole, visited Laban in a dream.

> Gen. 31:24 But God had come to Laban the Syrian in a dream by night, and said to him, "Be careful that you speak to Jacob neither good nor bad."

In Gen. 31:24, the warning to speak neither good nor bad to Jacob appears to be the reason Laban focuses on his daughters as the reason for running Jacob down. The question about taking his daughters away—as if the daughters, his grandchildren and a festive send-off was the reason for chasing them seven days—does not ring true, as stated in verses 25 through 28. Laban's statement is even less credible when you review the daughter's assessment of his concern for them in verses 14 through 16, but it does open a door for civil conversation. Verse 29 shows Laban's original intent—he brought enough men to hurt them, but God's dream turned his heart.

> Gen. 31:29 It is in my power to do you harm, but the God of your father spoke to me last night, saying, "Be careful that you speak to Jacob neither good nor bad."
>
> 30 And now you have surely gone because you greatly long for your father's house, but why did you steal my gods?"
>
> 31 Then Jacob answered and said to Laban, "Because I was afraid, for I said, "Perhaps you would take your daughters from me by force."
>
> 32 With whomever you find your gods, do not let him live. In the presence of your brethren, identify what I have of yours and take it with you." For Jacob did not know that Rachel had stolen them.

The gods mentioned in verse 30 did not show Laban anything because they could not. You might ask why Laban wouldn't abandon the idols and follow the God of Jacob's father, since God gave him a credible revelation. The answer is in the timing. Even though Laban's people aspired to serve God, the way to do that was not yet known to them. God was in the process of developing a nation from the loins of Laban's grandchildren, whose duty it would be to reveal God to the whole world.

Jacob, unlike us, did not have a written record of God's will to teach him, so he was taking life one revelation at a time. Jacob did not know then his life would become the written record for us to follow and his nation would deliver the Bible that blesses all the families of the earth.

The interesting thing to note is that from the end of the flood up to this time, all of the people that the principal people encountered had a general knowledge of God. The problem seems to be that they all invented different ways to express their devotion.

The images men make are simply not gods: The maker of a thing is greater than the thing made. The practice of making images is an error that creates an open door Satan can use to enter man's mind and have him worshipping the works of his hands, which is an indirect way of worshipping one's self. The gods Laban referred to in verse 30 were man-made images. The fact that they were not a part of the agreement and Rachel took them without Jacob's knowledge or consent put the whole company in a position they could not defend.

Verse 31 covers Jacob's total distrust of his father-in-law. After 13 years of marriage, 12 children, three satisfied contracts, and a 20-year service record, he believes Laban would have sent him away the same way he came, alone and poor.

In verse 32, Jacob would not have said they could execute the person found with Laban's gods if he knew his beloved Rachel had taken the images. The whole situation could have changed if the images had been found in Jacob's camp and, knowing Laban, you would have to say he would have found a way to turn a profit from it. Rachel hid the images in her camels saddle and told her father her monthly cycle prevented her rising up, so he searched her tent and the rest without success (Gen. 31:33–35).

Jacob, to the best of his knowledge is righteous, and he pours out his righteous wrath on his father-in-law in verses 36 through 42. Jacob defends himself, his service record, his right to everything he earned while with Laban and declares that God was right for rebuking him in verse 42.

> Gen. 31:42 "Unless the God of my father, the God of Abraham and the Fear of Isaac, had been with me, surely now you would have sent me away empty-handed. God has seen my affliction and the labor of my hands, and rebuked you last night."
>
> 43 And Laban answered and said to Jacob. "These daughters are my daughters, and these children are my children, and this flock

> is my flock; all that you see is mine. But what can I do this day to these my daughters or their children whom they have borne?
>
> 44 Now therefore, come, let us make a covenant, you and I, and let it be a witness between you and me."

The real Laban shines through his statement in verse 43. He saw Jacob as a non-person and considered that everything Jacob had was his. Laban's statement confirms Jacob's fears, as stated in verse 31. Although the women are Laban's daughters, they are Jacob's wives first and foremost. The women's children are Laban's grandchildren, but they are Jacob's children first and foremost. The livestock are not Laban's either; they carry the undisputable color that, by agreement, makes them Jacob's. The actions and words of Laban leave little doubt that he wanted to take everything that Jacob had earned during the 20 years he spent with Laban.

The God of Abraham, Isaac, and now Jacob, communicated his will to Laban, and now Laban is seeking a covenant of peace with Jacob in verse 44. The way God leads and directs the paths of these people through dreams and revelations should be a lesson the reader never forgets. The growth of Jacob, as demonstrated by his willingness to step out on what God reveals to him, should not go unnoticed either. The conditions of the covenant and Laban's peaceful departure are covered in verses 45 through 55.

CHAPTER 32

Jacob, by the grace of God, has made a successful break from his father-in-law. God is directing him back to Canaan where he must deal with his twin brother, Esau, and face the consequences of his and his mother's deception of Esau. The angels of God that met Jacob at the place he named Mahanaim must have given him a boost of confidence in verses 1 and 2. According to verses 3 through 5, Jacob attempts to curry favor with Esau through his messengers and make amends for stealing his birthright.

> **Gen. 32:3 Then Jacob sent messengers before him to Esau his brother in the land of Seir, the country of Edom.**
>
> **4 And he Commanded them, saying, "Speak thus to my Lord Esau, "Thus your servant Jacob says: "I have dwelt with Laban and stayed there until now.**
>
> **5 I have oxen, donkeys, flocks, and male and female servants; and I have sent to tell my Lord, that I may find favor in your sight."**

The birthright blessing is covered in Genesis 27:27–29. The birthright is not the Abrahamic covenant that God bestowed; it is a custom within the power of the father to bestow. A close review of this passage, as measured by the birthright covenant passage, will raise questions about how successful Jacob's theft was. Who is master over whom here, who is bowing to whom here; keep this in mind as we proceed through Genesis.

Verse 6 does not record the dialog between Esau and the messengers; this verse only says the messengers told Jacob that Esau was coming to meet him with 400 men. Jacob has no way of knowing whether his brother is coming as friend or foe the way his messengers report Esau's arrival. He can only assume 400 soldiers under the command of a man whose understandable desire to kill him 20 years earlier is a valid reason to be alarmed.

Verse 7 says "alarmed" was an understatement. Jacob was afraid and distressed. He divided the people and herds as a defensive move, making it obvious that he was bracing for an attack. Verse 8 confirms that if Esau attacks one company, the other has a chance to escape. The fact that Jacob takes steps to make a plan in case he has to escape is understandable under the circumstances. While they do not negate his faith, they may prove that his faith is not yet as strong as Abraham's was when he offered up Isaac.

The prayer covered in verses 9 through 12 shows a more mature, obedient responsible man who believes Esau might kill him, his wives and his children, verse 11. The fears and distress are genuine, but he still has faith in God's directive for him to return to his father's home. Verse 12 shows Jacob depending on what God said, "For you said I will surely treat you well," while he is actively working at trying to appease what he thinks is Esau's anger in verses 13 through 21.

The custom of giving gifts to a superior is to promote good will from the greater to the lesser person. By doing so, Jacob acknowledges Esau's superiority. The size of the gifts in prime livestock and Jacob's humility show a repentant, yet fearful, man seeking forgiveness and reconciliation. The way the gifts were delivered and statements Jacob had the servants make to Esau were carefully planned and designed to soften Esau's heart.

Jacob prevailed over Laban without a sword. Now, he is working to prevail over Esau in a similar way—without a sword. Jacob is already living the title the angel would bestow on him in Genesis 32:28, "For you have struggled with God and with men, and have prevailed." Jacob continued to prove his faith when he acted on God's call to return home, then added to it by his prayers and actions. Jacob also proved he could use wisdom to accomplish his goals in his dealings with men.

Jacob went to sleep in his camp that night after sending the reconciliation package to Esau, but according to verses 22 and 23, he was uncomfortable with the location. He got up that night and moved his immediate family across the ford of Jabbok, then sent them across a brook and he stayed between the ford and brook alone.

> Gen. 32:22 And he arose that night and took his two wives, his two female servants, and his eleven sons, and crossed over the ford of Jabbok.
>
> 23 He took them, sent them over the brook, and sent over what he had.
>
> 24 Then Jacob was left alone; and a Man wrestled with him until the breaking day.
>
> 25 Now when He saw that He did not prevail against him, He touched the socket of his hip; the socket of Jacob's hip was out of joint as He wrestled with him.
>
> 26 And He said, "Let me go, for the day breaks." But he said, "I will not let you go unless You bless me!"
>
> 27 So He said to him, "What is your name?" He said, "Jacob."
>
> 28 And He said, "Your name shall no longer be called Jacob, but Israel; for you have struggled with God and with men, and have prevailed."
>
> 29 Then Jacob asked, saying, "Tell me your name, I pray." And he said, "Why is it that you ask about My name?" And He blessed him there.

The man wrestling with Jacob until daybreak was no doubt an angel. The Bible does not record a conversation prior to the struggle, but it is obvious from verse 26 that Jacob knew he was not ordinary and that he believed the man could bless him.

Another notable point is taken from verses 25 and 26. The man touched Jacob's hip socket and knocked it out of joint as they struggled, but Jacob still would not let the man go until the man blessed him. This Jacob, the Jacob who is hanging onto the angel to secure a blessing, that protects his family and confirm ownership of the Abrahamic covenant, is a long way from Jacob, the birthright thief.

The name Israel means "Prince with God" in verse 28 and it signifies a new meaning to the man's character. He is no longer Jacob, the trickster, he is Israel, the Prince who has learned how to deal successfully with God and man and none of it was easy. At Genesis 35:9–13, the name Israel and the Abrahamic covenant would be confirmed by God. Jacob's sons would come to be known as the children of Israel. The group would later become the nation of Israel.

Jacob wanted to know the angel's name, but the angel did not tell him. It seems Jacob assumed he was wrestling with God because, at verse 30, he named the place, Penial, which translated means, "the Face of God."

> **Gen. 32:30 So Jacob called the name of the place Peniel: "For I have seen God face to face, and my life is preserved."**

Jacob is quoted as saying he saw God face-to-face and his life was preserved. Jacob was certainly impressed by the encounter with the angel who presented himself as a man, but that does not make his assumption a fact. The Bible does not say God was dealing with Jacob face-to-face here. God, himself, would later tell Moses that no man shall see his face and live (Ex. 33:20–23).

> **Ex. 33:20 But He said, "You cannot see My face; for no man shall see Me, and live."**
>
> **21 And the Lord said, "Here is a place by Me, and you shall stand on the rock.**
>
> **22 So it shall be, while My glory passes by, that I will put you in the cleft of the rock, and will cover you with My hand while I pass by.**
>
> **23 Then I will take away My hand, and you shall see My back; but My face shall not be seen."**

Chapter 33 of Exodus should clearly establish God's words and position on men seeing his face. Moses had a very close relationship with God. Moses' request to see God's glory in Exodus 33:18, which the other scriptures associate with seeing his face, was denied. The above scriptures show Moses was only allowed to see God's back. Exodus 33:20 is not an assumption. It is a direct quote from God and it says no man can see God's face and live, as is verified at Exodus 33:23.

The careful student should establish the facts of Jacob's encounter to understand that Jacob, not God, is making an unproven claim when he says he saw God face-to-face and lived. The distinction should be made so no one thinks the Bible is contradicting itself. I have seen people argue to the point of fighting over what the Bible says, without identifying the speaker, circumstances or context of a passage.

Jacob would limp on the leg the angel touched from that point and his descendants would refrain from eating that part of a butchered animal's thigh because the angel touched Jacob there.

CHAPTER 33

Chapter 33 of Genesis covers the reunion of Jacob and Esau. The Bible describes all the actions Jacob took to ease his opinion of Esau's anger and possible desire for revenge.

> Gen. 33:1 Now Jacob lifted his eyes and looked, and there, Esau was coming, and with him were four hundred men. So he divided the children among Leah, Rachel, and the two maidservants.
>
> 2 And he put the maidservants and their children in front, Leah and her children behind, and Rachel and Joseph last.
>
> 3 Then he crossed over before them and bowed himself to the ground seven times, until he came near to his brother.
>
> 4 But Esau ran to meet him, and embraced him and fell on his neck and kissed him, and they wept.

The story to this point is told from only Jacob's standpoint and the reader might think that Jacob's planning, praying and actions had changed Esau's heart. Jacob's actions definitely show the worries of a guilty conscience. God knew that Esau was not interested in vengeance over the birthright. The careless attitude he showed for it proves that things like a heritage or security for anyone but himself was not high on Esau's agenda.

Esau is a prosperous and powerful man, but he is a here and now man. God's foreknowledge of Esau's attitude put him in a position to know this; that is no doubt why God chose Jacob for this job before they were born. The loss of the wealth and power of the birthright seemed to be Esau's motivation for hatred long ago and, now, he had more of both when he met Jacob.

The theft of the customary birth right inheritance was not an issue now because their father was still alive. Esau, who was well on the way to becoming a king by his own hands before anybody can claim the physical inheritance, had no reason to be vengeful. Last, but not least, God, who changes the hearts of men, had no doubt changed Esau's heart before he ever called Jacob home.

The first response or action you see from Esau is in verse 4 when he runs to meet his twin brother with hugs, kisses and weeping from the joy of seeing him after over 20 years. The evidence tends to show that Esau was not the least bit interested in rehashing the past. The whole family came forward, bowing in humility in the order that Jacob had established in verse 3. They were hoping to find grace in his brother's sight, but verse 9 reveals what must have been Esau's feelings all along.

> **Gen. 33:9 But Esau said, "I have enough, my brother; keep what you have for yourself."**
>
> **10 And Jacob said, "No please, if I have found favor in your sight, then receive my present from my hand, inasmuch as I have seen your face as though I had seen the face of God, and you were pleased with me.**
>
> **11 Please, take my blessing that is brought to you because God has dealt graciously with me, and because I have enough. And he urged him, and he took *it*."**

Jacob urged Esau to take what he offered him. At first, Esau said, "I have enough, keep the livestock for yourself." Esau did not need or want Jacobs's wealth nearly as much as Jacob needed to ease his guilty conscience. Verses 10 and 11 show Jacob pleading with his brother to take the gift as Esau finally gives in and accepts it. Verse 12 shows Esau taking the lead in rebuilding the brotherhood that Jacob and Rebekah had destroyed. Esau told Jacob, "Let us go, and I will go before you."

In Genesis 33:13–15, Jacob makes an excuse for not going with his brother or accepting his men for protection. The fact that verse 16 shows

Esau leaving for Seir and that he is fully expecting Jacob, as promised in verse 14, to catch up with him there shows Jacob is still not ready (Gen. 33:17).

> **Gen. 33:17 And Jacob journeyed to Succoth, built himself a house, and made booths for his livestock. Therefore the name of the place is called Succoth.**

Jacob went to the area named Succoth and built a house for his family and shelters for his herds, after clearly telling Esau he would come to him at Seir. The Bible does not say how Esau took Jacob's deception, but the meeting established peace between them. Jacob has talked to Esau and can communicate with his brother again.

In summary, I don't want to leave the readers without a clear understanding of this situation. I have heard ministers try to put a positive spin on Rebekah and Jacob's deception of the other two members of their immediate family, but there is no way to do that. The act was wrong and the whole family bore the scars of it. Rebekah took God's answer to her prayers and misunderstood it to the point that she became an instrument that Satan used to create a rift between every member of the family. Understanding the Bible demands that you take all known information and measure it by the known standard that determines right and wrong. The person is not greater than or above the law.

The situation in which Jacob found himself was the situation in which he put himself. The things he thought he was stealing from Esau by taking the birthright (Gen. 27:27–29) were still Esau's at this point and would be throughout their lifetimes. The things God promised Jacob before birth through the Abrahamic covenant (Gen. 25:23) would be Jacob's. The only thing he stole was a hard time. The positive thing is how God worked through the error of Jacob to keep his word and bring some maturity to Jacob.

The Bible does not say much more about Isaac and Rebekah's marriage. Jacob, though reconciled to Esau, would never be comfortable in his presence. I know a lot of repetition has been used in this family's life, and I apologize for it, but every angle of their situation should be scrutinized to avoid making the same mistake. I say that because I have seen people get the idea that trickery and deception are acceptable ways to gain objectives because they did not understand how wrong Jacob, their hero, was.

Jacob would later move to the city of Shechem in the land of Canaan where he would buy a piece of property. God is clearly becoming an established power in their lives, as verse 20 says Jacob erected an altar there and called it El Elohe Israel. The words mean, "God, the God of Israel."

CHAPTER 34

Chapter 34 of Genesis illustrates another hard situation indirectly caused by the fact that Jacob was not at home and was uncomfortable around his brother; he is in the midst of strangers. Dinah, Leah's youngest child and the family's only daughter, was obviously craving female friends her own age, so she went out to visit some of the young women of the land.

> Gen. 34:1 Now Dinah the daughter of Leah, whom she had borne to Jacob, went out to see the daughters of the land.
>
> 2 And when Shechem the son of Hamor the Hivite, prince of the country, saw her, he took her and lay with her, and violated her.
>
> 3 His soul was strongly attracted to Dinah the daughter of Jacob, and he loved the young woman and spoke kindly to the young woman.
>
> 4 So Shechem spoke to his father Hamor, saying, "Get me this young woman as a wife."
>
> 5 And Jacob heard that he had defiled Dinah his daughter. Now his sons were with his livestock in the field; so Jacob held his peace until they came.

Shechem, Hamor the Hivite's son, saw Dinah, took her, lay with her and defiled her. The Bible does not mention that Shechem made any attempt at courtship or conversation with Dinah. The fact that his father was a Prince in the land and Jacob's family were newcomers must have given him the confidence to obey his lust, force himself on Dinah and defile her.

Verse 3 records an eerie scene. After raping her, the young man spoke kindly to her. He falls in love with Dinah. The Bible does not say how Dinah felt about Shechem's confessed love for her after he defiled her, but it is painfully clear that Shechem didn't get first things first.

Verses 6 through 12 lay out what should have been done before Shechem forced himself on Dinah. The honorable thing would have been to speak to his father and her father to see if there could be a marriage between them. Then, he should have asked for permission to speak to Dinah in the hope that she would like him. In verse 8, the attempt to make a marriage now was more of an insult than a genuine request for matrimony. The honor of the young woman had been compromised before her family had the chance to refuse the offer of matrimony.

> **Gen. 34:8 But Hamor spoke with them, saying, "The soul of my son Shechem longs for your daughter. Please give her to him as wife.**
>
> **9 And make marriages with us; give your daughters to us, and take our daughters to yourselves.**
>
> **10 So you shall dwell with us, and the land shall be before you. Dwell and trade in it, and acquire possessions for yourselves in it."**

Jacob had no reason to have confidence in the offers being made and there were questions about what the children of Hamor would do if the Israelites did not enter into an agreement with them. The offers of Hamor and Shechem would appear to have some possible advantages, but the fact that Shechem raped Dinah before the deal would always make it an unbalanced deal (Gen. 34:8–10).

Shechem happened to fall in love with Dinah after having his way with her, but if he had not come to love her, she would still have been a compromised maiden. The family of Dinah had a legitimate reason for outrage. The way the situation was handled would certainly raise questions under the legal systems most people live under today. At that time, Jacob's family had no courts to address the initial rape, and no neutral law to protect everyone's interest since Shechem's father was the law in that region.

Shechem's love of Dinah, as stated in verses 11 and 12, would be the weapon Jacob's sons would form and use against Hamor and the men of his city. Verse 13 sums up the brother's position.

> **Gen. 34:13 But the sons of Jacob answered Shechem and Hamor his father, and spoke deceitfully, because he had defiled Dinah their sister.**

They answered deceitfully; they lied to them. Why? Because Shechem had defiled Dinah, their sister. The deal could never work for that reason, so the outnumbered Israelites were looking for an advantage. The plan was obviously set before the meeting with Hamor and Shechem. They told them that an uncircumcised man is a reproach to the Israelites. If, they proposed, the Hamorites would submit to circumcision, the marriage of Dinah and Shechem could go forward, plus the possibility of other marriages would exist (Gen. 14–17). The proposal was accepted by the father and son.

> **Gen. 34:18 And their words pleased Hamor and Shechem, Hamor's son.**
>
> **19 So the young man did not delay to do the thing, because he delighted in Jacob's daughter. Shechem was more honorable than all the household of his father.**

The young man is so in love with his victim that he is willing to submit to circumcision. I say victim because her feelings and opinions have not been heard or considered yet, according to what is written here. As this young rapist is more honorable than all the household of his father (Gen. 34:19), then all in his father's house must be a treacherous bunch. A look at his honor shows a man who is willing to make sacrifices for a woman he falls in love with after he rapes her.

The honor of his father is seen in Genesis 34:20–24 as they sell the idea of circumcision to the other men in their village. The men are peaceable and let Jacob's group dwell in the land and trade (Gen. 34:21). There's no mention of the fact that they had purchased the land and had every legal right to be there. Verse 23 sheds more light on their respective honor.

> Gen. 34:23 Will not their livestock, their property, and every animal of theirs be ours? Only let us consent to them, and they will dwell with us."
>
> 24 And all who went out of the gate of his city heeded Hamor and Shechem his son; every male was circumcised, all who went out of the gate of his city.

Verse 23 brings the treacherous intentions of both men to light. I say both because both Hamor and Shechem are named. The spider may offer friendship to the fly long enough to get the fly in his web, then the fly is the spider's lunch. Verse 26 sheds some additional light on the honor of these men.

After the circumcision of the men, Dinah's brothers waited three days, came into the city and slaughtered all of the males. The verse says they took Dinah from Shechem's house and went out. The questions: When was Dinah taken to Shechem's house? Who took Dinah to Shechem's house? Had Dinah been at Shechem's house from the day he raped her? Was Dinah a prisoner at his house while they were talking to her family about marriage? Was she at his disposal to be used as he saw fit? The men were still sore from the circumcision and that had to take place before the marriage, so when and what circumstances put Dinah in Shechem's house if they were not yet married?

The idea of marriages between these two groups under these conditions may threaten their budding relationship toward God. Verses 27 through 29 show how the intent of Hamor and Shechem in verse 23 was reversed when the city was plundered. The Bible does not say how many men were killed or if Simeon and Levi had help, nor does it say what happened to the captives they took. Why? Because they defiled their sister. The opinions, doubts, offers, actions or statements cannot erase the cause. The young man who was the most honorable in his father's house should have put honor before lust and been willing to accept an answer of "No" from the young maiden with honor.

The statement of Jacob in verse 30 a might lead you to believe he did not love his daughter as much as his sons loved her.

> Gen. 34:30 Then Jacob said to Simeon and Levi, "You have troubled me by making me obnoxious among the inhabitants of

> the land, among the Canaanites and the Perizzites; and since I am few in number, they will gather themselves together against me and kill me. I shall be destroyed, my household and I."
>
> 31 But they said, "Should he treat our sister like a harlot?"

Verse 30 shows you the logic behind his statement. The people in the area outnumbered his group and he said, not thought, they will gather themselves together and kill us. The responsibility of leadership is always to save as many lives as possible. Leadership does not give him the luxury of vengeance regardless of his personal feelings. He must have been thinking that Dinah could survive with the man who wants her and we will not have to worry about being outnumbered. He did not know the full intentions of Hamor. The way he addressed the men of his city, you could safely say everything Jacob owned was potentially at risk.

The young man truly loved Dinah after raping her and he would be her protector and provider if they married. Jacob may have been thinking, "Since Shechem took Dinah's virginity, if we take her back, would she be a desirable wife to another man, subjected to a dishonorable marriage, no marriage or harlotry?"

The slaughter by the brothers may have been their only way out, given the full knowledge of Hamor's intentions. Verse 31 still raises a strong argument on the brothers' behalf, even though they did not know Hamor's full intentions. The bottom line is that they had stayed there for a good while, on land bought with their money, until Shechem's wrong actions forced their reactions. The Bible does not say whether the father's position or the sons' position was right or wrong; the Bible just tells you what happened. Jacob, the head of the family, would never feel right about the act and it would come up again just before his death.

CHAPTER 35

Chapter 35 of Genesis marks God's call to have Jacob return to Bethel in verses 1 through 5.

> Gen. 35:1 Then God said to Jacob, "Arise, go up to Bethel and dwell there; and make an altar there to God, who appeared to you when you fled from the face of Esau your brother."
>
> 2 And Jacob said to his household and to all who were with him, "Put away the foreign gods that are among you, purify yourselves, and change your garments.
>
> 3 Then let us arise and go up to Bethel; and I will make an altar there to God, who answered me in the day of my distress and has been with me in the way which I have gone."
>
> 4 So they gave Jacob all the foreign gods which were in their hands, and the earrings which were in their ears; and Jacob hid them under the terebinth tree which was by Shechem.
>
> 5 And they journeyed, and the terror of God was upon the cities that were all around them, and they did not pursue the sons of Jacob.

Chapter 28 of Genesis must be reviewed in it's entirety to understand the full significance of God's call to Jacob and the move to Bethel. When reading verse 2, understand that the known commandment to have no gods before the true God had not been given yet. The Living,

True God had not dealt extensively with anyone in that group except Jacob, so for them to have strange gods at that time puts them on par with the rest of the world.

God is, in fact, showing his power over the idols and winning the people at this point, as Jacob's statement in verse 3 proves. The altar to God and the fact that God answered in the many days that Jacob was distressed is evidence of God's power, as Jacob realizes and is bringing his immediate and extended family to realize. The idol gods are losing and a true conversion is taking place.

Bethel, as your review of Chapter 28 proves, was the name given by Jacob to the city of Luz at Genesis 28:19. The vow Jacob made several years earlier at that site must have made God's call to return to it sound like music to his ears. The faithfulness of God to keep his promise and facilitate Jacob's safe return with great wealth and no loss of life from enemies is continuing, as stated in verse 5. Jacob was sure the surrounding nations would destroy them, and they could have, except for the terror God put in their hearts. Jacob had the most powerful friend possible in the highest of places.

The people gave up the strange gods and Jacob put them away. Verses 6 and 7 mark the full return to Bethel and the open actions Jacob take in obedience to his faith. The altar sets a positive example and establishes submitting to God as a faith basis for the group to pass on to future generations of their nation.

Rebekah's nurse, Deborah, who had left Padan Aram to serve her before she married Isaac, died at Bethel and was buried under a terebinth tree. In verse 8, the place was named Allon Bachuth. It is not mentioned where Rebekah was at the time, but Deborah appears to have been with Jacob's group when she died.

God appeared to Jacob again and blessed him in Genesis 35:9–13.

> **Gen. 35:9 Then God appeared to Jacob again, when he came from Padan Aram, and blessed him.**
>
> **10 And God said to him, "Your name is Jacob; your name shall not be called Jacob anymore, but Israel shall be your name." So he called his name Israel.**
>
> **11 Also God said to him: "I am God Almighty. Be fruitful and**

multiply; a nation and a company of nations shall proceed from you, and kings shall come from your body.

12 The land which I gave Abraham and Isaac I give to you; and to your descendants after you I give this land."

13 Then God went up from him in the place where He talked with him.

The blessing confirms Jacob's new name, Israel, repeats the Abrahamic covenant, specifies the promised land, then blesses him and his offspring on a perpetual basis again. This happened in Bethel, the same Bethel where God had made that promise many years and 12 children earlier. The dream and promise God gave Jacob at Genesis 28:12–15 is being fulfilled and taking shape. The importance of Israel, Christ and the Bible for all of the families of the earth from generation to generation would prove that out. The Bible does not tell us how long Jacob stayed at Sheehem or Bethel, so we cannot put an accurate age to his most tragic personal loss up to that point.

Gen. 35:16 Then they journeyed from Bethel. And when there was but a little distance to go to Ephrath, Rachel labored in childbirth, and she had hard labor.

17 Now it came to pass, when she was in hard labor, that the midwife said to her, "Do not fear; you will have this son also."

18 And so it was, as her soul was departing (for she died), that she called his name Ben-Oni; but his father called him Benjamin.

19 So Rachel died and was buried on the way to Ephrath (that is Bethlehem).

20 And Jacob set a pillar on her grave, which is the pillar of Rachel's grave to this day.

The group had left Bethel and was nearly at Ephrath, which would later be named Bethlehem, when Rachel went into hard labor with her second child. The child was born, but Rachel died there. The name his mother gave him while dying was Ben-Oni which meant, "Son of my Sorrow." Israel, his father, renamed him Benjamin, which meant, "Son of the Right Hand." Rachel was buried near Bethlehem where centuries later, King Herod would slaughter the inhabitants' children in an attempt to cut off the Messiah.

In verses 21 and 22, the group moved on and settled beyond the tower of Eder.

> **Gen. 35:21 Then Israel journeyed and pitched his tent beyond the tower of Eder.**
>
> **22 And it happened, when Israel dwelt in that land that Reuben went and lay with Bilhah, his father's concubine; and Israel heard about it.**

While living there, Reuben, Jacob's first-born and the oldest son of Leah, lay with Bilhah, who had been Rachel's maid. Bilhah was given to Jacob by Rachel for a wife and is the mother of Reuben's half-brothers, Dan and Naphtali, as stated in Genesis 35:25.

The Bible says Israel heard about it, but he apparently kept it to himself until later in his life. The Bible does not say why Jacob did not act on it then, but looking at Jacob's earlier way, avoiding confrontations, thinking first, then acting only when necessary, may have a lot to do with it. The disrespect of the act could have created violence between innocent family members who were impacted by it, so Jacob apparently tabled it, but he never forgot it. Chapter 49 of Genesis records Jacob's last words and prophecies concerning his twelve sons and their offspring. The adulterous act of Reuben would shape the character of his tribe, as Jacob would point out in Genesis 49:1–4.

The twelve sons of Jacob and their mothers are named in verses Genesis 35:23–26. Isaac and Jacob were reunited in verse 27.

> **Gen. 35:27 Then Jacob came to his father Isaac at Mamre, or Kirjath Arba (that is, Hebron), where Abraham and Isaac had dwelt.**
>
> **28 Now the days of Isaac were one hundred and eighty years.**

The Bible does not say how old either man was at this reunion, but according to verse 28, Isaac lived 180 years, so they should have had quite a few years together before he died. The Bible does not say how their time was spent, but it does identify the place with some of the promised land where Abraham and Isaac lived. The twins, Esau and Jacob (Israel), buried their father at a ripe old age.

CHAPTER 36

Chapter 36 of Genesis covers the genealogy and royal lines of Esau and identifies Esau as the father of the Edomite nation. Verses 6 and 7 say that Esau and Jacob dwelt in Canaan at the same time and all indications show a good relationship between them.

> **Gen. 36:6 Then Esau took his wives, his sons, his daughters, and all the persons of his household, his cattle and all his animals, and all his goods which he had gained in the land of Canaan, and went to a country away from the presence of his brother Jacob.**
>
> **7 For their possessions were too great for them to dwell together, and the land where they were strangers could not support them because of their livestock.**
>
> **8 So Esau dwelt in Mount Seir. Esau is Edom.**

Esau left Canaan because the country could not support the number of servants, herds and belongings the brothers had acquired. They had the same problem Abraham and Lot had before they split. Their cups are running over so abundantly that the problem is not where to get wealth, but where to keep all of the wealth.

Esau is the most powerful and wealthy of the two men and his nation would become prominent first. Jacob's nation would be born after 400 years in slavery and is still a prominent player on the world scene because of God's blessing. Esau's Edom would not stand the test of time and is no longer standing as a nation.

The peace the brothers seemed to achieve late in life could and should have been theirs all along. The main opposition to it came from their mother as Satan used her as a weapon that hurt both sons, her husband and herself.

The lessons we can learn from them is to always apply Godly principals in every situation. Satan has already outwitted the best of us when he can draw us away from using Godly principals in every facet of our lives. Rebekah and Jacob opened a door for Satan when they started using falsehood and deceit to obtain something that they already had.

Rebekah would have been wiser to work as a dutiful wife, a happy, non-controlling, proud mother and an obedient servant of God who is content with what He had shown her. God was in control of what he had shown her long before she saw it. Her job, like ours, is to understand it, then accept it.

CHAPTER 37

In Chapter 37 of Genesis, Joseph is introduced as the 17-year-old favorite of his father.

> Gen. 37:2 This is the history of Jacob. Joseph, being seventeen years old, was feeding the flock with his brothers. And the lad was with the sons of Bilhah and the sons of Zilpah, his father's wives; and Joseph brought a bad report on them to his father.
>
> 3 Now Israel loved Joseph more than all his children, because he was the son of his old age. Also he made him a tunic of many colors.
>
> 4 But when his brothers saw that their father loved him more than all his brothers, they hated him and could not speak peaceably to him.

Verse 3 says Joseph was the favorite because he was the son of Jacob's old age, but his full brother, Benjamin, was actually the youngest. The fact that Joseph was Rachel's first-born, and not the one she died giving life to, probably had a bearing on the favoritism, but the narrative may prove that Joseph had something to do with this also.

The family has weathered many storms. Now, they are back in Canaan, Isaac is still alive and the whole family is continuing to prosper. The land Jacob bought in the city of Shechem (Gen. 33:18–19) was still Jacob's grazing lands (Gen. 35:12), as were many other places near other towns.

Verse 2 tells us that Joseph was working with Dan, Naphtali, Gad and Asher, feeding a flock, and the older brothers did something that they should not have done. Joseph told their father and it would earn him a reputation among his brothers as a talebearer. On the contrary, the reputation he would earn from his father, the owner of the flock and his employer, would be as a loyal, obedient and dutiful servant.

The coat of many colors that Jacob made for Joseph in verse 3 is only one sign of his choice of Joseph as his favorite. Verse 4 reveals how his brothers felt about their father's greater love for Joseph, so he must have demonstrated it in many other ways. The end result is that the brothers could not speak peaceably with Joseph. The lessons Jacob should have learned from seeing his parents play favorites between Esau and himself either didn't take or don't seem to be on his mind now.

The beauty of having this blessed Bible is the power of analysis it gives us so we can study the actions of others. The other sons of Jacob might not know of the trickery of Laban, their grandfather, when he substituted Leah for the beloved Rachel. The other sons of Jacob might not know or understand how the maids became wives during the sisters' childbearing competition. The fact that Joseph is the first-born of the only wife that Jacob really wanted is not a factor in the minds of the other sons either.

The other sons know they are just as much the sons of Jacob as Joseph and they want to be dealt with on that level. The other sons are exactly right. The father as head and overseer has the responsibility to set a fair, non-discriminatory standard within the family. The standard should be fair in its distribution of love, raising, feeding, trust, discipline, punishment and so on. The standard set by the leader should be followed if it is a right standard—a person who rejects a right standard puts themselves in the wrong.

The Bible says Jacob made differences between the brothers that may not have been because of their actions. By doing so, Jacob violated the standard. The problems that would enter Jacob's family, through him giving in to the emotions of his past when all of his children needed impartial love, are going to haunt him the rest of his life. Treating all of his children equally would not have altered God's choice of Joseph as a dreamer and deliverer. It would not have changed the report that his brothers earned, but it could have taken away the hatred the brothers felt for Joseph because the standard-setter had made all of them inferior to him.

In verses 5 through 11, the dreams Joseph had did not do much to improve his relationship with his brothers. The second dream even drew a rebuke from his father in verse 10. The Bible does not say Joseph was boasting or gloating about the dreams. He was simply relating what he had seen.

I would not call him spoiled for that. He only dreamed the dreams—he did not interpret them. The dreams would come true, but Joseph didn't know that then. A wiser and older Joseph would have never mentioned the dreams, given the climate in his family.

Verses 12 through 14 describe an action that Jacob had every right to take.

> Gen. 37:12 Then his brothers went to feed their father's flock in Shechem.
>
> 13 And Israel said to Joseph, "Are not your brothers feeding the flock in Shechem? Come, I will send you to them." So he said to him, "Here I am."
>
> 14 Then he said to him, "Please go and see if it is well with your brothers and well with the flocks, and bring back word to me." So he sent him out of the Valley of Hebron, and he went to Shechem.

He sent his younger son to check on the older sons who envied and hated him because he was openly their father's favorite. The flip side is that their father trusted Joseph because he did not have an affair with one of his wives or destroy the men of Shechem or earn the evil report he made on four other sons. The father should have thought the issue through and saw that he may have been putting Joseph in harm's way. The fact that Jacob was not wrong for sending Joseph does not quench the evil in his other sons' hearts.

The situation could have been handled with more wisdom, but who would have thought their hatred would be that intense. In any society, you can be in the right for carrying your legal money anywhere you wish. Wisdom, however, would tell you not to take a pocketful of money into the seediest section of your community because you know your rights are not enough to stop the greed of a group that will kill you for the money.

Jacob certainly should have done this job himself. Satan's power over the flesh is driving this machine. With Jacob's older sons, Satan was using the same tools of envy and hatred that he used on Cain, who slew Abel for doing right. The point I am making is that the father should not have been the initiator of the favoritism game at all. Obviously, he could not see the effect it would have on his other sons, but thankfully, we can analyze the story and see this for ourselves.

The above-named facts are true, but they still don't justify what Joseph's brothers are planning in the upcoming verses (Gen. 37:18–20).

> Gen. 37:18 Now when they saw him afar off, even before he came near them, they conspired against him to kill him.
>
> 19 Then they said to one another, "Look, this dreamer is coming!
>
> 20 Come therefore, let us now kill him and cast him into some pit; and we shall say, "Some wild beast has devoured him. We shall see what will become of his dreams!"

The plan to kill Joseph in verse 18 was made before he could say why he was there. I wonder if the whole group had earned another evil report. Jacob had sent Joseph to Shechem to get a report on their activities there, so it is obvious that they were supposed to be there.

In verse 17, the man who found Joseph wandering around there said he heard them say they were going to Dothan, some 15 to 20 miles farther away. Why were they in Dothan and were they there on legitimate business or were they goofing off? The Bible doesn't say if they were away from their assigned location without justification; they knew Joseph was not going to lie for them.

The hatred over two dreams Joseph related and they interpreted hardly seems to be a motive for murder, but verses 19 and 20 identify the dreams as their reason. The plot to kill Joseph did not have the support of all of the brothers. Two brothers would actually work to deliver him, while trying to appear as if they were with the majority.

> **Gen. 37:21 But Reuben heard it, and he delivered him out of their hands, and said, "Let us not kill him."**
>
> **22 And Reuben said to them, "Shed no blood, but cast him into this pit which is in the wilderness, and do not lay a hand on him that he might deliver him out of their hands, and bring him back to his father.**

Reuben had to think up the plan to deliver Joseph very quickly because the plan to kill him was hatched from the time he came into view until the time he reached them. Reuben alone knew he would come back later and free Joseph if he could keep the other brothers from committing the actual murder.

In keeping with Reuben's plan, verses 23 through 25 show that the brothers grabbed Joseph, took his tunic or coat of many colors, threw him into a pit or empty cistern and sat down to eat. A company of Ishmaelites carrying spices down to Egypt came by. Like Reuben, Judah came up with another plan to get Joseph out of harm's way. The plan of Judah was then carried out as laid out in verses 26 through 28, "Let us be free of his blood, he is our brother so we will sell him instead."

> **Gen. 37:26 So Judah said to his brothers, "What profit is there if we kill our brother and conceal his blood?**
>
> **27 Come and let us sell him to the Ishmaelites, and let not our hand be upon him, for he is our brother and our flesh." And his brothers listened.**
>
> **28 Then Midianite traders passed by; so the brothers pulled Joseph up and lifted him out of the pit, and sold him to the Ishmaelites for twenty shekels of silver. And they took Joseph to Egypt.**

The idea of making a profit on a person that they hated enough to murder must have appealed to them. A look at Judah's plan does not give Joseph as much as Reuben's would have, but Judah did not know Reuben's plan, so he is using what is available to save Joseph's life. The end result is that Joseph is sold for 20 shekels of silver, which was no doubt divided among the men there. The intentions of Reuben were manifested in verses 29 and 30.

> **Gen. 37:29 Then Reuben returned to the pit, and indeed Joseph was not in the pit; and he tore his clothes.**
>
> **30 And he returned to his brothers and said, "The lad is no more; and I, where shall I go?"**

Reuben returned to the pit and was distressed when he did not find Joseph. The concern he had was most certainly for his younger brother, but he may also have had some concerns over his responsibilities as the first-born child as well. The statement he makes after he returns to the brothers camp is, "The lad is no more, where shall I go?" This leads you to think Reuben believes he will not be very welcome at his father's house if Joseph's absence cannot be explained.

The Bible does not say whether the others ever told Reuben they had sold Joseph, or where he was when they sold him. He must have bought into some kind of deception to become a part of their unified effort to deceive their father in verses 31 through 33. The tunic or coat of many colors was dipped in goat's blood and taken to Jacob for identification. Verse 32 says they sent the tunic—no doubt, "they" meaning the brothers—and they brought it to their father, claiming to have found it.

> **Gen. 37:31 So they took Joseph's tunic, killed a kid of the goats, and dipped the tunic in the blood.**
>
> **32 Then they sent the tunic of many colors, and they brought it to their father and said, "We have found this. Do you know whether it is your son's tunic or not?"**
>
> **33 And he recognized it and said, "It is my son's tunic. A wild beast has devoured him. Without doubt Joseph is torn to pieces."**

The Bible does not say which brothers sent the coat or which brothers brought the coat, but verses 32 and 33 show their clever preplanned approach: "We found this tunic; you tell us if it's your son's tunic." The brothers who brought the bloody tunic are denying by their statement that they had ever seen Joseph at all. The father, by identifying the garment, is left to draw his own conclusion about Joseph's fate. The bloody tunic convinces Jacob that some evil beast had eaten Joseph and, without doubt, the father has convinced himself that his son has been torn to pieces. The brothers designed the deception with such clever precision that they did not have to admit or deny anything about Joseph's disappearance.

Jacob has lost his favored wife, Rachel, and their favored son, Joseph, in a very short span of time. The idea of comforting him was out of the question, as he makes clear in verses 34 and 35, "I will go down into the grave to my son mourning." The pain of losing Joseph a short time after losing Rachel must have been devastating.

Joseph was sold in Egypt to Potiphar, an officer of Pharaoh and captain of the guard.

CHAPTER 38

The story of Judah, Jacob's son, as told in Chapter 38 of Genesis gives some vital information about marriage customs in those days. The nationality of all the wives of the sons of Jacob are not known here, but it is assumed that none of them came from Abraham's homeland. Verse 2 says Judah's wife was a Canaanite woman named Shua.

Shua, the wife of Judah, bore him three sons—Er, Onan and Shelah (Gen. 3–5). Tamar, the daughter-in-law of Judah and Shua, would emerge as one mother of the tribe of Judah and hers would be a story of perseverance.

> Gen. 38:6 Then Judah took a wife for Er his firstborn, and her name was Tamar.
>
> 7 But Er, Judah' s firstborn, was wicked in the sight of the Lord, and the Lord killed him.
>
> 8 And Judah said to Onan, "Go in to your brother's wife and marry her, and raise up an heir to your brother."
>
> 9 But Onan knew that the heir would not be his; and it came to pass, when he went in to his brother's wife, that he emitted on the ground, lest he should give an heir to his brother.
>
> 10 And the thing which he did displeased the Lord; therefore He killed him also.

Tamar began as the wife of Er, Judah's oldest son, but before he fathered children with her, God killed him because he was so wicked. The duty of a husband's brother was apparently accepted by Judah's people long before it became Bible law (Deut. 25:5–10), because he instructed and expected Onan to perform this rite.

The idea might sound like a pleasant task to some, but the reality is that the husband's brother has to maintain or establish the dead brother's child and household. He cannot claim the child or property as his own; it goes on forever as his brother's property and family. He is a surrogate father with a responsibility for his brother's name and no rights or privileges in that name.

Verse 9 says Onan knew the heir or person would not be his, so instead of impregnating Tamar, he spilled the semen on the ground. Verse 10 says the selfishness of Onan in this act so displeased God that God killed him also.

Judah had produced and raised two men that were too sorry for God to allow them to live. The Bible does not say if Judah knew why they died, he just knew they died during their involvement with Tamar.

Verse 11 shows that Judah probably blamed Tamar for his son's deaths. The obedience to custom is so strong in him that he said he would follow through on the husband's brother custom when Shelah, his youngest son, was grown. Judah sent Tamar back to her father's house as a widow-in-waiting until Shelah was grown, "Lest he also die like his brothers." This shows some of the fears and superstitions Judah had in regard to Tamar.

Tamar, the daughter-in-law of Judah is in a dire situation for an honorable woman. She is twice widowed, and not legally free to remarry. Tamar must be thinking, "the father of the groom is thinking of me as a black widow, the groom may be afraid of me and the wedding is shaky at best and leaning toward impossible." The sons of Judah died because they had no earthly value to God. God killed them, but Tamar knows that she is being blamed for their deaths.

Verse 12 records the death of Judah's wife over the process of time. It does not say how much time or how old Shelah was at this time, though he appears to be an adult. At verse 13, the mourning time ended and Judah went to Timnah to check on his sheep shearers there. The same Hirah, the Adullumite, who he was visiting when he met his wife, was with him. Tamar found out where Judah was going. She makes a desperate and extremely dangerous move in Genesis 38:14–18.

> Gen. 38:14-18 And she put her widow's garments off from her, and covered her with a vail, and wrapped herself, and sat in an open place, which is by the way to Timnath; for she saw that Shelah was grown, and she was not given unto him to wife.
>
> 15 When Judah saw her, he thought her to be an harlot; because she had covered her face.
>
> 16 And he turned unto her by the way, and said, Go to, I pray thee, let me come in unto thee; (for heknew not that she was his daughter in law.) And she said, What wilt thou give me, that thou mayest come in unto me?
>
> 17 And he said, I will send thee a kid from the flock. And she said, Wilt thou give me a pledge, till thou send it?
>
> 18 And he said, What pledge shall I give thee? And she said, Thy signet, and thy bracelets, and thy staff that is in thine hand. And he gave it her, and came in unto her, and she conceived by him.

The plan she put together did not get the husband's brother to impregnate her; her plan got the husband's father to impregnate her, without him knowing her identity. Tamar, as a widow in that family, was under the authority of Judah, the head of the family. Any unchaste act could bring a sentence of death from the head of the family. The pregnancy of Tamar was discovered about three months after the seduction of Judah. In verse 24 Judah's sentence on her was death by fire.

> Gen. 38:24 And it came to pass, about three months after, that Judah was told, saying, "Tamar your daughter-in-law has played the harlot; furthermore she is with child by harlotry." So Judah said, "Bring her out and let her be burned!"

The plan of Tamar must go by the numbers now or she is dead. In verses 25 and 26, the items she took from Judah in pledge are presented to him and he has no valid case against her. In fact, he declares that she is more righteous than him. Judah had promised to follow through on the husband's brother custom when Shelah came of age, but his fears prevented his following through on it. There are no further sexual relations between them.

The encounter between Judah and Tamar produced twins. The twin boys, Perez and Zerah, would be named with Shelah as the heads of the families of Judah in Numbers 26:20. Tamar proved that she was not cursed or the cause of Er and Onan's deaths by successfully bearing children with Judah, who did not die as a result of it. The act secured her place in that family with property and inheritance security through her children. The Bible does not say whether Shelah married Tamar or if she ever married again. Shelah married and fathered children, but no wife is named.

CHAPTER 39

In Chapter 39 of Genesis, the narrative turns back to Joseph's life after some of his brothers sold him into slavery. Potiphar, captain of the guard in Egypt who bought Joseph from the Ishmaelites, is no doubt a wealthy, privileged man, as stated in verses 1 and 2. Joseph's lifestyle and surroundings had changed drastically, but instead of losing his composure and going berserk at 17 years old, he appears to have been remarkably level-headed from the beginning of the ordeal.

Some commentaries seem to think of and project Joseph as spoiled; needless to say, they cannot prove that from the Bible. Joseph's brothers spoke of him as a fun-spoiling little snitch, when in truth he was honestly carrying out the orders of his father. Israel must have thought Joseph was the most honest and dependable of his sons, even though he was his favorite, or Israel would not have been wise to trust him to make reports on the others.

The God of his father was with Joseph in Egypt, blessing and prospering his every act (Gen. 39:2–6).

> Gen. 39:2 The Lord was with Joseph, and he was a successful man; and he was in the house of his master the Egyptian.
>
> 3 And his master saw that the Lord was with him and that the Lord made all that he did to prosper in his hand.
>
> 4 So Joseph found favor in his sight, and served him. Then he

made him overseer of his house, and all that he had he put under his authority.

5 So it was, from the time that he had made him overseer of his house and all that he had, that the Lord blessed the Egyptian's house for Joseph's sake; and the blessing of the Lord was on all that he had in the house and in the field.

6 Thus he left all that he had in Joseph's hand, and he did not know what he had except for the bread which he ate. Now Joseph was handsome in form and appearance.

Joseph, the dreamer, was gifted with extraordinary honesty and an ability to manage and organize things. The Bible does not say how long it took for him to go from being a worker in Potiphar's house to being overseer, but verse 5 says God blessed Potiphar through Joseph. The blessings got enough of his master's attention to secure the promotion. Potiphar was wise enough to see God's blessings coming to him through Joseph and he did not allow the negatives like envy, hatred or egotistical pride to stop him from giving Joseph unlimited power. God reciprocated by blessing Potiphar in the house and in the field.

Verse 6 sums up the character of Joseph. Potiphar grew to trust Joseph enough to put all of his wealth in Joseph's hands and did not bother to keep account of his growing wealth. Joseph, a Godly, well-favored person earned that trust by not skimming any profits or diverting funds or services for his own use.

He exhibited the same quality around his father when he told his father the truth about his brothers, even though he could have been more popular with them if he had lied for them. The reward for lying for his brothers may have made him a working part of their group, but he chose honesty. It nearly got him killed and it did get him sold into slavery.

The situational ethics of our time would dictate that Joseph use every honest or dishonest opportunity to get the most profit out of every endeavor, without caring what it cost others. Honesty demands that you seek and serve the highest good of whoever you are in service to. Joseph chose honesty and God loved him for it.

Receiving short-time gratification for giving in to the desires of the flesh is not worth losing the eternal glory of bringing the flesh under the control of the spirit and walking the spiritual path. In verses 7 through 9, Joseph would suffer again for choosing the right path to follow when someone in his environment is driven by the flesh and tries to entice him to do the wrong thing.

> Gen. 39:7 And it came to pass after these things that his master's wife cast longing eyes on Joseph, and she said, "Lie with me."
>
> 8 But he refused and said to his master's wife, "Look, my master does not know what is with me in the house, and he has committed all that he has to my hand.
>
> 9 There is no one greater in this house than I, nor has he kept back anything from me but you, because you are his wife. How then can I do this great wickedness, and sin against God?"

Verse 7 says, "after these things," meaning after Joseph's honest reputation and authority was established. Some time after Joseph established his honest reputation, Potiphar's wife cast her eyes on Joseph and said, "Lie with me." The position of Joseph is made very clear to her in verses 8 and 9—he refused. Joseph tells her that his master has put everything he has in Joseph's hands, a fact that would stir up jealousy among the other servants. Joseph tells Potiphar's wife, "No one who serves him is greater than I. Everything he has, but you, his wife, is available for my use. How then can I do this great wickedness and sin against God?"

Joseph is in his mid- to late-twenties here and his priorities are still in the right place. He proves his love and respect for his fellow man and absolute devotion to God by his actions. Jesus Christ would sum up the law and prophets in two statements from Matthew 22:36–40: *"Love the lord your God with all of your heart, soul and mind,"* and *"Love your neighbor as yourself."*

Joseph's mind and spirit had already reached this point over 400 years before Moses received the law at Mt. Sinai and over 1700 years before Christ's statement, as recorded by Matthew. The wife of Potiphar was seeking to serve her own lustful desires while obviously giving herself over to Satan as a tool he uses to destroy Joseph one way or the other.

Gen. 39:10 So it was, as she spoke to Joseph day by day, that he did not heed her, to lie with her or to be with her.

11 But it happened about this time, when Joseph went into the house to do his work, and none of the men of the house was inside,

12 that she caught him by his garment, saying, "Lie with me." But he left his garment in her hand, and fled and ran outside.

13 And so it was, when she saw that he had left his garment in her hand and fled outside,

14 that she called to the men of her house and spoke to them, saying, "See, he has brought in to us a Hebrew to mock us. He came in to me to lie with me, and I cried out with a loud voice.

15 And it happened, when he heard that I lifted my voice and cried out, that he left his garment with me, and fled and went outside."

16 So she kept his garment with her until his master came home.

Verse 10 shows Potiphar's wife literally stalking Joseph, day after day. Verse 11 raises these questions: Why was no one else in the house on this day when Joseph went to do his routine duties? Where were the others on a routine workday? If Joseph was in charge of the whole operation and he did not send them elsewhere, who did? The text does not answer the questions, but it is possible that Potiphar's wife engineered the situation. The woman simply was not taking "No" for an answer.

Verse 12 says she grabbed his clothes, saying, "Lie with me." The physical attack moved her up from a stalker to an attempted rapist. Joseph was just as committed to doing what was right as he ran out of the clothing she had grabbed and ran out of the house. The thing could have ended there if the woman had the will to leave him alone, but apparently, she was not going to take rejection from a slave.

Verses 13 through 18 show the lengths this woman would go to in order to get back at Joseph. The evidence she would use against him should have raised enough questions to afford Joseph a trial if he was not a slave and of a different race. The reputation of Joseph should have led someone to ask why a person with his intelligence would leave his garment with someone he is attempting to force himself on after they began to scream.

The woman's statement in verse 15 would play out like Joseph was saying, "I'm here to rape you, but since you are screaming, I will run away, but here is some of my clothing that you can use to incriminate me."

The lying woman of class had a say and Joseph, the honest slave, was never asked anything. He is being punished again for doing the right thing. Potiphar accepts his wife's statement without question and gives himself over to anger. In verses 19 and 20, the place where he imprisoned Joseph is referred to as the place where the King's prisoners were kept.

Most people would call Joseph foolish for not keeping the plush position he earned by accepting the moments of stolen pleasure with his master's wife. Joseph simply was not that kind of person. The payoff for following spiritual honesty and rejecting fleshly deception would begin while Joseph was in prison, as stated in verses 21 through 23.

> **Gen. 39:21 But the Lord was with Joseph and showed him mercy, and He gave him favor in the sight of the keeper of the prison.**
>
> **22 And the keeper of the prison committed to Joseph's hand all the prisoners who were in the prison; whatever they did there, it was his doing.**
>
> **23 The keeper of the prison did not look into anything that was under Joseph's authority, because the Lord was with him; and whatever he did, the Lord made it prosper.**

The above verses say the Lord was with Joseph, showing him mercy and giving him favor in the sight of the keeper of the prison. The keeper of the prison may have heard about Joseph from Potiphar or some of his people. He may have observed him in action and come to the conclusion that Joseph was a genius in all manner of planning and management skills.

The bottom line is that God blessed Joseph and used him as a blessing to the people around him, even making the worst-case scenario, prison, into a prosperous endeavor. In prison, Joseph had risen to a rank that was second only to the head, as he had in Potiphar's house and in his own father's house. This is because he was a servant of God in all things first and, in his dealings with men, he was obedient, loyal, hard working, trustworthy, unselfish and excellent in management.

CHAPTER 40

In Chapter 40 of Genesis, the events surrounding the butler and baker who served the King of Egypt would give Joseph a chance to use yet another gift God had given him. God's gift would ultimately free him and set his feet on the path to greatness.

Joseph did not interpret the two previous dreams about the sheaves bowing before him and the sun, moon and stars bowing to him, as mentioned earlier (Gen. 37:5–11). Joseph is about to move from dreamer to interpreter. The Bible does not detail the transition, but Joseph clearly identifies God as the giver of this knowledge.

> Gen. 40:7 So he asked Pharaoh's officers who were with him in the custody of his lord's house, saying, "Why do you look so sad today?"
>
> 8 And they said to him, "We each have had a dream, and there is no interpreter of it:" So Joseph said to them. "Do not the interpretations belong to God? Tell them to me, please."

The two officers sent to this prison by the King handled and served his food and drink. Without today's forensic science, you could assassinate a king back then by poisoning him and not raise suspicion. The Bible does not say what the two men are charged with or suspected of doing. The chief butler would later refer to it in Genesis 41:10 as a time when Pharaoh was angry with his servants. The two of them could have been imprisoned for anything from trying to poison the king, to giving him indigestion, or something completely different. The facts are not known about how they offended the king, but verse 1 says they did and verse 4 shows Joseph being charged with guarding them.

In verses 5 through 8, the Bible says that both officers had a dream the same night. The following morning, Joseph noticed their demeanor and asked them why they were so sad. The men told Joseph about the dreams and their sadness was because there was no interpreter. He told them in verse 8 that interpretations belong to God and Joseph, a young man who is still trusting God and seeking to serve others, asks them to tell him their dreams.

The chief butler's situation would be dealt with first in verses 9 through 13. The telling of the dream in verses 9 through 11 appears to end in fruitful service to Pharaoh.

> Gen. 40:11 Then Pharaoh's cup was in my hand; and I took the grapes and pressed them into Pharaoh's cup, and placed the cup in Pharaoh's hand."
>
> 12 And Joseph said to him, "This is the interpretation of it: The three branches are three days.
>
> 13 Now within three days Pharaoh will lift your head and restore you to your place, and you will put Pharaoh's cup in his hand according to the manner when you were his butler.
>
> 14 But remember me when it is well with you, and please show kindness to me; make mention of me to Pharaoh, and get me out of this house.
>
> 15 For indeed I was stolen away from the land of the Hebrews; and also I have done nothing here that they should put me into the dungeon."

The interpretation in verses 12 and 13 support the dream, but even more significant is what appears to be Joseph's absolute faith in the interpretation, as he asked the butler to remember him when the butler is back in power. Joseph is treating the interpretation from God like a promise that is already on its way. From his standpoint, it would soon be a solid reality. Joseph exhibits the faith of his great-grandfather, Abraham.

The desire to be out of prison is well-stated by Joseph in verses 14 and 15. The Bible does not show even one deviation from Godly service on Joseph's part, but the fact that he has been innocent from the beginning of his story does not change the predicament he is in right now. Joseph is not the kind of man who falls into a trap of self-pity. He would be the best he could be, no matter what his position.

Verse 16 says when the chief baker saw that the butler's interpretation was good, he told Joseph his dream.

> Gen. 40:16 When the chief baker saw that the interpretation was good, he said to Joseph, "I also was in my dream, and there were three white baskets on my head.
>
> 17 In the uppermost basket were all kinds of baked goods for Pharaoh, and the birds ate them out of the basket on my head."
>
> 18 So Joseph answered and said, "This is the interpretation of it: The three baskets are three days.
>
> 19 Within three days Pharaoh will lift off your head from you and hang you on a tree; and the birds will eat your flesh from you."

The interpretation of the baker's dream was not the same as the butler's, but it would no doubt be in line with his actions, as death would be his earnings. The dreams and interpretations transferred accurate foreknowledge from God of an upcoming fact. The knowledge could have given the chief baker the time to flee if he was not in custody already, while the chief butler would be able to ease his troubled mind. The facts of each man's actions as measured by the law would be the difference, but foreknowledge could have prepared each man to deal with the inevitable.

Verse 23 says the butler forgot Joseph after he was freed.

> Gen. 40:21 Then he restored the chief butler to his butlership again, and he placed the cup in Pharaoh's hand.
>
> 22 But he hanged the chief baker, as Joseph had interpreted to them.
>
> 23 Yet the chief butler did not remember Joseph, but forgot him.

CHAPTER 41

Chapter 41 of Genesis opens two full years after the chief butler is released in accordance with Joseph's interpretation of his dream. Joseph is about 30 years old now after being sold by his brothers at age 17. The Pharaoh's dreams, as identified in verses 1 through 7, would open the way for Joseph to be heard.

> Gen. 41:1 Then it came to pass, at the end of two full years, that Pharaoh had a dream; and behold, he stood by the river.
>
> 2 Suddenly there came up out of the river seven cows, fine looking and fat; and they fed in the meadow.
>
> 3 Then behold, seven other cows came up after them out of the river, ugly and gaunt, and stood by the other cows on the bank of the river.
>
> 4 And the ugly and gaunt cows ate up the seven fine looking and fat cows. So Pharaoh awoke.
>
> 5 He slept and dreamed a second time; and suddenly seven heads of grain came up on one stalk, plump and good.
>
> 6 Then behold, seven thin heads, blighted by the east wind, sprang up after them.
>
> 7 And the seven thin heads devoured the seven plump and full heads. So Pharaoh awoke, and indeed, it was a dream.

8 Now it came to pass in the morning that his spirit was troubled, and he sent and called for all the magicians of Egypt and all the wise men. And Pharaoh told them his dreams, but there was no one who could interpret them for Pharaoh.

The wise men and magicians throughout all of Egypt could not interpret the dream and ease Pharaoh's troubled spirit in verse 8. The chief butler, who is still a trusted servant after reinstatement, remembers Joseph now. The time of his own tribulation, along with the accuracy of Joseph's interpretation of his dream, is recounted in verses 9 through 13. Joseph prepares himself to meet royalty as quickly as possible after being summoned in verse 14. Upon his arrival, Pharaoh reveals the situation to Joseph and in verse 15, says, "I have heard it said of you that you can understand a dream, to interpret it." Joseph's answer in verse 16 is amazing in its simplistic honesty.

Gen. 41:16 So Joseph answered Pharaoh, saying, "It is not in me; God will give Pharaoh an answer of peace."

The young man who has been in captivity for 13 of his 30 years has a chance to be heard by the one man who could release him, but he does not put on a self-promotion show. In verse 16, Joseph says, "It is not in me. God will give Pharaoh an answer of peace." The average person would try to give themselves some of the credit for many reasons, one being the possibility that Pharaoh would credit God and then return them to jail.

Joseph was putting God on the pedestal and presenting himself as an obedient servant who is continuing to dance with the one that brought him this far. The dream is told to Joseph in verses 17 through 24. In verse 25, Joseph speaks again and again; he gives God the glory.

Gen. 41:25 Then Joseph said to Pharaoh, "The dreams of Pharaoh are one; God has shown Pharaoh what he is about to do:

The Bible does not say what type of history the Egyptians had with the true God, but Pharaoh's dream is the beginning of something good that God gave him. The vital end of the gift would travel down Jacob's ladder, using Joseph as the conduit that would deliver it. The statement, "God has shown Pharaoh what he is about to do," brings the value of dreams, true interpretations, prophecies and visions into focus.

Mankind, with all of the things we think we can do, cannot do anything against the powers that God controls. A heeded warning, however, could be the difference between life and death. The two views of the dream bore witness to two segments of the same situation; therefore, the dream is one.

The interpretation, as explained in verses 26 through 32, showed seven fertile, bumper crop years, followed by seven years of intense famine that God would bring about shortly. Joseph, the slave and current convict in Egypt, advises Pharaoh to seek out a man who is discerning and wise to prepare Egypt (Gen. 41:33–36). The man would have many overseers whose objective would be to gather twenty percent of the land's yield in the good years and store it for the seven years of famine.

The statement in verse 35, "and store up grain under the authority of Pharaoh, and let them keep food in the cities," makes it plain that Pharaoh would bankroll the effort. While the details of the deals with grain and livestock sellers are not disclosed in these verses, future events show that Pharaoh would support the idea.

The time of the king's dream would no doubt come with Egypt living a prosperous life. The undertaking proposed by Joseph, based on no visible evidence of a famine, would take a lot of faith, money, and effort on Egypt's part. Joseph had literally presented himself as a living sacrifice to God's interpretation because failure would cost Pharaoh money plus credibility, and could easily cost Joseph's life. Verse 37 shows a merger between wisdom and faith.

> **Gen. 43:37 So the advice was good in the eyes of Pharaoh and in the eyes of all his servants.**
>
> **38 And Pharaoh said to his servants, "Can we find such a one as this, a man in whom is the spirit of God?"**
>
> **39 Then Pharaoh said to Joseph, "Inasmuch as God has shown you all this, there is no one as discerning and wise as you.**
>
> **40 You shall be over my house, and all my people shall be ruled according to your word; only in regard to the throne will I be greater than you."**

41 And Pharaoh said to Joseph, "See, I have set you over all the land of Egypt."

42 Then Pharaoh took his signet ring off his hand and put it on Joseph's hand; and he clothed him in garments of fine linen and put a gold chain around his neck.

43 And he had him ride in the second chariot which he had; and they cried out before him, "Bow the knee!" So he set him over all the land of Egypt.

44 Pharaoh also said to Joseph, "I am Pharaoh, and without your consent no man may lift his hand or foot in all the land of Egypt."

45 And Pharaoh called Joseph's name Zaphnath-Paaneah. And he gave him as a wife Asenath, the daughter of Poti-Pherah priest of On. So Joseph went out over all the land of Egypt.

46 Joseph was thirty years old when he stood before Pharaoh king of Egypt. And Joseph went out from the presence of Pharaoh, and went throughout all the land of Egypt.

The advice sounded good to the king and his court. The dream has traveled through a God-led interpretation to believing hearts that will move it forward to working hands. Whose hands are qualified to do this new type of work? The wisdom and authority of a king is a powerful tool among people. The King of Egypt uses these tools to perfection in the preceeding verses.

The King recognizes Joseph as a man in whom the spirit of God dwells. The fact that he could not find anyone else but Joseph to interpret his dream had to be noticed as well. The King of Egypt disregards the social and racial differences between Joseph and himself as, "convict and king, Hebrew and Egyptian," and proceeds on the basis of wisdom. In verse 39, the King says, "Inasmuch as God has shown you all this, there is no one as discerning and wise as you." In other words, you are the one. Joseph would trade for Pharaoh, giving him full ownership of the food stores.

God is about to bless Joseph beyond his wildest dreams. Joseph, as a slave, was falsely jailed as a sexual degenerate at one point, but now he is about to become the second most powerful man in Egypt, with authority over everyone there except the king. The 13 hard years are over in a day as God moves Pharaoh to act. At 30 years of age, Joseph has come this far by faith—and it is only the start.

The changing of Joseph's name may be evidence of Egyptian citizenship. Accepting an Egyptian wife who would be the mother of his children certainly showed that Joseph was willing to live among the Egyptians, as stated in verse 45. The faith of these parties prompted actions that put a famine rescue team on the move while there is no evidence of a famine, just faith.

The Bible and history would justify that faith (Gen. 41:47–57). Verse 47 says the ground brought forth abundantly in the seven years of plenty and Joseph made the most of it. The nation may have questioned the actions of Joseph's team during the plenteous years—since it would look like the good times would go on and on—but faith in the unseen times ahead was driving Joseph. The two sons of Joseph, Manasseh and Ephraim, were born during the plenteous years (Gen. 41:50–52). The famine came right on schedule and it was not limited to Egypt.

Verse 54 says it was in all lands, but in all the land of Egypt, there was bread. The Bible does not say how long it was before all the land of Egypt was famished, or whether the average Egyptians laid up anything during the plenteous years. The people cried to Pharaoh for bread and he sent them to Joseph, instructing them to follow his directives. The times were bad for everyone except the King of Egypt. He must have been elated over his wise decisions and his faith in Joseph is obvious.

The food was sold to the people in Egypt and all of the surrounding nations. The power to sell the food proves Pharaoh owned it and gives credibility to the idea that he was purchasing the twenty percent during the plenteous years. The food stores were earning money from Egyptians and from all of the surrounding nations as well. The investment of faith and money is returning an excellent profit in both ways.

CHAPTER 42

Jacob heard about the food stores in Egypt and sent ten sons down to Egypt to buy grain. Verse 2 (part b) shows how desperate the situation was, "that we may live and not die." Verse 4 shows Jacob protecting Benjamin, Rachel's youngest son and Joseph's full brother.

> Gen. 42:4 But Jacob did not send Joseph's brother Benjamin with his brothers, for he said, "Lest some calamity befall him."
>
> 5 And the sons of Israel went to buy grain among those who journeyed, for the famine was in the land of Canaan.
>
> 6 Now Joseph was governor over the land; and it was he, who sold to all the people of the land. And Joseph's brothers came and bowed down before him with their faces to the earth.

The situation with Joseph over twenty years earlier no doubt makes Jacob even more protective of Benjamin, who is in his twenties now. Verse 5 say Joseph's brothers traveled in a caravan from Canaan because the famine was also throughout that land and there were an unspecified number of people going to Egypt to buy grain.

Joseph saw the fulfillment of his first dream in verse 6 when his ten older brothers bowed before him with their faces to the earth. The end of the seven plenteous years would have made Joseph 37 years old. Joseph said in Genesis 45:6 that the famine was in its second year when he revealed himself to them, so he is about 39 years old, give or take a few months.

The reason his brothers could not recognize him is not clear. Maybe his appearance changed that much over the twenty years. More than likely he was dressing and speaking like the Egyptians and may have been wearing the facial make-up that Egyptian royalty used then. Whatever the case, verses 7 and 8 show that Joseph knew them, but they did not know him.

The situation Joseph is in with his brothers now may be the most trying situation yet. Joseph, who has never meant or done harm to anyone, is face-to-face with his brothers who did mean and harmful things to him, and now they are under his power.

In verse 9 Joseph remembers the dream about the sheaves bowing, and then he accuses them of spying the land to find weaknesses. Joseph knows they are not spies, so it is obvious that he is dealing with them in a way that will not allow a swift purchase and return trip to Canaan. The next few Chapters will show Joseph initiate a cat-and-mouse type game that will allow him to get some information and, possibly, to answer some questions.

The first accusation of spying makes them say they are all one man's sons and, of course, they claim their honesty, in verses 11 through 17.

> Genesis 42:11 We are all one man's sons; we are honest men; your servants are not spies."
>
> 12 But he said to them, "No, but you have come to see the nakedness of the land."
>
> 13 and they said, "Your servants are twelve brothers, the sons of one man in the land of Canaan; and in fact, the youngest is with our father today, and one is no more."
>
> 14 But Joseph said to them, "It is as I spoke to you, saying, "You are spies!"
>
> 15 In this manner you shall be tested: By the life of Pharaoh, you shall not leave this place unless your youngest brother comes here.
>
> 16 Send one of you, and let him bring your brother; and you shall be kept in prison, that your words may be tested to see

whether there is any truth in you; or else, by the life of Pharaoh, surely you are spies!"

17 So he got them all together in prison three days.

The second accusation of spying, in verse 12, makes them give him more family history. Twelve sons in all, ten are here, the youngest is in Canaan with our father and one is no more. The third accusation of spying comes with a test. For the first part of the test, Joseph tells them they cannot leave until one of them brings the youngest brother to Egypt. Then he puts all of them in jail for three days without sending anyone for Benjamin.

On the third day, he changes the conditions in their favor and points out the fact that he fears God. He told them that if they were true men, they would allow one brother to be left as a hostage until the other nine return with Benjamin.

Since the others needed to get food back to their homes, they did not have a bargaining position at all. They accepted the offer in verses 19 and 20. Joseph no doubt designed the charade so he could hear them discuss him, as in verses 21 through 24.

Gen. 42:21 Then they said to one another, "We are truly guilty concerning our brother, for we saw the anguish of his soul when he pleaded with us, and we would not hear; therefore this distress has come upon us."

22 And Reuben answered them, saying, "Did I not speak to you, saying, "Do not sin against the boy"; and you would not listen? Therefore behold, his blood is now required of us."

23 But they did not know that Joseph understood them, for he spoke to them through an interpreter.

24 And he turned himself away from them and wept. Then he returned to them again, and talked with them. And he took Simeon from them and bound him before their eyes.

The brothers thought Joseph could not understand them because he used an interpreter to talk to them, so they were focusing openly on what they thought was the cause of their distress. The fact that they sold Joseph after being talked out of killing him has no doubt haunted them all of this time. "We are guilty. We saw the anguish of his soul. We would not heed his pleas not to be killed or sold. This is the cause of our distress," they thought and said.

At Genesis 37:21–22, Reuben, the oldest who had tried to deliver Joseph from the time he heard the plot, speaks now about what must have been a touchy subject from the time it happened. Reuben reminded them that he warned them not to sin against the boy and they would not listen. Now the payment for it is due.

The first phase of Joseph's plan shows him that even the guilty brothers still carried the deed on their conscience and that Reuben had fought to deliver him from the beginning. The emotion of the situation overcame Joseph, as he had to turn aside and cry before taking Simeon as the lone hostage. The accusations of spying are about to initiate other encounters that would allow Joseph to take a close look at their relationship with Benjamin and their feelings toward him.

Joseph commanded his workers to fill their sacks with corn and put every man's money back in his sack along with provisions for the trip. The men left carrying bags that they had not packed.

> **Gen. 42:27 But as one of them opened his sack to give his donkey feed at the encampment, he saw his money; and there it was, in the mouth of his sack.**
>
> **28 So he said to his brothers, "My money has been restored, and there it is, in my sack!" Then their hearts failed them and they were afraid, saying to one another, "What is this that God has done to us?"**
>
> **29 Then they went to Jacob their father in the land of Canaan and told him all that had happened to them, saying:**

Verse 27 says one of them opened his sack to feed his donkey and found his money in his sack's mouth. Verse 35 says that as the others emptied their sacks at home in Canaan after telling Jacob about their episode in Egypt, they found the money in their sacks also and were afraid. The Bible does not say it, but it appears as if Joseph had the money placed in the sacks so that the money in one sack could be easily found, while the other sacks would have to be emptied to reveal each man's money.

The specifics are not clear on that action, but after the first man's money is found, their reactions are crystal clear (Gen. 42:28–29). Hearts failed, they are afraid, they begin to falsely question God, and yet, the man who found the money did not take it back to Egypt: They went home. In verses 30 through 34, they recount the high points of their trip and tell about the delivery of Benjamin being demanded to prove their honesty and secure the vital rights to do business in Egypt.

The famine would last another five years, so they had quite a few problems to iron out. The brothers accused God of doing something to them when the first brother found his money. It was hard to decide who to accuse after the other eight found their money, as stated in verse 35. The fear they felt now may be a sampling of what Joseph felt when he was in that pit wondering what his brothers were going to do to him.

Jacob is surveying his situation and coming to a conclusion of his own in verses 36 through 38.

> Gen. 42:36 And Jacob their father said to them, "You have bereaved me: Joseph is no more, Simeon is no more, and you want to take Benjamin. All these things are against me.
>
> 37 Then Reuben spoke to his father, saying, "Kill my two sons if I do not bring him back to you; put him in my hands, and I will bring him back to you."
>
> 38 But he said, "My son shall not go down with you, for his brother is dead, and he is left alone. If any calamity should befall him along the way in which you go, then you would bring down my gray hair with sorrow to the grave."

Jacob grieves that Joseph is no more and Simeon is no more. It sounds like he is writing Simeon off as dead already. To Jacob, the idea of trading Benjamin for Simeon was the farthest thing from his mind. Reuben's offer in verse 37 does show dedication, but it is not wise for Jacob to hold his own grandchildren as surety. The idea of killing them makes even less sense because they would be all that is left of Reuben if he does not get back.

Jacob may also be thinking, "If you could not get home with Simeon now, why would I send my surviving son of Rachel to buy more grain? The grain we are talking about buying is from people who can prove you stole the first load, since every one of you brought all of your money back with the grain."

The greater part of why Joseph was hated and sold by his brothers may be clearly understood from previous incidents and verse 38. The statement, "My son shall not go down with you for his brother is dead and he is left alone," says a lot. The absolute bias in Jacob's statement, when he says to his other sons that Benjamin is alone without Joseph, shows a selfish old man discriminating against his children because of who their mother is. The dedication to and memory of his dead Rachel has become a tool that Satan is using through him to drive a wedge between his sons.

I cannot imagine how small this must have made his other sons feel. To some degree, the brothers are bearing the scars for what their grandfather, Laban, did to Jacob, who, by some opinions, was receiving his just rewards for what he tried to do to Esau. The situation with Rachel and Leah was trickery on Laban's part, but when Jacob accepted it, he should not have played favorites among his sons.

The son's knowledge and sense of honesty and fair play comes from him, the father, spiritual leader, teacher and provider. Simeon is in trouble at this point because Jacob won't risk sending Benjamin to gain his release. Verse 4 explains why he did not send him the first time and Jacob is certain it would kill him if something happened to him. The fact that he would still have ten sons, one daughter, three wives and a good bit of money left, even in a famine, never enters his mind.

CHAPTER 43

In Chapter 43 of Genesis, Jacob and his sons had no way of knowing how long the famine would last, so they couldn't know that they would have to go back to Egypt.

> Gen. 43:1 Now the famine was severe in the land.
>
> 2 And it came to pass, when they had eaten up the grain which they had brought from Egypt, that their father said to them, "Go back, buy us a little food."
>
> 3 But Judah spoke to him, saying, "The man solemnly warned us, saying, You shall not see my face unless your brother is with you.
>
> 4 If you send our brother with us, we will go down and buy you food.
>
> 5 But if you will not send him, we will not go down; for the man said to us, "You shall not see my face unless your brother is with you."
>
> 6 And Israel said, "Why did you deal so wrongfully with me as to tell the man whether you had still another brother?"
>
> 7 But they said, "The man asked us pointedly about ourselves and our family, saying, Is your father still alive? Have you another brother? And we told him according to these words. Could

we possibly have known that he would say, "Bring your brother down?"

8 Then Judah said to Israel his father, "Send the lad with me, and we will arise and go, that we may live and not die, both we and you and also our little ones.

9 I myself will be surety for him; from my hand you shall require him. If I do not bring him back to you and set him before you, then let me bear the blame forever.

10 For if we had not lingered, surely by now we would have returned this second time."

The Bible did not say how long it was before the food ran out, but according to verses 1 and 2, Jacob wanted and needed them to go back to Egypt and buy more food. But for the charade, poor Simeon would have spent the rest of his life in Egypt if they had not run out of food.

Judah speaks to his father this time and tells him, "We cannot do business in the land if we don't bring our youngest brother. Send Benjamin and we go, don't send Benjamin and we don't go," in verses 3 through 5. Simeon has not seen his family since he left for Egypt the first time and the other brothers can only foresee the same fate befalling them if they go back to Egypt without Benjamin.

The stress and strain of the situation is no doubt taking its toll on everyone. In verse 6, Jacob wants to know why they told the man in Egypt that they had another brother. In verse 7, they respond that the man asked them pointedly—how could they know he would tell them to bring the youngest brother down to Egypt? Judah takes responsibility for Benjamin's return. The need is obvious.

Judah does not offer his children as Reuben did. Judah said he would bear the blame forever if he does not bring his youngest brother back. He then closes by saying they would have already completed the second trip if they had not lingered. Jacob accepted reality and agreed to send Benjamin, but he sought an edge by employing the tactic he used while trying to soften Esau's heart upon his return home. "A gift may soften this man's heart also," he thought.

The best fruits, balm, honey, spices, myrrh, nuts, almonds, double the amount needed to buy the food, and now the original money become an issue. Hopefully, it was an oversight. The trade goes beyond the fair market value of the food. It is an attempt to get Benjamin, Simeon and the others back safely with more food and also ease the fear that came with the return of the first money, at verses 11 through 14.

The brothers stood before Joseph with Benjamin now and they were compelled to have lunch with Joseph at his house.

> Gen. 43:18 Now the men were afraid because they were brought into Joseph's house; and they said, "It is because of the money, which was returned in our sacks the first time, that we are brought in, so that he may make a case against us and seize us, to take us as slaves with our donkeys."
>
> 19 When they drew near to the steward of Joseph's house, they talked with him at the door of the house,
>
> 20 and said, "O sir, we indeed came down the first time to buy food;

To say that they are afraid is an understatement at this point. The money in their sacks comes back to haunt them again. This time, they think they will all be made slaves and their animals will be taken away also. The brothers approached the steward who was in charge of the lunch arrangements at Joseph's house and told him about the original money being in their bags. They told him this without being asked about it, so fear and a guilty conscience must have been eating away at them. The brothers, thinking they are in for a hard time, find out that this steward had collected their money at first and he credits the God of their fathers as the reason it was returned. The steward releases Simeon after telling them not to be afraid, verse 23.

The brothers are no doubt feeling better about their situation now; they are in Joseph's house. Their animals are provided for and they are preparing the gift for Joseph in verses 24 and 25. After Joseph's arrival, the luncheon proceeded with the presentation of gifts, civil conversation about their father and Joseph being overcome with emotion again after seeing Benjamin. The twelve brothers were all together, but eleven of them did not know that yet.

The actual serving of the meal went well also, with Benjamin being shown favoritism in the amount of food he was given.

> Gen. 43:32 So they set him a place by himself, and them by themselves, and the Egyptians who ate with him by themselves; because the Egyptians could not eat food with Hebrews, for that is an abomination to the Egyptians.
>
> 33 And they sat before him, the first-born according to his birthright and the youngest according to his youth; and the men looked in astonishment at one another.
>
> 34 Then he took servings to them from before him, but Benjamin's serving was five times as much as any of theirs. So they drank and were merry with him.

The larger portion for Benjamin did not seem to strike any cords of jealousy in the group as they ate, drank heavily and made merry. The way Joseph handled serving the meal makes it obvious that he wanted to see how the group felt about Benjamin. He would also have been looking to see if they had outgrown their jealous hearts.

The favoritism his father showed him was unwise, yet Joseph still earned some prestige by his honesty. However, the other brothers' jealousy was the driving force of his problems.

CHAPTER 44

Verses 1 through 6 in Chapter 44 of Genesis cover Joseph's order to put every man's money in the mouth of his sack, along with as much food as each could carry. Joseph's silver cup was to be put in Benjamin's sack.

The brothers woke up, after a night of feasting and heavy drinking, to a sense of relief at having eased their fears, and joy of having Simeon released. Confident in their success, the brothers took the sacks, which were packed and loaded by someone else again, and went on their way without checking the contents again. They were later overtaken by Joseph's men just outside the city and accused of stealing (Gen. 44:7–13).

> Gen. 44:7 And they said to him, "Why does my lord say these words? Far be it from us that your servants should do such a thing.
>
> 8 Look, we brought back to you from the land of Canaan the money which we found in the mouth of our sacks. How then could we steal silver or gold from your lord's house?
>
> 9 With whomever of your servants it is found, let him die, and we also will be my lord's slaves.
>
> 10 And he said, "Now also let it be according to your words; he with whom it is found shall be my slave, and you shall be blameless."

> 11 Then each man speedily let down his sack to the ground, and each opened his sack.
>
> 12 So he searched. He began with the oldest and left off with the youngest; and the cup was found in Benjamin's sack.
>
> 13 Then they tore their clothes, and each man loaded his donkey and returned to the city.

The brothers found the money in their sacks the first time and, for reasons that I don't understand, they rode away with full sacks that they didn't see filled the second time. The denial and assertions the second time are based on their absolute knowledge that they did not steal anything, but they could have truthfully made the same claim about the first trip. The argument: "Why would we steal this money after bringing back the first money we found in our sacks?"

Verse 9 says whoever has the cup should die and the rest would become slaves, as stated by the accused men. The confidence they showed was not tempered with the wisdom of past experiences. The offer of death for the cup-holder and slavery for the rest should have been based on them actually packing, loading and guarding the sacks. Joseph's servant accepted their words, but not the severity of the punishment they spoke on themselves in verse 10, "The one with the cup shall be the servant the rest shall be blameless." The men opened their sacks and Joseph's servant found the cup where he had put it.

The brothers reloaded their animals and returned to Joseph's house to find that he was still at home. Of course, he was at home—the entire situation was designed for a purpose. The next encounter will reveal Joseph's purpose (Gen. 44:16–17).

> Gen. 44:16 Then Judah said, "What shall we say to my lord? What shall we speak? Or how shall we clear ourselves? God has found out the iniquity of your servants; here we are, my lord's slaves, both we and he also with whom the cup was found."
>
> 17 But he said, "Far be it from me that I should do so; the man in whose hand the cup was found, he shall be my slave. And as for you, go up in peace to your father."

Joseph accuses them and Judah declares that God had found out about their iniquity. The entire statement of Judah, in verse 16, seems to be riddled with guilt related to Joseph. The steward said he put the money in their sacks the first time, so there is no reason for guilt about that. The sacks, which were loaded by others the second time and never checked by the brothers, were found to contain Joseph's cup and every man's money (verse 1). There is no need for guilt about that. They may have thought that the steward would not repeat his actions, maybe they are afraid to accuse him or maybe they thought the iniquity God knew about could only be tied to the selling of Joseph. They knew that none of them stole the cup or money, yet they are confessing guilt.

Judah declares that they are all his servants along with Benjamin, the one who had the cup, but Joseph isolates Benjamin as the one deserving slavery and the others were set free. Joseph's purpose seems clear enough now. He would put Benjamin in a position where they can be rid of Rachel's other son, if their hatred is still as strong as it was. He could see if their hearts and attitudes had changed with time. The answer he was looking for would come from Judah, the future head of the tribe of Judah and the brother who got them to sell Joseph instead of killing him (Gen. 44:18–34).

Judah asked for permission to speak in verse 18, then recounts their actions from the first meeting with Joseph up to the present. The statement does not bring a confession about what actually happened to Joseph, only a repeat of what they allowed their father to assume after returning Joseph's bloody coat, in verse 28. The concern for their father if Benjamin didn't return, and a possible understanding of why and how Jacob favored Rachel's children, can be seen again in verses 27 through 29.

> Gen. 44:27 Then your servant my father said to us, 'You know that my wife bore me two sons;
>
> 28 and the one went out from me, and I said, "Surely he is torn to pieces"; and I have not seen him since.
>
> 29 But if you take this one also from me, and calamity befalls him, you shall bring down my gray hair with sorrow to the grave.'

Jacob refers to Rachel as his wife and her two sons as his sons in a way that leaves no doubt that the three of them were favored by him. The brothers may have found out over time about the deception of Laban and the competition of the sisters giving Israel their handmaids to produce children. The competition and deception is reality that exists through the lives, attitudes and actions of human beings now, and returning to a level playing field will take a lot of understanding and adjustment. The favoritism, while still unwise, may be understood and accepted by the brothers now, who no doubt have families of their own.

The speculation about what the ten brothers are thinking or feeling is swallowed up by the fact that Judah follows through on his promise to be surety for Benjamin and asks to take his place as a slave.

> Genesis 44:32 For your servant became surety for the lad to my father, saying, "If I do not bring him back to you, then I shall bear the blame before my father forever."
>
> 33 Now therefore, please let your servant remain instead of the lad as a slave to my Lord, and let the lad go up with his brothers.
>
> 34 For how shall I go up to my father if the lad is not with me, lest perhaps I see the evil that would come upon my father?"

The reality of his willingness to give it all up to become the liberator of Rachel's son and savior of his father must have satisfied Joseph. The charade had produced some positive results.

CHAPTER 45

Chapter 45 of Genesis opens with our understanding that the statement and request of Judah was enough for Joseph. The Egyptians were told to leave and Joseph made himself known to his brothers in verses 1 through 8.

> Gen. 45:1 Then Joseph could not restrain himself before all those who stood by him, and cried out, "Make everyone go out from me!" So no one stood with him while Joseph made himself known to his brothers.
>
> 2 And he wept aloud, and the Egyptians and the house of Pharaoh heard it.
>
> 3 Then Joseph said to his brothers, "I am Joseph; does my father still live?" But his brothers could not answer him, for they were dismayed at his presence.
>
> 4 And Joseph said to his brothers, "Please come near to me." So they came near. Then he said: "I am Joseph your brother, whom you sold into Egypt.
>
> 5 "But now, do not therefore be grieved or angry with yourselves because you sold me here; for God sent me before you to preserve life.
>
> 6 For these two years the famine has been in the land, and there

are still five years in which there will be neither plowing nor harvesting.

7 And God sent me before you to preserve a posterity for you in the earth, and to save your lives by a great deliverance.

8 So now it was not you who sent me here, but God; and he has made me a father to Pharaoh, and lord of all his house, and a ruler throughout all the land of Egypt.

In verse 2, Joseph wept so loud the Egyptians heard it. Joseph asked if his father was still alive when he told his brothers who he was a second time. They couldn't answer. The Bible says they were dismayed at his presence and there is no way of knowing what other thoughts would have been going through their minds upon learning this.

The reader can only imagine how surprised the speechless brothers must have looked and felt, at verse 3. The other thing that might be hard to imagine is what Joseph did in verses 4 through 8. Instead of taking some type of revenge, Joseph, the man they bowed to and reverenced, is alone in the room with his 11 brothers telling them, "I am Joseph, your brother whom you sold into Egypt." He is concerned about their physical and emotional well-being as he tells them, "Don't be angry or grieved with yourselves; God sent me before you to preserve life."

The wisdom of Joseph at his age is remarkable. He can see God's purpose for his life. The desire to take revenge on his brothers is the farthest thing from his mind. Joseph is trying to comfort them and remove the well-earned guilt from their conscience by telling them God had control over the situation. The statement Joseph makes in verse 8, "So now it was not you who sent me here, but God," might make most people wonder what Joseph means. Is he saying God was in the midst of the brothers, helping plot his downfall? Of course not, that is just not the way he meant it.

The brothers would later meet with Joseph after their father's funeral to remind him that their father wanted him to forgive them for the evil they did to him (Gen. 50:15–19). The statement of Joseph in verse 20 shows how he meant it.

Gen. 50:20 "But as for you, you meant evil against me; but God

meant it for good, in order to bring it about as it is this day, to save many people alive.

The brothers acted from evil hearts that God did not inspire when they meant to kill him, but God meant it for good, using two of the brothers to convert the lemon they gave Joseph into lemonade. Why? To save many people alive. Joseph could have gone to Egypt by way of a different, possibly more noble route, but this is the route he was forced to take and the route on which God prospered him.

God was obviously working behind the scenes to save Joseph and see that he got to Egypt, which had the size, wealth and power to equip his deliverer for this major life-saving effort. Joseph is just too full of God's love to be plotting vengeance against men whose conscience was already whipping them.

The way Joseph went to Egypt as a powerless slave might have been useful to God so he could be tested, prepared and elevated from humility to power with first-hand knowledge at each level. Verses 9 through 15 show a scene that is the exact opposite of the exiled victim rising to power and taking vengeance on all who raised a hand against him. The man, Joseph, is greater than the emotions that drive most people, a man whose heart has been touched in a way that leads him to love those who hate him and to reflect Christ, even before Christ lived.

The reuniting, forgiving, weeping and talking ends shortly after Joseph tells them to hurry and bring his father and their families into Egypt. The land of Goshen was best suited for shepherds. Joseph seemed to have thought this out beforehand, when in verse 10, he said, "You shall dwell in Goshen and you and all that you have will be near me." The news of Joseph and his brothers reached Pharaoh and verses 16 through 20 clearly show how Pharaoh received the whole family of Joseph.

The open honesty of Joseph is paying big dividends now. With five years of famine left, any family with a lot of livestock and no rain to produce water and grass might lose all of it. The Nile River flooded its banks in Egypt each year, leaving fertile ground for agriculture and pasture for livestock, even if it did not rain in the area. Livestock could survive there when all around it would be a dust bowl. The land of Goshen was the best in the country for shepherds and Joseph, having traveled throughout the country, knew it.

The invitation of Pharaoh adds certification and a royal quality to Joseph's invitation when, in verse 18, the Egyptian king says, "I will give you the best of the land of Egypt, you will eat the fat of the land." Verses 19 and 20 show the King of Egypt commanding his friend Joseph to use Egyptian wagons to transport the people and disregard goods; the best goods of Egypt were theirs for the taking.

The relationship between Joseph and the Pharaoh may be one of the most honorable and trusting in scripture. God made Joseph a man who would always give his best effort and it continued with Pharaoh, who would reciprocate in kind. Verse 24 is yet another reflection of Joseph's character.

> **Gen. 45:24 So he sent his brothers away, and they departed; and he said to them, "See that you do not become troubled along the way."**
>
> **25 Then they went up out of Egypt, and came to the land of Canaan to Jacob their father.**
>
> **26 And they told him, saying, "Joseph is still alive, and he is governor over all the land of Egypt." And Jacob's heart stood still, because he did not believe them.**
>
> **27 But when they told him all the words which Joseph had said to them, and when he saw the carts which Joseph had sent to carry him, the spirit of Jacob their father revived.**
>
> **28 Then Israel said, "It is enough. Joseph my son is still alive. I will go and see him before I die."**

The brothers are going back home with wealth, good news, a promising future and no doubt a good reason for finger pointing and arguing between themselves about Joseph and what they did not tell their father twenty two years earlier. Joseph, upon sending them back for the rest of the clan says, "See that you do not become troubled along the way." After forgiving them, Joseph is advising and hoping they will forgive each other, themselves and bury the past, then enjoy God's blessings with a clear conscience.

Verse 26 say Israel did not believe their story about Joseph and his success. The picture fixed in his mind is of Joseph being dead. The brothers, as stated earlier, never said they saw Joseph dead. They gave Israel the bloody garment and he assumed an evil beast had eaten Joseph (Gen. 37:32–33). Now they are telling their father that Joseph is alive, but they still don't give absolute proof by telling him what they did. The doubts are replaced by what his ears hear and what his eyes see. It's enough, though, and Israel is off to Egypt to see Joseph.

CHAPTER 46

In Chapter 46 of Genesis, Israel departed with everyone tied to him in tow. The company stopped at Beersheba and Israel offered sacrifices and worshipped the God of his fathers. The land Jacob is leaving is the land promised to his descendants from Abraham forward. The trip back to it after leaving Laban was long, drawn out and dangerous, so even with the incentives to go into Egypt, Jacob must be wondering how and when his descendants would get back. The amount of trouble and hostility they might encounter regaining control of it may also be a concern of Jacob, when you study the answers provided in the vision that follows.

> Gen. 46:2 Then God spoke to Israel in the visions of the night, and said, "Jacob, Jacob!" And he said, "Here I am."
>
> 3 So He said, "I am God, the God of your father; do not fear to go down to Egypt, for I will make of you a great nation there.
>
> 4 I will go down with you to Egypt, and I will also surely bring you up again; and Joseph will put his hand on your eyes."
>
> 5 Then Jacob arose from Beersheba; and the sons of Israel carried their father Jacob, their little ones, and their wives, in the carts which Pharaoh had sent to carry him.
>
> 6 So they took their livestock and their goods, which they had acquired in the land of Canaan, and went to Egypt, Jacob and all his descendants with him.

The Lord said, "Don't be afraid to go down to Egypt." He will transform the handful of people into a nation of more than three million people over an extended period in Egypt, and then bring them back to the promised land. Jacob accepts the night visions as true communications from God and he knows the nation's immediate and distant future is in safe hands.

Jacob knows he will die in the presence of Joseph, "and Joseph will put his hand on your eyes, or literally close your dead eyes," in Egypt. The next verses show an invigorated Jacob leaving Beersheba with God's blessing to accept Joseph and Pharaoh's invitation.

Verses 8 through 27 follow the genealogy of the sons of Israel. The existing males are numbered through their mothers, as stated in verses 15, 18, 22, and 25. Verse 27 counts seventy people of Jacob going into Egypt. The reader must understand that they are being counted here by heads or potential heads of households, hence only the males are counted. Verse 7 identifies a larger number.

> **Gen. 46:7 His sons and his sons' sons, his daughters and his sons' daughters, and all his descendants he brought with him to Egypt.**

The daughters who marry would become a part of their husband's people, as Dinah would have been a Shechemite and as the wives of Israel's sons became Israelites. They are not counted, but the wives, daughters and mothers are in the group that went down to Egypt, along with herdsmen, servants and other employees. I cannot say exactly how many human beings went with Israel, but I have seen people nearly come to blows arguing that only seventy went to Egypt. Verses 15, 18, 22, 25 and 27 do not present a contradiction as they relate to verse 7; it only needs the clarification that verse 26 presented here.

Jacob was the last man known of Abraham's descendants to get a wife from among Abraham's kindred. The twelve sons seemed to take wives from among the people where they lived. As stated in Chapter 38, Judah married a Canaanite woman and fathered other children by Tamar, his daughter-in-law whose clan is not named there. Joseph's wife was Egyptian. Some of the brothers may have taken wives from among the Shechemite captives after killing the men of Shechem in Chapter 34. It is simply unknown at this point where all of their wives came from, but it is safe to say they came from their travels and possibly from among their employees. The point being labored here is that Jacob's sons would people the nation with wives from various places, proving race or nationality was not a hindrance to salvation or God's grace.

The meeting of Joseph and Israel in Goshen was a smashing success.

> Gen. 46:29 So Joseph made ready his chariot and went up to Goshen to meet his father Israel; and he presented himself to him, and fell on his neck and wept on his neck a good while.
>
> 30 And Israel said to Joseph, "Now let me die, since I have seen your face, because you are still alive."

Israel's spirit had to soar when he finally saw, touched and spoke with Joseph after thinking he was dead. Joseph's next objective is to secure the land of Goshen as their dwelling place. It had been mentioned earlier, but now it's time to put the deal in place.

> Genesis 46:33 So it shall be, when Pharaoh calls you and says, 'What is your occupation?'
>
> 34 that you shall say, "Your servants' occupation has been with livestock from our youth even till now, both we and also our fathers," that you may dwell in the land of Goshen; for every shepherd is an abomination to the Egyptians."

I cannot say with certainty why shepherds were an abomination to the Egyptians, unless you assume situations similar to the old American West range wars existed. Egyptians appear to be big on farming, as you see Jacob having livestock and sending to Egypt for grain. The livestock grazed on land the farmer wanted to use to grow produce. The farmer took irrigation waters that the cattlemen needed for livestock, hence the conflict. There may have been sheepherder/cattleman issues also.

The relationship between Joseph and the king was strong enough to bridge this gap, or any other gap. Joseph's advice to his family is to tell the King they deal in livestock and have for generations. The king had already opened the best lands in Egypt to them and he would be wise enough to know they could not change life-long professions easily.

Goshen was the best area in the country for their profession, so that was their allotted land in Egypt.

CHAPTER 47

In Chapter 47 of Genesis, Joseph takes five of his brothers before the King. He tells the King that his family, their herds, flocks and provisions have completed the trip from Canaan to Egypt and are currently in Goshen.

> Gen. 47:1 Then Joseph went and told Pharaoh, and said, "My father and my brothers, their flocks and their herds and all that they possess, have come from the land of Canaan; and indeed they are in the land of Goshen."
>
> 2 And he took five men from among his brothers and presented them to Pharaoh.
>
> 3 Then Pharaoh said to his brothers, "What is your occupation?" And they said to Pharaoh, "Your servants are shepherds, both we and also our fathers."
>
> 4 And they said to Pharaoh, "We have come to dwell in the land, because your servants have no pasture for their flocks, for the famine is severe in the land of Canaan. Now therefore, please let your servants dwell in the land of Goshen."
>
> 5 Then Pharaoh spoke to Joseph, saying, "Your father and your brothers have come to you.
>
> 6 "The land of Egypt is before you. Have your father and brothers dwell in the best of the land; let them dwell in the land of

Goshen. And if you know any competent men among them, then make them chief herdsmen over my livestock."

The formal request for a specific area is being made now as the King asked the five-brother delegation about their occupation and found out that they were shepherds. Verse 4 confirms how devastating the famine was in Canaan and the surrounding areas. The land of Goshen is the area they requested. The pastures of Canaan had dried up and the fact that they went straight to Goshen with their herds even before the request proves how valuable the area was and it may also suggest they made it in the nick of time.

Pharaoh, speaking to his Prime Minister, Joseph, follows through on their coalition of honor. He tells them, "The whole of Egypt is before you, you can dwell in the best of the land, if the land of Goshen is best-suited for you, then the land of Goshen is yours." Joseph's plan to put his people on the land best suited for them is now confirmed by the king, who also wants to have some of their best shepherds supervise his herdsmen and no doubt produce him some prime livestock.

The job Joseph had done in Egypt gave the King confidence in the whole group. The slave who became Prime Minister had carried himself in such a positive way that his whole family was given the most select portion of a foreign land.

Verses 7 through 10 record Jacob's meeting with the King of Egypt. Jacob blessed the King when he entered and when he left. If this passage covers all that was said, the meeting was brief, at verses 8 and 9.

Gen. 47:8 Pharaoh said to Jacob, "How old are you?

9 And Jacob said to Pharaoh, "The days of the years of my pilgrimage are one hundred and thirty years; few and evil have been the days of the years of my life, and they have not attained to the days of the years of the life of my fathers in the days of their pilgrimage."

Jacob told the king he was one hundred and thirty years old. If Joseph was thirty-nine or forty years old, it would mean Jacob was ninety or ninety-one years old when Joseph was born, and even older when Benjamin was born.

Verses 11 and 12 show a good working relationship in Jacob's family. The statement to Pharaoh, "few and evil are the years of my life," is so much improved now that I hate to be the one to say Jacob's unneeded deception of Esau put him on the trail of tears he had to travel. God gets the glory for blessing and carrying him when and where he could not carry himself. The message to the reader remains the same: There is no right way to do what is wrong. Even when God blesses you through a hard situation, you may still have to face the consequences of your actions.

The famine was getting worse, but Jacob was no doubt elated over his personal situation and new surroundings. The famine was doing what famines do—drying up farmlands, creating crop failures, causing poverty among the populace and the only life they had was the one provided by Joseph's interpretation.

Genesis 41:56 through 57 records how the storehouses were opened and the fifth part of grain previously collected according to Joseph's advice was in service now (Gen. 41:34–36). The expense of buying, processing and storing the fifth part of the land was Pharaoh's in the plenteous years. The profit for selling the stored grain in the famine years was Pharaoh's, as demonstrated by Joseph at Genesis 47:14, when he faithfully brought the money earned into Pharaoh's house.

> **Genesis 47:14 And Joseph gathered up all the money that was found in the land of Egypt and in the land of Canaan, for the grain which they bought; and Joseph brought the money into Pharaoh's house.**

Verse 14 also says Joseph gathered up all the money in Egypt and Canaan and all of this wealth was in Pharaoh's hand. The best investment the King of Egypt ever made was the power and authority he bestowed on Joseph. The investment is about to pay even greater profits for the king and the people, according to verses 15 through 26.

The famine continued after the people of Egypt and Canaan spent all of their money and Joseph traded for their livestock that year, in verses 15 through 17. The second year after the money failed, the people were back and in need of bread, grain and seed. Their money was spent surviving the famine, their livestock and herds were spent on surviving the famine, and now all they had left to trade was their land and the service of their bodies. Joseph traded on the basis of the people's request in verse 19 and, according to verse 20, he faithfully delivered all of the land of Egypt to Pharaoh.

The faithful interpreter of dreams, who had no ambition to use his popularity and power to project himself over his benefactor, had truly saved many lives. The wisdom of the king had put him in a position where he not only governs, but also owns the land of Egypt and the service of the people.

The financial worth of the king is uncountable. The personal satisfaction and national pride of being the nation to help other nations survive the famine should make this noble king extremely happy. Egypt would become an even greater nation because of it.

The human objectives for most people would have been met, but Joseph is not most people. Loyalty, unselfish service, obedience, management and wisdom are only a few of his character traits. The next move he makes is designed to use every inch of the land for the common good and demonstrate his unselfish love for all people.

> Gen. 47:21 And as for the people, he moved them into the cities, from one end of the borders of Egypt to the other end.
>
> 22 Only the land of the priests he did not buy; for the priests had rations allotted to them by Pharaoh, and they ate their rations which Pharaoh gave them; therefore they did not sell their lands.
>
> 23 Then Joseph said to the people, "Indeed I have bought you and your land this day for Pharaoh. Look, here is seed for you, and you shall sow the land.
>
> 24 And it shall come to pass in the harvest that you shall give one-fifth to Pharaoh. Four-fifths shall be your own, as seed for the field and for your food, for those of your households and as food for your little ones."
>
> 25 So they said, "You have saved our lives; let us find favor in the sight of my lord, and we will be Pharaoh's servants."
>
> 26 And Joseph made it a law over the land of Egypt to this day,

that Pharaoh should have one-fifth, except for the land of the priests only, which did not become Pharaoh's.

The people had put their land and lives in Pharaoh's hand for food. The relocation described in verse 21 had the noblest objective imaginable. Joseph was about to manage Egypt in a way that would create wealth in the midst of a famine. Wow.

The priests' lands were not purchased and the state provided their food. The 22nd verse may be one of the first major biblical proofs that there were differences in the way religious and political objectives were dealt with, even back then, before God's law through Moses.

The rest of the people who sold their land to survive were subjected to the massive relocation program. Verses 23 and 24 set up the arrangement between Joseph, representing the governing body, and the people, for themselves. The famine, not Joseph or Pharaoh, made all people equally poor. The only source of life they had was provided by Joseph's wisdom through the grace of God. The opportunities to feast on the people's misfortune for a greedy, abusive man would be endless, but not for Joseph—Joseph is God's man. The people, who are penniless, are moved into all usable areas of the land and outfitted with livestock, seed, day-to-day provisions and equipment to sow the land.

Verse 24 separates the man of God from the man of greed. Unlike the sharecropper situations in some nations where the objective is to keep people so poor that they can never prosper, Joseph's plan gives the worker 80 percent of the gross yields. The famine would have left them with 100 percent of nothing. Now, through Joseph, they have 80 percent, minus zero investment on possibly larger farms than they had. The question in your mind might be, "How did the people feel about this proposed arrangement?" Verse 25 says it all: "You have saved our lives. We will be Pharaoh's servants."

People who would have been dead from starvation are about to become as wealthy as their will to work can make them, while in a famine. Joseph made the 80 percent, 20 percent split a law for the whole country, with the priesthood being the only exception. How would you feel about that deal?

The Israelites prospered in the land of Goshen and grew in numbers, as stated in verse 27. Jacob had lived in Egypt for 17 of his 147 years when he sent for Joseph to secure a promise regarding his last rites.

> Gen. 47:29 When the time drew near that Israel must die, he called his son Joseph and said to him, "Now if I have found favor in your sight, please put your hand under my thigh, and deal kindly and truly with me. Please do not bury me in Egypt,
>
> 30 but let me lie with my fathers; you shall carry me out of Egypt and bury me in their burial place." And he said, "I will do as you have said."
>
> 31 Then he said, "Swear to me." And he swore to him. So Israel bowed himself on the head of the bed.

The Bible does not say how Jacob knew that his death was near, but unlike Isaac, his father, who thought his death was near scores of years before it occurred, Jacob's death truly was at hand.

The promise from Joseph to bury him in the same cemetery that Abraham and Isaac were buried in was of the utmost importance to Jacob, as stated in verses 29 and 30. Joseph said, "I will do as you have said." The act of Joseph putting his hand under Jacob's thigh was a physical manifestation of the solemn oath Jacob wanted from Joseph and he gave it to his father.

The task would be massive and a lesser man might tell a dying old man anything to soothe his mind while he was alive, then do what is simple or economical when he died—not Joseph. Joseph's word was like money in the bank, even before he swore to honor his father's request.

CHAPTER 48

In Chapter 48 of Genesis, the Bible does not say how much time passed between the time Joseph agreed to fulfill his father's funeral request and the time he heard his father was sick, but it was probably the same year. The first verse says Joseph took his sons, Manasseh and Ephraim, to his father's home when he heard about his sickness.

> Gen. 48:1 Now it came to pass after these things that Joseph was told, "Indeed your father is sick"; and he took with him his two sons, Manasseh and Ephraim.
>
> 2 And Jacob was told, "Look, your son Joseph is coming to you"; and Israel strengthened himself and sat up on the bed.
>
> 3 Then Jacob said to Joseph: "God Almighty appeared to me at Luz in the land of Canaan and blessed me,
>
> 4 and said to me, 'Behold, I will make you fruitful and multiply you, and I will make of you a multitude of people, and give this land to your descendants after you as an everlasting possession.
>
> 5 And now your two sons, Ephraim and Manasseh, who were born to you in the land of Egypt before I came to you in Egypt, are mine; as Reuben and Simeon, they shall be mine.
>
> 6 Your offspring whom you beget after them shall be yours; they will be called by the name of their brothers in their inheritance.

Jacob sat up on his bed to receive Joseph and his two sons, then began to recount some of the high and low points of his life. The appearance and blessing at Luz in the land of Canaan is where he started (Gen. 28:11–19). He recounted God's promise of the Abrahamic covenant and the promised land of Canaan as their permanent home in verses 3 and 4.

The blessing described here occurred while Jacob was fleeing from Esau because of the confusion he and his mother created from trying to steal something Jacob already had, something God gave him before he was born. I have never read where Jacob came to understand the above truth in his lifetime, so he may have lived and died thinking he had stolen something he was born to own.

Verses 5 and 6 take an interesting turn. Ephraim and Manasseh would be Jacob's in the same way that Reuben and Simeon were his. Jacob, speaking as the spirit, gives him the word that he is doubling Joseph's tribal inheritance through his first two sons (1 Chron. 5:1–2).

> **1 Chron. 5:1 Now the sons of Reuben the first-born of Israel; he was indeed the first-born, but because he defiled his father's bed, his birthright was given to the sons of Joseph, the son of Israel, so that the genealogy is not listed according to the birthright;**
>
> **2 yet Judah prevailed over his brothers, and from him came a ruler, although the birthright was Joseph's.**

The verses in Chronicles show the fulfillment of the prophetic statement of Jacob in Genesis. The Bible and history verify that both Ephraim's and Manasseh's offspring would become tribes with the sons of Jacob, even though they were natural grandsons. The chief ruler would come through Judah and be referred to as the "Lion of the tribe of Judah," proving again that seniority is not an automatic qualifier for spiritual blessings.

The point should also be made that race is not the determining factor in service to God, for those who think Ishmael was not the chosen child because his mother was Egyptian. The sons of Joseph have an Egyptian mother and they are included in a most extraordinary way. The situation with Ishmael was created by Sarah's doubt and Abraham's failure to consult God before acting on his wife's request. God still loved, protected and blessed Ishmael in a mighty way and God loves and blesses people from all races in all times.

Verse 6 says Jacob told Joseph, "The children you father after the two that are as mine and destined to become tribes of Israel shall be yours and shall be called after the name of their brothers in their inheritance." The Bible does not name any children of Joseph beyond Ephraim and Manasseh, but this verse appears to make their existence or future existence obvious. They, meaning any other offspring of Joseph's, will be called by the name of their brothers in their inheritance, who are Ephraim and Manasseh. The obvious meaning is that all other children of Joseph's would inherit tribal lands and titles as the children of Ephraim or Manasseh.

Verse 7 is where Jacob reflects on what must have been the hardest day of his life, the death of his beloved Rachel. The place where Rachel is buried is near the town that was Ephrath at the time, but would later be named Bethlehem, the same Bethlehem where Jesus Christ would be born and King Herod would murder all of the children up to two years old in an attempt to prevent the birth of the Messiah. The act fulfilled the prophecy (Jer. 31:15) of Rachel weeping for her murdered children. Joseph's two sons, now in their late teens to early twenties, are presented to Jacob. Afterward, he wanted them to come forward for his blessing.

> **Gen. 48:8 Then Israel saw Joseph's sons, and said, "Who are these?"**
>
> **9 And Joseph said to his father, "They are my sons, whom God has given me in this place," And he said, "Please bring them to me, and I will bless them."**

The blessing of the young men would be inspired by God and would prove once again that there is no seniority system involved in God's blessings or choices. The boys were pushed toward Jacob by Joseph in a way that Manasseh, the firstborn would be at Jacob's right hand, which was indicative of greater power. Ephraim, the youngest, would be at Jacob's left hand, as stated in verse 13.

Verse 14 shows Israel's reversal of Joseph's intentions.

> **Genesis 48:14 Then Israel stretched out his right hand and laid it on Ephraim's head, who was the younger, and his left hand**

on Manasseh's head, guiding his hands knowingly, for Manasseh was the first-born.

15 And he blessed Joseph, and said: "God, before whom my fathers Abraham and Isaac walked, The God who has fed me all my life long to this day,

16 The Angel who has redeemed me from all evil, Bless the lads; Let my name be named upon them, And the name of my fathers Abraham and Isaac; And let them grow into a multitude in the midst of the earth."

Israel apparently crossed his arms and put his right hand on the younger son's head and his left hand on the older boy, guiding his hands knowingly and leaving no doubts about his intentions. Israel blessed Joseph first, then blessed the grandsons after the order of his natural sons in verses 15 and 16. Joseph's displeasure with his father's hand placement may have been out of respect for the first-born custom, as his statement in verse 18 bears out.

Gen. 48:17 Now when Joseph saw that his father laid his right hand on the head of Ephraim, it displeased him; so he took hold of his father's hand to remove it from Ephraim's head to Manasseh's head.

18 And Joseph said to his father, "Not so, my father, for this one is the first-born; put your right hand on his head."

19 But his father refused and said, "I know, my son, I know. He also shall become a people, and he also shall be great; but truly his younger brother shall be greater than he, and his descendants shall become a multitude of nations."

20 So he blessed them that day, saying, "By you Israel will bless," saying, "May God make you as Ephraim and as Manasseh!" And thus he set Ephraim before Manasseh.

21 Then Israel said to Joseph, "Behold, I am dying, but God will be with you and bring you back to the land of your fathers.

22 Moreover I have given to you one portion above your broth-

ers, which I took from the hand of the Amorite with my sword and my bow."

The blessing bestowed here had nothing to do with man's customs—it was part of the establishment of the nation that started the Abrahamic Covenant. God knew which one of the boys would grow to be the greater nation before he gave the knowledge to Israel, who conveys the knowledge to Joseph. Joseph is living proof of the fact that God is not a respecter of customs or persons, as he, the 11th of 12 sons, was chosen for the work he did without regard for who was born first.

The man, Israel, closes with a blessing for Joseph that would become a reality when Israel becomes a nation, at verses 21 and 22. God would truly be with Joseph throughout his life and he would return soon to the land of his fathers to bury his father, Israel. The return Israel is talking about, however, is the symbolic spiritual return when Joseph's bones are brought out of Egypt hundreds of years later.

The whole purpose of the Abrahamic covenant is to build a nation that will serve God and bring the word or light of God to all of the families of the earth. The individual building blocks or people would be as useful to God as their willingness to live a faithful life, a life that looks toward a faithful heritage instead of a greedy selfish life that seeks individual pleasures of the here and now. God has used and still uses his right to choose people who will value the future by the way they live in the present. If we are willing to look, the Bible will show us what God values by the choice and character of his human building blocks.

CHAPTER 49

In Chapter 49 of Genesis, Jacob calls his sons together to tell them what would befall them in the last days.

> **Gen. 49:1 And Jacob called his sons and said, "Gather together, that I may tell you what shall befall you in the last days:**
>
> **2 "Gather together and hear, you sons of Jacob, and listen to Israel your father."**

When Jacob says "the last days," he does not refer to the final days of the individual lives of these men. The words apply for the tribes each man would head that would make the nation Israel. Israel's words are prophecies from God and show how the character of each man affects the whole group of those he fathered.

For example, the character of Ham, who looked at and spoke of his father Noah's nakedness, is magnified through his son, Canaan. Canaan was the father or head of the Canaanite lands that God would eventually give to the Israelites with the stern warning of Deuteronomy 18:9–22. Canaan's character, as influenced by his father Ham, would permeate the lives of his nation in such a negative way that centuries later, they would have no earthly value to God. The bottom line is that clay has to be useful to the potter or it is thrown away.

Reuben, the first-born, would show a lot of character in trying to save Joseph. Telling his brothers their act against Joseph was why they were charged with being spies in Egypt, and later offering his sons for

Benjamin's return, showed conscience and duty. But the disrespectful affair with Bilhah, his father's concubine would swallow up his good traits and blemish his tribal heritage forever, as stated in verses 3 and 4.

In verses 5-7, the actions of Simeon and Levi over the rape of Dinah in Chapter 34 are called to memory and noted as the defining acts in their character that would reflect on their nations. The dividing mentioned in verse 7 no doubt refers to Simeon's tribe nearly being absorbed by the tribe of Judah after they reached the promised land.

Judah, whose plan to sell Joseph moved Joseph from death's door to the path of greatness, would have the most memorable heritage. King David and the King of Kings, Jesus Christ, would come through his tribe (Gen. 49:8–12).

The rest of the brothers would hear an overview of their tribe's future, with the Bible and history proving these things to be true. Judah and Joseph would have more positive things said about them than the other sons would, but all of their offspring would be under God's covenant through Abraham. They would be God's representative nation in a world filled with nations that do not know him. Verse 28 identifies these 12 individuals as the original 12 tribes of Israel.

> **Gen. 49:28 All these are the twelve tribes of Israel, and this is what their father spoke to them. And he blessed them; he blessed each one according to his own blessing.**

The blessing their father spoke unto them is from God and is in line with each man's character. It is not based on perfection or righteousness of the person. It's based on God's grace.

Verses 29 through 32 cover the charge, or order, of Jacob to all of his sons concerning his funeral arrangements. The burial site is well known to these men because their great-grandfather, Abraham, who bought and established the site as a cemetery, is buried there with great-grandmother Sarah. Isaac and Rebekah, their grandparents on their father's side, are buried there. Leah, the mother of six natural sons, two legal sons through her maid and Israel's only daughter, is buried there also. The request of Israel is difficult, but not unreasonable. The sons have the wealth, authority and ability to fulfill their father's last request and he has a right to be buried with the other patriarchs.

Jacob, named Israel by the Angel of God, who was introduced in Chapter 25 and is a major character up to this point, drew his feet up into the bed and breathed his last. The body literally died and his soul was gathered unto his people.

> **Gen. 49:33 And when Jacob had finished commanding his sons, he drew his feet up into the bed and breathed his last, and was gathered to his people.**

Life beyond the grave appears to be an accepted, if not clearly understood, concept even back then. Jacob's life is a look at the changes a man's bad judgement can put him through and the distance God will go with that man to make him a useful servant that fulfills his destiny.

The careful reader who rightly divides the word of truth will look at Jacob's failures and triumphs for what they are and not be caught up in the idea that being a Jacob-like trickster is divine. The mother-inspired trouble that Jacob experienced was not necessary. God's prophecy in Genesis 25:23 would have still been fulfilled concerning Jacob's future nation. Without his trickery, he could have done it in peace and security and never had to deal with Laban from the disadvantaged position he created.

The statement Jacob makes upon his first meeting with Pharaoh at Genesis 47:9, "Few and evil have been the days of the years of my life," did not have to happen. The lesson for us is simple enough: Do it God's way the first time and don't give trouble a place to bloom.

CHAPTER 50

Verses 1 through 14 in Chapter 50 of Genesis cover the elaborate funeral of Jacob or Israel. The Egyptian participation was quite extensive from the start. It included a forty-day embalming and seventy-day mourning process while still in Egypt. Joseph, speaking through the household of Pharaoh, sought and was heartily given permission by Pharaoh to leave the country and bury his father in Canaan.

> Gen. 50:5 My father made me swear, saying, "Behold, I am dying; in my grave which I dug for myself in the land of Canaan, there you shall bury me." Now therefore, please let me go up and bury my father, and I will come back."'
>
> 6 And Pharaoh said, "Go up and bury your father, as he made you swear."

Joseph, with all of his power, wealth and over 25 years of loyal service to Pharaoh, the Egyptian people and his own people, may still legally be a slave who was promoted directly from the prison without being legally freed. In Genesis 41:37–46, Pharaoh gives Joseph wealth, power, a mission and even a wife, but he does not give him freedom or the permission to leave Egypt and not look back.

The request for permission and promise to return makes sense when you understand the above statements. Joseph's word has been his bond from childhood and that's the lifelong power of their relationship. The highest-ranking Egyptians and Elders, along with a great company of Jacob's family, made the impressive trip. The guilty conscience of

Joseph's brothers got the best of them when they returned from the funeral.

> Gen. 50:15 When Joseph's brothers saw that their father was dead, they said, "Perhaps Joseph will hate us, and may actually repay us for all the evil which we did to him."
>
> 16 So they sent messengers to Joseph, saying, "Before your father died he commanded, saying,
>
> 17 Thus you shall say to Joseph: "I beg you, please forgive the trespass of your brothers and their sin; for they did evil to you. Now, please, forgive the trespass of the servants of the God of your father." And Joseph wept when they spoke to him.
>
> 18 Then his brothers also went and fell down before his face, and they said. "Behold, we are your servants."
>
> 19 Joseph said to them, "Do not be afraid, for am I in the place of God?
>
> 20 But as for you, you meant evil against me: but God meant it for good, in order to bring it about as it is this day, to save many people alive.
>
> 21 Now therefore, do not be afraid; I will provide for you and your little ones." And he comforted them and spoke kindly to them.

Jacob was dead and they assumed Joseph would take revenge on them now. Jacob had apparently found out what they did to Joseph after arriving in Egypt, because the brothers lean on the promise for safety their father commanded in verses 16 and 17. Their problem was looking at Joseph through their own eyes and seeing what they would do if they were in his shoes.

Joseph had long since forgiven them and they seemed to forget that, unlike most of them, Joseph was intensely honest from his childhood. The whole situation became a means to God's ends. The evil they meant, as pointed out in verse 20, was clearly redirected by God for good to save a multitude of lives. Joseph forgave them. If they repented, God forgave them. Now, all they needed to do was forgive each other and themselves, put it behind them and enjoy God's blessings and grace.

The problem too many people have after repentance and forgiveness of the sins we commit is how to put them down and move on. The brothers of Joseph got final confirmation from him that he was not lurking in the shadows, waiting for their father to die so he could take revenge, and they appear to move on. The words of Joseph in verse 21 say it all: "I will provide." He comforted them and spoke kindly to them a second time. They did not then, and never did have, a reason to fear Joseph.

Joseph was in his mid- to late-fifties when Jacob died. Verse 22 say Joseph died at 110 years old. Joseph saw a lot of envy, lust, hatred, violence and treachery directed at him because he did what was right in God's eyes. The bitter acts against him never changed his desire to do God's will. He never allowed anyone to drag him down to their level; he always stayed on the moral high ground. The picture painted in verses 23 through 26 reflects a tranquil, fruitful life for Joseph and his people. The grandchildren of Ephraim and Manasseh are brought up on Joseph's knees, as stated in verse 23.

> **Genesis 50:24 And Joseph said to his brethren, "I an dying; but God will surely visit you, and bring you out of this land to the land of which He swore to Abraham, to Isaac, and to Jacob."**
>
> **25 Then Joseph took an oath from the children of Israel, saying, "God will surely visit you, and you shall carry up my bones from here."**
>
> **26 So Joseph died, being one hundred and ten years old; and they embalmed him, and he was put in a coffin in Egypt.**

The oath Joseph took from the children of Israel in verse 25, about his funeral in Canaan after God's visit, makes the assignment a generational obligation over the 300 or so years before the exodus. When Joseph died, he was embalmed, Egyptian-style, and placed in an unburied coffin in Egypt.

SUMMARY

In writing this book as a Bible-based commentary on Genesis, I have tried to keep the reader focused on what God is teaching humanity, based on what the Bible says, and bring humanity out of the idea that the Bible's sole function is to allow people to fit it into their own personal views.

A careful look at key points of scripture will leave no doubt that there is an ongoing plan of salvation and a return to eternal service to the Creator for those people who accept the terms of God's plan. The reader will profit most by learning to limit speculation and build their faith by acting on what can be proven from the Bible.

The life assurance policy that God pays claims on is contained in his word, the Bible. A religious faith one was born into and follows without ever measuring it by scripture, or whatever else, will leave a person with an invalid life assurance policy when they suffer their greatest loss—death.

The whole Bible must be accepted as inspired and carefully studied to put every part in its proper place. A prophecy is a prophecy. It is useful knowledge for an appointed time, but in and of itself, it should not be the foundation of a church denomination. A careful examination of most religious denominations will reveal the human input and emphasis on certain areas of the Bible that cannot be questioned.

The problem comes when other denominations do the same thing with other parts of the Bible and they create opposing positions on parts of the whole, when all should have been built on the whole Bible to start with. Accept and implement the whole Bible as your guide, then put the emphasis on teaching the whole Bible to each generation and you will eventually establish the one church that Paul refers to at Ephesians 4: 4–6.

> **Eph. 4:4 There is one body and one spirit, just as you were called in one hope of your calling;**
>
> **5 one Lord, one faith, one baptism**
>
> **6 one God and Father of all, who is above all, and through all, and in you all.**

The power of the one church can be more effective in the war against sin than the many churches that are at war with each other over denominational differences. The strategy of Satan to divide and conquer works best when churches and nations that claim God's law as law fail to show evidence of their claim by the way they live.

A nation that is wise enough to establish a Constitution from the Bible must never forget that the Bible is the parent of that Constitution. If issues arise over how the children perceive the human constitution, wisdom demands a return to the parent (the Bible) for a truth that settles issues.

Governments are a God-ordained necessity. They keep order, establish civil laws, punish crimes and should exalt honesty. In times and areas where not only the quantity of sin and crime abound, but also the quality of sin and crime reaches a repulsive peak, governments can assess harsher penalties and build bigger and stronger prisons in the hope of changing people.

The reality of that hope can be seen in judicial systems in our country and around the world. We see prison and jail overcrowding, court systems that cannot keep up with criminal cases and prisoners who merit incarceration being released early because taxpayers can't afford to build more prisons. The whole situation needs a different approach. Cages, which criminals make a necessity, can contain, control and warehouse people for a time. God, through his revealed will from his written word, can change the heart and mind of a criminal, then establish a moral compass that leads that person away from habitual sin and crime.

The best solution is not better prisons, but better people who don't need to be in prison. God has provided the formula for that.

A nation that God sets on a hill and illuminates with the light of his word as a moral compass for the world that fails God on issues, truths, deeds, realities and evidence of loyalty to God, has lost that compass and is disqualifying themselves as useful tools to God. The worst thing that a God-claiming nation can do is to allow any ungodly system, belief tool, lie or weapon that Satan has put in play against it to prosper. The wisest thing that same nation can do is to table all other issues until they settle the issue of who they are committed to.

If they honor God with visible evidence of that, in actions and deeds, then many of the other problems within their society will be self-solving. If not, they have poured up the cup of God's wrath that they or their children will one day drink, because it does not matter how smart and intellectually elite man thinks he is, he cannot match wits with Satan and win. Jesus Christ is the only man born of a woman that has defeated Satan and his victory is your reward for joining him.

Christ brings us back to the Bible, which is like all other books—it conveys the thinking of and communication from its author, who is God, regardless of which human tool He used as the pen to write it. The only true interpretation is the author's, as Peter points out at 2 Peter 1: 20–21.

> **2 Pet. 1:20 knowing this first, that no prophecy of scripture is of any private interpretation,**
>
> **21 for prophecy never came by the will of man, but holy men of God spoke as they were moved by the Holy Spirit.**

Understand what God said and why God said it, and you have harnessed the power of it. People often get into trouble with how they perceive and apply what they think they have learned from the Bible. For example, I've seen people argue about how a particular passage of scripture served a specific need they had that happened to be different from the need it satisfied for another person.

The argument ensues with each claiming that a particular Bible passage has a different meaning. The truth is that the Bible still means what God, the author, meant for it to say. The argument is over how each person served their specific need by applying the wisdom of the passage to their own situation.

A doctor may prescribe one specific medication for 100 different people with 100 different ailments. That should never create confusion about the medicine. The doctor's job is to know the properties and healing powers of the medicine and how it applies to each person's illness, without changing the ingredients in the medicine. The informed Christian who applies the mental, spiritual, physical, psychological and soul-soothing healing powers of a passage of scripture to their life must realize that each person alive could do the same with that passage of scripture. It could serve a different need or set of circumstances for each person without changing the meaning of the Bible.

If the saints are to judge the world, then they must understand that the power of the word is in knowing the proper time and application for your specific need. This comes with better understanding and knowledge that is developed by studying the Bible for yourself.

Human history has taught and will continue to teach mankind that God's way is the way. Honor God as an individual, group, or nation, and He will exalt your efforts at the appointed time.

THE END

ISBN 141203874-X

9 781412 038744